THE CAMPAIGN OF 1870–1871

OPERATIONS OF
THE FIRST ARMY

UNDER GENERAL VON MANTEUFFEL

COMPRISING THE PERIOD FROM THE CAPITULATION
OF METZ TO THE FALL OF PERONNE

*COMPILED FROM THE OFFICIAL WAR DOCUMENTS OF
THE HEAD-QUARTERS OF THE FIRST ARMY BY*

COUNT HERRMANN VON WARTENSLEBEN

COLONEL IN THE GENERAL STAFF

TRANSLATED by COL. C. H. VON WRIGHT

CHIEF OF GENERAL STAFF, 8TH ARMY CORPS

WITH TWO MAPS

The Naval & Military Press Ltd

Published by

The Naval & Military Press Ltd
Unit 5 Riverside, Brambleside,
Bellbrook Industrial Estate,
Uckfield, East Sussex,
TN22 1QQ England

Tel: +44 (0) 1825 749494
Fax: +44 (0) 1825 765701

www.naval-military-press.com
www.nmarchive.com

In reprinting in facsimile from the original, any imperfections are inevitably reproduced and the quality may fall short of modern type and cartographic standards.

PREFACE.

IT IS CHARACTERISTIC of the first period of the German-French war—the campaign against the *Imperial Army*—that, notwithstanding the great breadth of front on which the French troops assembled in the first instance, still both sides aim at the greatest possible co-operation of all their forces. In consequence, a series of mighty blows, dealt for the most part in rapid succession, soon decide the fate of the campaign, the importance and mutual connection of these different actions being from the very beginning plainly evident to the public in general.

In the later period—the war against the *Republic*—the case is different. Here we see the armies on both sides engaged in separate campaigns, each more or less depending on the other.

The unexpected length of the resistance offered by Paris, and the astonishing capability of the hostile country to furnish fresh forces, cause the operations to be pushed farther and farther westward from the German frontier. It is true, Head-Quarters at Versailles still combine the different operations to the attainment of one joint purpose, but the impulse thus given is often not outwardly perceptible. Therefore, the impression produced by this second period of the great war is often one of apparent confusion, particularly to such as are at a distance from the seat of the operations.

The general plan of the war, and the particular tasks allotted to the different armies fix the main direction of their operations; their subsequent measures then depend on orders or directions from higher quarters, and, as far as these allow, on the reports sent in from subordinates, as well as on other information received and on the general aspect of affairs. This is not only the case with the commander-in-chief, but also, more or less, with every leader of troops who is placed in a position to form self-dependent resolutions. These materials in their totality afford the ever-changing, often indistinct, picture of the momentary state of affairs. Without obtaining some general insight into the latter, no impartial judgment can be formed, no instructive criticism is possible.

For these reasons an early publication of the special history of each single campaign cannot fail to excite general interest.

We now give a survey of the campaign of the 1st Army, from the capitulation of Metz to the fall of Péronne. The narrative is founded on the head-quarter war-documents; much that it describes was personally witnessed by the author. We by no means profess to give anything perfect, but merely wish to afford materials which we think will, from the reasons alluded to above, not be unwelcome; at the same time we would recall to the memory of all participators in the campaign of the 1st Army, the eventful time we passed together. May each fellow combatant, even though not personally mentioned, recognize in these pages his own share in the jointly attained success.

With regard to the view taken of the subject, and the way it is treated, we refer in general to the preface to 'The Operations of the South Army.'

CONTENTS.

INTRODUCTION.
Situation of the 1st Army previous to its march from the Moselle PAGE 1

FIRST PERIOD.
MARCH OF THE 1ST ARMY FROM THE MOSELLE TO THE OISE.

CHAPTER I.
From Metz to Rheims (November 7th to November 15th) . . . 17

CHAPTER II.
From Rheims to Compiègne—Positions on the Oise (November 16th to November 23rd) 36

SECOND PERIOD.
OPERATIONS IN PICARDY AND NORMANDY UP TO THE TAKING OF ROUEN.

CHAPTER III.
Advance towards Amiens—Reconnoitring Actions at Quesnel and Mézières—Action of the Advanced Guard at the Luce—Capitulation of Thionville (November 24th to November 26th) 49

CHAPTER IV.
Battle of Amiens (November 27th) . 62

CHAPTER V.

Capitulation of La Fère—Occupation of Amiens—Surrender of the Citadel —Formation of the 1st Army preparatory to its march upon Rouen— German Civil Administration established in the department 'de la Somme' —State of affairs of the VIIIth Army Corps (November 27th to November 30th) . . . . PAGE 74

CHAPTER VI.

March to Normandy—Action at Buchy—The 1st Army enters Rouen (December 1st to December 6th) . . . 89

THIRD PERIOD.

OPERATIONS ON THE SEINE AND THE SOMME, FROM THE ENTRANCE INTO ROUEN TO THE BATTLE OF THE HALLUE.

CHAPTER VII.

Military position of the 1st Army in December, in general and in particular —State of affairs at Rouen—Operations of Flying Columns on both banks of the Seine (December 7th to December 11th) 102

CHAPTER VIII.

Arrangements made for forming the 1st Army in two groups at the Seine and the Somme, and first steps taken to carry them out—Actions at the Rille—Reconnaissances in the direction of Hâvre (December 9th to December 14th) 114

CHAPTER IX.

Events at the Somme and in front of the Ardennes Fortresses during the first half of December—Surprise of Ham—General Faidherbe's advance upon La Fère—Capitulation of Montmédy 122

CHAPTER X.

Concentration of the greater part of the 1st Army in the direction of Amiens (December 13th to December 22nd) 128

CHAPTER XI.

Battle of the Hallue . . 146

FOURTH PERIOD.

OPERATIONS AND ACTIONS FROM THE BATTLE OF THE HALLUE UNTIL THE FALL OF PÉRONNE.

CHAPTER XII.

Advance of the VIIIth Army Corps to Bapaume—Investment and Bombardment of Péronne—Actions at Longpré, Busigny, &c.—Surprise of Souchez—Advance of the Enemy towards Rouen—Actions at the Seine—Storming of the 'Chateau Robert le Diable' (December 25th to December 31st)

PAGE 168

FINAL CHAPTER.

Capitulation of Mézières on the 1st and of Rocroi on the 6th of January—The 14th Infantry Division leaves the 1st Army—Defeat of the French on the left bank of the Seine on the 4th of January—Advance of the French Army of the North to raise the siege of Péronne—Battle of Bapaume—Operations of Count Lippe's Cavalry Division against Vervins (January 2nd to January 6th)—General von Goeben assumes the command of the 1st Army—Capitulation of Péronne on the 9th January . . 191

APPENDIX.

1. Remarks on the measures taken to provision the 1st Army and complete its ammunition 208
2. Order of Battle of the 1st Army at the time of leaving the Moselle (November 7th) 220
3. Order of Battle of the 1st and VIIIth Army Corps 224
4. Forces composing the French Army of the North . . 226

THE

OPERATIONS of the FIRST ARMY

UNDER

GENERAL von MANTEUFFEL.

INTRODUCTION.

SITUATION OF THE 1ST ARMY PREVIOUS TO ITS MARCH FROM THE MOSELLE.

AFTER the battle of Gravelotte the 1st Army formed part of the large army investing Metz, under command of Prince Frederick Charles. Its formation was as follows:—

Commander-in-chief: General of Infantry, Von Steinmetz.
Chief of the Staff: Major-General von Sperling.
1st Army Corps: General of Cavalry, Baron von Manteuffel.
VIIth Army Corps: General of Infantry, Von Zastrow.
VIIIth Army Corps: General of Infantry, Von Goeben.
3rd Reserve Division: Lieut.-General von Kummer.
1st Cavalry Division: Lieut.-General von Hartmann.
3rd Cavalry Division: Lieut.-General, Count von der Groeben.
Inspector-Gen. of 'Etappen': Lieut.-General von Malotki.

About the middle of September General Steinmetz was appointed Governor-General of Posen. From this moment the 3rd Army Corps and the independent divisions for the time being attached to the Army, received all orders referring to tactics direct from Head-quarters of the Army of Investment, but the previous formation of the Ist Army was still maintained in all questions of administration and other matters. The Chief of the Staff had been *ad interim* in command of the 29th Infantry Brigade since the 10th September. In this position he fell ill, in consequence of the fatigue of outpost duty, and did not rejoin the army until the beginning of December at Rouen; his duties as Chief of Staff were meanwhile fulfilled by the Quartermaster-General, Colonel Count Wartensleben.

The district in front of Metz in which the Army was distributed, and which it had to defend, was frequently changed, according as the general military situation made it necessary to reinforce either one or the other front of the line of investment, and according to the number of available troops. In addition to the Ist Army, the IInd, IIIrd, IXth, and Xth Army Corps of the IInd Army formed the Army of Investment, to which at the commencement, part of the 'Etappen' troops of the Ist Army, and for a time, the XIIIth (Meklenburg) Army Corps also, belonged. The details of this, as well as of the actual defensive positions against Metz, do not come within the limits of this narrative. During the first period of the investment only the Ist Army Corps, General Kummer's Division, the 3rd Cavalry Division, and a small portion of the VIIth Army Corps, were on the right bank of the Moselle; all the rest of the troops were on the left bank of the river; later the Ist Army held, in the main, the ground on the right, the IInd, that on the left bank.

The following outlines of the districts which the different Army Corps occupied from the 1st October to the capitulation of Metz will suffice to render the account of the measures taken for the advance of the army more intelligible to the reader.

The VIIIth Army Corps, with the 3rd Cavalry Division attached to it, in the district between the river Seille and the Saarbrücken railway. Head-quarters at Chérisey. Line of defence, Pouilly—Mercy le Haut.

The VIIth Army Corps from the right wing of the VIIIth, to

Distribution of the forces investing Metz.

the Saarbrücken high-road. Head-quarters, Puche. Line of defence, Ars Laquenexy—Montoy.

The Ist Army Corps, with half of the 1st Cavalry Division attached to it, in the district on both sides of the Saarbrücken high road. Head-quarters, St. Barbe. Line of defence, Noisseville—Failly. The other half of the 1st Cavalry Division was in front of Thionville.

The 3rd Reserve Division (General Kummer), at that time attached to the Xth Army Corps, was on the left bank of the Moselle. Head-quarters, Maizières. Line of defence, Amelange—Fèves.

The Xth Army Corps of the IInd Army held the ground between the Ist Army Corps and General Kummer's Division. Immediately adjoining the latter, on the left bank of the Moselle, the IIIrd Army Corps was stationed, next to it the IXth, which reached to the Upper Moselle. The IInd Army Corps was principally between the Moselle and the Seille.

Ever since the 7th September, Prince Frederick Charles's Head-quarters had been at Corny, south of Metz; near to them was the Staff of the Ist Army in Jouy aux Arches. The Inspections-General of 'Etappen' of the Ist and IInd Armies were at the Saarbrücken railway in the neighbourhood of Herny and Courcelles. All supplies for both armies were conveyed by this line of railway, on which each had its own separate terminus—one Herny, the other Courcelles. The lines of communication from the Army of Investment to the Prussian frontier were but short, whereas those of the other armies lengthened considerably as they advanced, and required more protection westward of the Moselle; the 'Etappen' troops of the Ist and IInd Armies were, therefore, by degrees withdrawn from their original destination; the greater part of those of the Ist Army were as early as October already with General Gayl's Corps in front of Verdun.

By the second half of October it became very evident that affairs were rapidly drawing to a crisis at Metz; on the 23rd of this month, therefore, orders were issued from Head-quarters at

4 *Arrangements in anticipation of the Capitulation.*

Versailles, making alterations in the formation of the Ist and IInd Armies, and pointing out the tasks which would fall to each in the ensuing period. These instructions, addressed to Headquarters of the Army of Investment, arrived at Corny on the 27th October; they contained, in the first instance, certain points to be held in view when the expected capitulation should take place: in particular, orders that the prisoners should be sent to Germany by two main routes, viz., by way of Saarlouis—Call—Cologne, and from Courcelles per rail over Saarbrücken. They then proceed to say:

'With regard to the future employment of the forces now before Metz, His Majesty's commands are as follows:

'The Ist Army (Ist, VIIth, and VIIIth Army Corps, 3rd Reserve Division) will garrison Metz, besiege Thionville and Montmédy, take charge of the captured army and send the prisoners off under escort of the Landwehr troops. A return of the latter is not to be expected for the present, as there are no other troops momentarily available to guard the prisoners at home; other Landwehr battalions may perhaps be brought up later. Two army corps at least of the Ist Army will march to the line St. Quentin—Compiègne, the leading troops of which will start immediately after the capitulation has taken place.

'The IInd Army (IInd, IIIrd, IXth and Xth Army Corps with the Ist Cavalry Division) will march with the utmost rapidity by way of Troyes in the general direction of the Middle Loire. Both armies will march on a broad front, in order to facilitate their subsistence and to hasten their advance to the utmost.

(Signed)   'MOLTKE.'

In the meantime the negotiations carried on with Marshal Bazaine had made such progress that the final conclusion of the capitulation was momentarily impending. Head-quarters of the Army of Investment therefore made the following preparatory arrangements as soon as the above-mentioned instructions arrived from Versailles.

The VIIth Army Corps and 3rd Reserve Division were ordered by Prince Frederick Charles to remain at Metz, under command of General Zastrow, and to undertake the sieges. This general was specially entrusted with the direction of all measures relating to the transport of the prisoners and with all arrangements at Metz and in front of Thionville. General Kummer was appointed provisionally Governor of Metz, but soon afterwards, on his division being broken up, he assumed the command of the 15th Division.

The 1st Cavalry Division was transferred from the Ist to the IInd Army, and ordered to march on the 29th to the neighbourhood of Briey; General Strantz took for the time the command of the troops before Thionville. On the 28th the following troops of the VIIIth Army Corps were despatched to reinforce the corps besieging Verdun: the 60th Infantry Regiment, 8th Rifle Battalion, and a company of pioneers. They reached the neighbourhood of Verdun on the 30th, and were placed under the orders of General Gayl, whose Head-quarters were at Charny. The 3rd Cavalry Division moved to the north of Fresnes on the 28th.

On the evening of the 27th the capitulation was signed at Chateau Frescati. Prince Frederick Charles then issued the following proclamation :—

'Soldiers of the First and Second Armies!

'You have fought battles, and blockaded your vanquished enemy for seventy days in Metz; seventy long days, most of which have increased, but none diminished, the honour and glory of your regiments. You left no means of escape unto your brave enemy until he should lay down his arms. That moment has now arrived.

'To-day, at last, this army of still full 173,000 of France's best men—more than 6 whole army corps, including the Imperial Guard—with 3 marshals of France, above 50 generals, and more than 6,000 officers, has capitulated, together with Metz itself, a fortress never before taken.

'With this bulwark, thus restored to Germany, immense stores of cannon, arms, and implements of war have fallen into the hands of the victor.

'You have won these bloody laurels by your bravery in the two days' battle of Noisseville, and in actions round about Metz, more numerous than the surrounding villages after which you name these combats.

'Willingly and gratefully I acknowledge your bravery, but not only this; I esteem, if possible, more highly still your obedience, and the equanimity, the cheerfulness, the devotion with which you have borne privations of many kinds. This is the characteristic of the good soldier.

'The great and memorable success of this day was prepared by the battles we fought before we invested Metz, and—let us gratefully remember—by the King himself, by the corps which left here with him, and by all those comrades who met their death, either on the battle-field, or in consequence of illness contracted here. This in the first instance opened the way to that great work which you now see, by God's help, completed, the downfall of France's might.

'The ultimate results of to-day's event are incalculable.

'Soldiers! who have been assembled for this purpose under my command before Metz, you will now soon part to fulfil different duties.

'I bid farewell, therefore, to the generals, officers and soldiers of the 1st Army, and of General Kummer's Division, and wish them good luck and further success.'

According to the Convention of Frescati, the hostile army left its camps round Metz at midday of the 29th, whilst we at the same time took possession of the forts St. Julien, Queleu, St. Privat, St. Quentin, and Plappeville, as well as of the town itself. The French troops came out unarmed, having previously laid down their arms and colours. The corps marched separately, in six different directions, to points where the Army

Corps of the Army of Investment were drawn up in readiness to receive their prisoners; the latter were then conducted to six large camps previously prepared for them. Thus the VIth French Corps (Canrobert) marched to Ladonchamps, and was there received by the Xth Prussian Army Corps; in like manner the IVth Corps (Ladmirault) was received by the IIIrd at Amanvillers; the Corps of Guards (formerly Bourbaki) by the IInd at Tournebride; the IInd (Froissard) by the VIIIth at Thiebault; the garrison troops, composed chiefly of 'Gardes mobiles,' by the VIIth at Grigy; the IIIrd (Lebœuf) by the Ist at Bellecroix. It was a dull, cold and wet October day; ever since midday the rain had poured down, at times in torrents. The feelings of friend and foe were serious, for, high as the spirits of the conquerors rose at the sight of the enormous success won by their steady perseverance, still they could not suppress the emotion which the human heart must feel on seeing a brave and vanquished foe going to meet the sad and uncertain lot of captivity. We believe that all who were present on this memorable occasion experienced more or less these varied emotions.

Prince Frederick Charles, accompanied by the head-quarters staffs of both armies, was present at the surrender, in the neighbourhood of Tournebride, where the reports of the enemy's troops were tendered to the Commanding General of the IInd Prussian Army Corps; the filing past of the French lasted until the evening. The whole act passed over in a manner worthy of the occasion, and amidst profound silence, for, out of respect for the feelings of the enemy, not a drum was beaten. For the present the French officers were allowed to return to Metz, whilst the soldiers were marched off to the camps prepared for them. Many a touching scene of farewell between the French leaders and their troops will still dwell in the memory of those present.

The capitulation of Metz took place at a moment when it had become very desirable that the Ist and IInd Armies should be available for operations in the field, in order to guard the army in front of Paris against the fresh hostile forces that had been organised in the meantime. Although the latter had not as yet assumed the offensive, still accounts and symptoms tended to show that such might soon be expected, especially from the direction of the Loire, and perhaps from the west also. At that moment the enemy's preparations in the north were less apparent, but even here some detachments of the Army of the Meuse met with much resistance in the directions of Rouen, Amiens, and St. Quentin, and from such superior numbers that they could not overcome it. The Army of Investment before Paris might, therefore, soon be called upon to face superior forces in two different directions. Under these circumstances the 'instructions' of the 23rd October had pointed out the necessity of expediting the advance of the Ist and IInd Armies to the utmost. Their march was, however, unavoidably delayed for some days, owing to the effective strength of the VIIth Army Corps and the 3rd Reserve Division having been so reduced by sickness and by casualties on the battle-field, that it did not nearly suffice to garrison Metz, and at the same time guard and escort a number of prisoners that far exceeded all expectations. The following rough calculation will make this evident:

As a rule, 100 prisoners require as escort 10 infantry, and 1 cavalry soldier. If we take this number as basis, and treble it, so as to be able to relieve guard during the period of watching the prisoners in their camps, we find that 173,000 prisoners require in round numbers 55,000 men to guard them. This was at that time about the whole effective strength of the 1st Army, including the Landwehr.

The preparatory arrangements made by Head-quarters of the Army of Investment for the reception and transport of the prisoners, were based on the following considerations:

The prisoners will, for the moment, be distributed in six large camps (this was effected on the 29th). The two eastern camps (Ars-Laquenexy—VIIth Army Corps, and St. Barbe—Ist Army Corps), will be the starting-points from which their march will commence in the two main directions prescribed by the Versailles orders— Saarbrücken and Saarlouis—the former per rail from Courcelles, the latter per foot march by the Boulay road. In either direction a batch of 10,000 prisoners will start daily, commencing on the 30th. The western camps to transfer one such échelon daily to the central, and these the same number to the eastern camps, so that the west camps would be the first, the east camps the last to be evacuated. The 1st Army will undertake all arrangements for the subsistence of the prisoners, the IInd will provide in like manner for the inhabitants of Metz.

We have already mentioned that the IInd Army occupied the ground on the west front of the investment; its camps of prisoners were, therefore, the first to be cleared. Besides, it soon became evident that the *town* of Metz was still provided with sufficient provisions, the want of which had only been felt by the *Army*. Thus the IInd Army was in this respect also soon set free from all trammels, and was able to start for its new destination, the Loire, as early as the 2nd November. This was in accordance with the Versailles instructions, and at the same time adapted to the general military situation, for at this time it was principally from the Loire that the army before Paris was menaced. On the other hand, the arrangement of all affairs at Metz now devolved upon the 1st Army, which was thus detained there for several days longer.

One whole division of the VIIth Army Corps had to be detailed as garrison of Metz and the forts. This was necessary to maintain order in the place, for about 20,000 convalescent soldiers were still in the town, many of them wandering about the streets, besides 6,000 officers with their servants. Added to this, during the first few days some irregularity occurred in the railway transport of the prisoners on the Saarbrucken line, so that the flow of what was called the south stream of prisoners was checked in the beginning; this caused an overcrowding of the east camps, as the west camps were cleared in the prescribed order. In the beginning of November, therefore, about the time the IInd Army started, the troops of the 1st Army were employed in the following manner:

One division of the VIIth Army Corps garrisoned Metz and the forts. The Landwehr battalions of General Kummer's Division, and part of the 'Etappen' troops, were escorting prisoners on the route Boulay-Saarlouis. General Blankensee's Brigade (19th and 81st Regiments) were similarly employed on the south (Saarbrücken) route.

Other detachments of the Army were, in pursuance of higher orders, either sent, as we have heard, to Verdun, or were absent on other duties, as will be presently shown.

The remainder (about 3 brigades of the VIIIth, and 1 of the VIIth Army Corps) guarded the camps, and garrisoned the nearest stations on both lines of the prisoners' march.

The whole force of the Intendance and of the Inspection-General of 'Etappen' was necessary to fulfil the arduous task imposed upon them. The subsistence of so many prisoners trebled the daily rations, added to which, the necessary stores had to be provided for the coming march.

We have thus briefly sketched the circumstances under which the transport of the prisoners was effected, and which resulted from the preparatory arrangements made by the Head-Quarters of the Army of Investment. It will be seen that that part of the 1st Army which was intended to undertake operations in the field could not start until the central camps were entirely, and the east camps so far evacuated that the troops destined to remain at Metz would suffice to guard them.

In order to resume the thread of our narrative, we must now turn back for a few days.

A royal order of the 27th October placed the command of the 1st Army, now that it had again to act independently, in the hands of the senior Corps Commander, General Manteuffel. Our previous account will have shown what the general situation of the Army was when he entered on his command on the

30th at Jouy aux Arches. It must be added that during the first period of the operations, General Manteuffel fulfilled the duties of his previous as well as of his present command, because the troops of the 1st Army Corps had in the commencement to be detached on many very varied duties.[1]

The presence of French partisan troops in the Argonnes had become evident for some time previous from attacks made upon detached posts, and had been reported to Versailles by the Government-General of Rheims. On the 29th General Moltke telegraphed to the Commander-in-Chief of the 1st Army to the same effect, and pointed out how desirable it was that troops should soon be sent to that district. In consequence, the 33rd Regiment and 2 batteries of the VIIIth Army Corps were despatched to Fresnes, where they were to join the 3rd Cavalry Division. With a view to clearing the Argonnes of the enemy, the commander of this division, General Count Groeben, was instructed to advance with these reinforcements to the neighbourhood of Clermont, St. Ménehould, and Varennes, where he was to wait until the Army came up, and then join it.[2]

On the evening of the 31st another telegram arrived at Jouy from Versailles, ordering a division of the 1st Army Corps to start in all haste 'for the purpose, if necessary, of reinforcing the detachment in front of Mézières.' We have seen how completely all forces of the 1st Army were at that time absorbed by the transport and guarding of the prisoners, for which duty they even scarcely sufficed. The execution of this new order was, however, rendered possible by Prince Frederick Charles placing a brigade (General Diringshofen) of the Xth Corps at

---

[1] As an eye-witness of the fact, we mention here, that General Manteuffel had a fall with his horse on the 6th September, a few days after his victory at Noisseville, and fractured a bone of his foot, which had to be bandaged daily during the whole of the autumn and winter campaigns. To ease his weak foot, the General was obliged to use a walking-stick, and could not mount his horse without assistance. Nevertheless, although sixty-three years of age, he performed almost all marches on horseback, long and fatiguing as many of them were.

[2] The IXth Army Corps of the IInd Army was also charged with an expedition to the Argonne mountains.

the disposal of the Ist Army, to take charge of the camp at St. Barbe for a few days. This brigade did not return to Corny until the 5th November, and then followed the IInd Army, which, as we have heard, had already started on the 2nd. Thanks to this arrangement, the 1st Division (General Bentheim) became available; it was moved on the 2nd November to Woippy, on the left bank of the Moselle, and marched on the 3rd by way of Briey, Stenay, Le Chêne towards Réthel, where it was to arrive on the 12th, if not required to reinforce the troops at Mézières. The division was ordered to march on a broad front, so that the troops might find sufficient provisions in their village quarters. The three days' rations carried by the men were only to be touched in case of need. Requisitions were forbidden, but it was permitted to purchase provisions. These arrangements were in accordance with the instructions which at that time regulated all marching in such districts as were under German administration.

General Moltke's telegram of the 31st also stated that the Ist Army would, in addition, be charged with the continuation of the siege of Verdun. We pass over the measures taken by Head-quarters of the Army for this purpose, because they were not carried out, as Verdun had capitulated already on the 8th November.

Whilst constant care was devoted to the orderly guarding and transport of the prisoners, and to the replenishment of the exhausted store of provisions, still the main point held in view was to hasten the departure of the Army from the Moselle as much as possible. For this reason orders were issued on the 3rd November, that such troops of the Ist and VIIIth Army Corps as were released from guarding prisoners, were to be moved to the valley of the Moselle immediately.[1] The Ist

---

[1] In consequence of the relative positions of the camps, the VIIIth Army Corps was able to commence this movement sooner than the Ist; parts of the latter were detained until the 6th of November in the north camp at St. Barbe, and at the first marching station on the Boulay road.

Sieges of the Ardennes fortresses. 13

Army Corps was to take the region north of the line Plappeville—Metz; the VIIIth that south of the line St. Quentin—Metz. The town itself was, as the reader knows, garrisoned by the VIIth Army Corps.

A telegram from the King's Head-quarters, dated November 5th, ordered another brigade to be despatched on the 9th per rail to Soissons, for the purpose of besieging La Fère, for which the necessary siege-guns, with artillerymen and pioneers, were ready at Soissons. La Fère lay on the future line of march of the Ist Army Corps; General Manteuffel therefore detailed the 4th Infantry Brigade (General Zglinitzki) with 1 squadron and 1 battery of the Corps, for the expedition. The detachment was accompanied by an officer of the General Staff and also by an official of the Intendance Department, and half a provision park, in order to ensure about a week's supply of provisions. It marched first to Pont à Mousson, where it was to take the rail; we shall find it later before La Fère.

In the meantime General Zastrow, having undertaken the special direction of the transport of the prisoners, the latter progressed more regularly than during the first few days. The Governor-General of Coblenz, General Herwarth von Bittenfeld, also afforded great assistance, by providing for the relief and immediate return of the troops of the Line escorting them. Thanks to these endeavours, and to the astonishing efforts made by the troops employed on guard and escort duty, affairs at Metz now became more settled, and on the 4th General Manteuffel was able to report to Versailles, that he would on the 7th commence his march from the Moselle with the part of his army destined for operations in the field. Exclusive of the troops already sent forward, this part of the Army consisted of 3 brigades of the VIIIth, and 1 of the Ist Army Corps, with the Corps Artillery of both corps.

On the 6th the following instructions were given to General Zastrow respecting the destination and tasks of the remainder of the Army:—

'The period of my departure with the 1st and VIIIth Army Corps now approaching, I give Your Excellency the following instructions regarding the task which you will have to undertake when the troops now escorting prisoners return :

'They will be :

'1. The settlement of all matters at Metz, and the providing for the security of the district round about the town, and further to the rear ; the latter in connection with the Inspector-General of " Etappen," and on an understanding with the civil authorities installed by the Governments-General.

'2. The organisation of an Army Reserve out of such troops as do not belong to the VIIth Army Corps, which Reserve is to be sent after me as soon as possible.

'3. The taking of Thionville and Metz.

'Ad. N. 1.

'The Governor of Metz[1] will be subordinate to General Zastrow. Their relative positions will be analogous to those of the commanding general of an army corps and the governor of a fortress. The arrangement of affairs at Metz will therefore be in general the duty of the Governor. General Zastrow will, however, maintain the supreme authority there, and will fix the strength of the garrison and also that of such troops as may be necessary to organise flying columns for the security of the neighbouring district, in which case General Zastrow will place himself in communication with the Inspector-General of " Etappen." It will be the duty of the latter to provide for the security of the actual lines of communication, for which purpose the " Etappen" troops now employed in escorting prisoners will be again placed at his orders as soon as they have accomplished this duty. It cannot yet be decided whether or when the " Etappen " troops now with General Gayl's detachment (4 battalions, 2 squadrons, 1 battery) can be again placed at the

---

[1] General von Loewenfeld had been recently appointed to this post.

disposal of the Inspector-General of "Etappen," because they joined that detachment in pursuance of higher orders.[1]

'Ad. N. 2.

'The Army Reserve will be placed under command of General Schuler von Senden, and will consist of General Blankensee's Brigade (19th and 81st Regiments), the 3rd Reserve Hussar and 1st Reserve Dragoon Regiments of General Strantz's Brigade, which general will take command of the two regiments; and lastly of 3 reserve batteries of General Kummer's former division. These troops will march from Thionville and Metz and meet at Briey, upon which they will immediately follow the route of the 1st Army Corps by way of Réthel and rejoin the Army with the utmost expedition. The branches of administration of General Kummer's late division will be attached to the Reserve. As far as possible these troops will be fed in their quarters, but the Inspection-General of "Etappen" will provide the detachment with a sufficiently large and laden wagon-park, with respect to which General Schuler will communicate with the Inspection. There will then remain at General Zastrow's disposal—over and above the troops of the VIIth Army Corps, and without counting the siege-artillery companies and batteries of Captain Schulze—still 2 battalions of the 72nd Regiment; 2 Reserve Cavalry regiments, and 3 batteries of General Kummer's Division.

'Ad. N. 3.

'General Zastrow will fix the proper moment for commencing the attack on Thionville and Montmédy, and will also decide whether to attack both places at once, or first Thionville and then Montmédy, merely investing the latter slightly until the former is taken. At the same time due attention must be paid to Longwy, which must not be overlooked. General Zastrow will decide upon these questions according to the number of

---

[1] The Versailles orders of the 31st which assigned other duties to the 'Etappen' troops, had not arrived at this time.

troops available for the purpose, and will, I am sure, agree with me that it is certainly of great importance to gain possession of Thionville as soon as possible, but also that the surest way of doing so will be to commence the attack from the very beginning with forces sufficient to command success.

(Signed) 'MANTEUFFEL.'

We shall now follow the operations of the 1st Army, dividing them into four principal periods, and stating the directions which were given by His Majesty's Head-quarters for each period, upon which the operations themselves were based.[1]

---

[1] The order of battle of the 1st Army, as it was at this time, will be found in Appendix No. 1.

FIRST PERIOD.

MARCH OF THE 1ST ARMY FROM THE MOSELLE TO THE OISE.

(NOVEMBER 7TH TO NOVEMBER 23RD.)

CHAPTER I.

From Metz to Rheims.

(NOVEMBER 7TH TO NOVEMBER 15TH.)

THE march to the Oise was undertaken in pursuance of the often-mentioned instructions of the 23rd October, ordering the 1st Army to advance to the line of St. Quentin—Compiègne—immediately after the capitulation, and with a force of at least two army corps. We have already shown that the unexpectedly great number of prisoners at Metz prevented the 1st Army from starting *immediately*. This and other reasons to which we have alluded in the introduction rendered it impossible to carry out the Versailles orders *literally*.

The Commander-in-Chief, however, and his commanding generals regarded it from the beginning as their first duty to hasten the march to the utmost and to raise the effective strength of the Army of Operation to its greatest possible height. Compared with this, the sieges which were now already or which might in future be entrusted to the Army must be of secondary consideration. Following up this idea, the siege of Thionville was postponed in order to employ the whole strength of the VIIth Army Corps, in the first place, at Metz, and secondly as escort of prisoners, so as to set the Ist and VIIIth Army Corps free sooner than would have otherwise been feasible. With the same view, the reserve detachment of General Schuler von Senden was ordered to be sent after the Army as soon as possible; these two points settled, the third paragraph of the instructions we have cited above left it to General Zastrow to fix the time for commencing the siege of the fortresses. An Army order of the 5th November, giving instructions for the march of the Army, also sets forth this main idea:

'I know that since the capitulation of Metz the troops have had even more fatiguing duty than during the period of investment, and I would gladly have granted them a few days of well-earned repose. His Majesty, however, deems it important that the Army should commence its march as soon as possible. It will, in consequence, start on the 7th instant, according to the subjoined route. The march will be performed on as broad a front as the necessity for guarding against any attacks of the enemy's free corps will permit, so that the troops may be furnished with good quarters. During the march all places will be searched for arms, which, when found, are to be confiscated.[1] Although the greater part of the country we have to pass through has been already traversed by Prussian troops, and some points are permanently occupied, still attempts have been made to organise a partisan war, particularly in the Argonnes district. The security of the cantonments, the trains, etc., must be particularly attended to. No officer must forget that we are in the face of an enemy. I especially direct attention to the many cases in which single companies and squadrons have been

---

[1] Afterwards a telegram arrived from Versailles on the 8th of November, commanding the destruction of all arms found, and the trial by court-martial of all inhabitants in whose possession arms should be discovered after having been ordered to give them up. These orders were carried out in such manner that the arms were not destroyed in the presence of their owners, so as to spare their feelings. The measure had the desired effect. A quantity of arms was found in the villages and woods, and the whole tract of country between the Marne and the Ardennes railway was from that time pacified and tolerably safe.

surprised—sometimes successfully—when feeling themselves secure, because they were marching or quartered along an "Etappen" road. If, in spite of our precautions, the inhabitants should be guilty of hostile acts against the troops, either by favouring franc-tireurs or committing other excesses, the officers in command will immediately take most severe reprisals and make the "maires" and "communes" responsible.[1]

'The Commander-in-Chief will accompany the march of the advanced guard, which will always detail a battalion as guard for Head-quarters. During the march the latter will be always accompanied by a squadron, which will canton in the neighbourhood of the Commander-in-Chief's quarters. The country between the routes of the Ist and VIIIth Army Corps will be scoured by the cavalry of both corps, which will keep up the communication between both. The 3rd Cavalry Division will perform this duty hereafter, as soon as it has rejoined the Army.'

(Here follow instructions regarding the daily issue of orders and the subsistence of the troops.)

(Signed) 'MANTEUFFEL.'

The route affixed to these orders assigned to the Ist Army Corps the road already taken by the 1st Division, viz.: Briey—Damvillers—Vouziers—Réthel, and then by way of Laon towards St. Quentin; the VIIIth Army Corps was to march by Fresnes and Etain, and then, passing round Verdun, over Clermont—Rheims—Soissons to Compiègne. As soon as the 3rd Cavalry Division joined, westward of the Argonnes, it was to keep between both corps and about half a day's march ahead of them, in the direction of Ville sur Tourbe—Neufchatel—Chauny. The Army was to reach the line Réthel—Rheims, by the 16th, the line St. Quentin—Compiègne, on the 22nd. In the district about to be crossed by the Army the only opposition to be expected was, at the most, that of franc-tireurs, but none on

---

[1] Similar orders had been already given to the 1st Division when it commenced its march towards Réthel on the 2nd.

the part of regular troops; it was therefore from the very commencement of the march possible and advisable to fix the daily stations of both Army Corps up to the time of reaching the Oise. Of course there was always the possibility of its becoming necessary to make alterations, and some were made, for instance, by omitting some halts, so that Compiègne was already reached on the 20th.

If we said that no serious opposition to the march of the Army was to be expected on this side of the Oise, it must be borne in mind that almost the whole of this district was under the administration of the Government-General of Rheims, viz.: the departments Ardennes, Aisne, Marne, Seine et Marne, Aube, Seine et Oise; in the beginning also the Meuse department, which lies on both banks of the Meuse, but this department was transferred to the Government-General of Lorraine by a royal order of the 4th November. Verdun and the Ardennes were, to be sure, still in the hands of the enemy, but a corresponding display of troops had already very much diminished their power of molesting our 'Etappen' roads. When the Army left Metz the following intelligence had been received on this subject: General Gayl's detachment, then belonging to the Government-General of Rheims, had been reinforced by troops of the VIIIth Army Corps and raised to the strength of 10 battalions, 3 squadrons, and 3 field batteries; the greater part of this force was in front of Verdun, holding a region of 9 miles circumference round the fortress and reaching southwards to Dugny, northwards to beyond Charny. There were no practicable bridges over the Meuse within this region, and the water was too high to admit of fording the river. The 1st Army was therefore compelled to make a still greater circuit round the fortress. Parts of General Gayl's detachment and other troops of the Government-General were stationed as follows: 5 companies and 2 squadrons east of Stenay, watching Montmédy; one company in each of the towns of Commercy, Étain, Clermont, and Suippe; 2 battalions in Sédan; and a strong detach-

Operations of the first Army under General von Manteuffel.

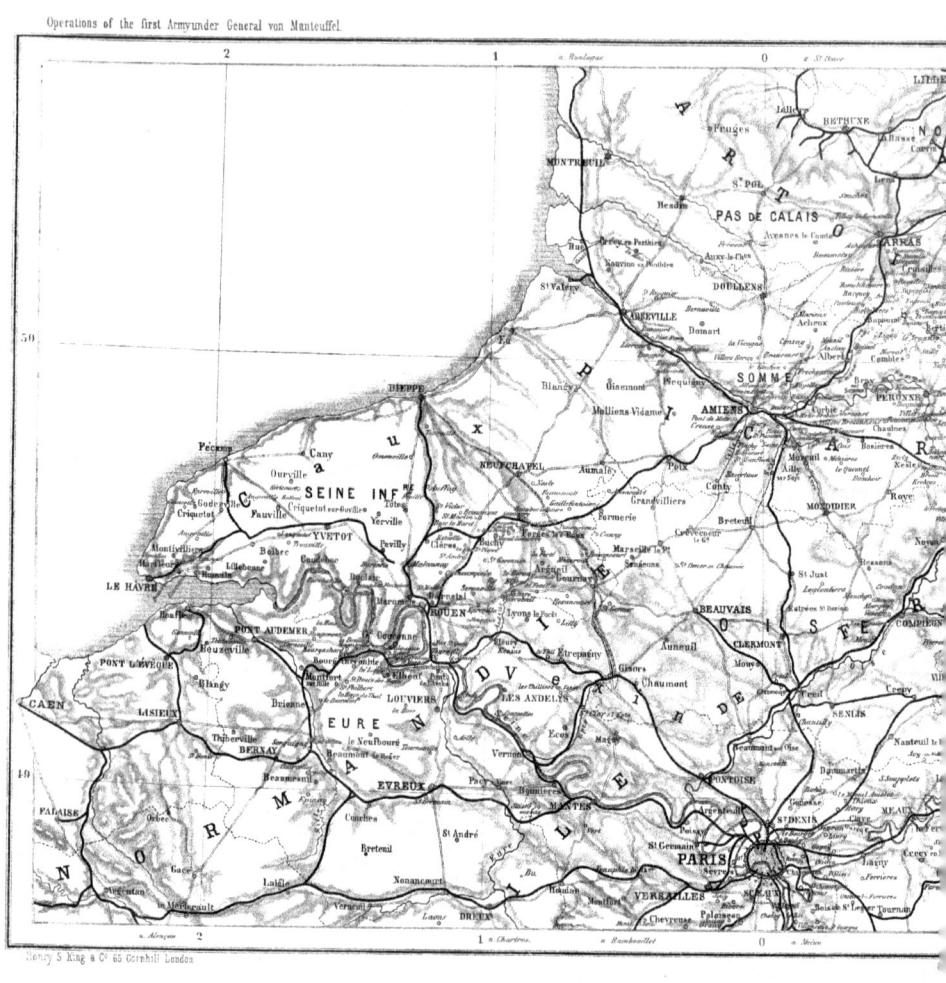

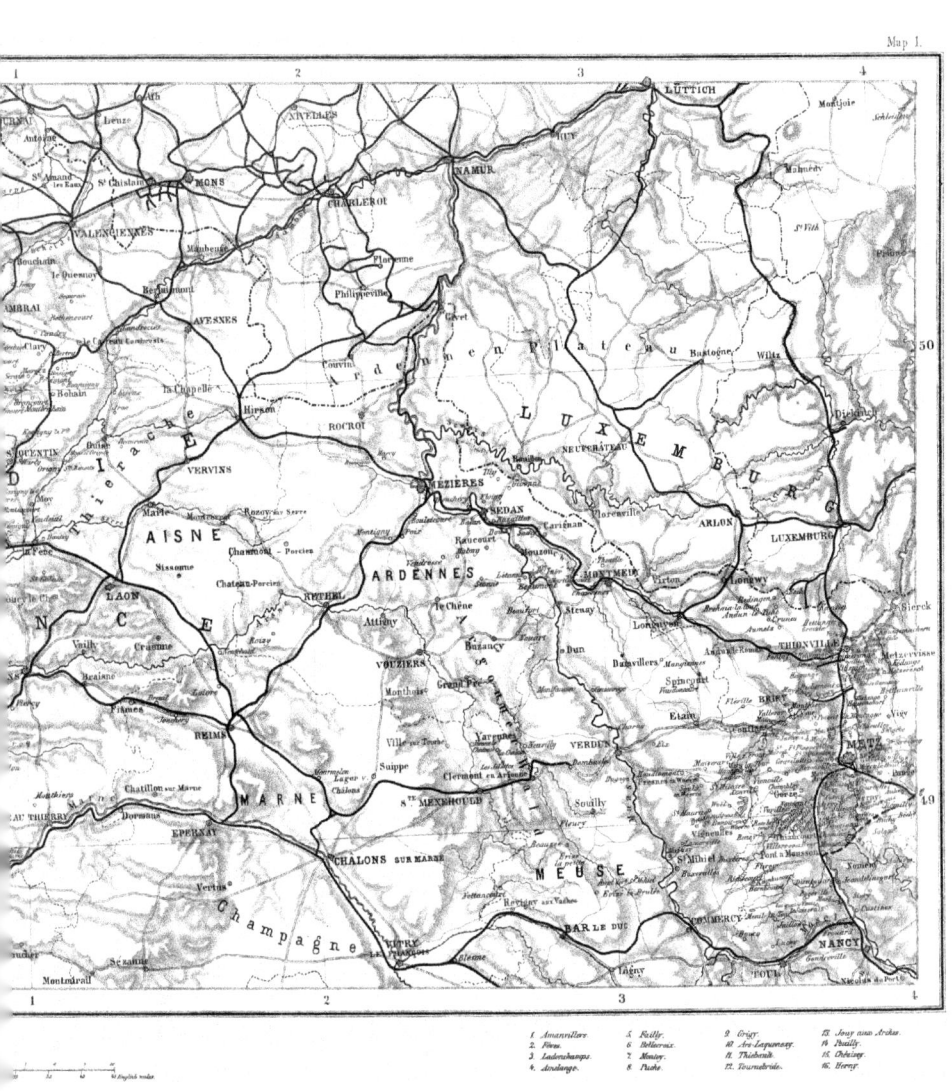

ment of the Brandenburg Landwehr Division in front of Mézières. The 3rd Cavalry Division, reinforced by infantry and artillery, had already commenced its operations in the Argonnes. Detachments of the troops of the Government-General in front of Mézières, viz.: 4 battalions, 2 squadrons, and 1 battery under Colonel Arnoldi, were also operating in the same direction by the Vouziers and Grand Pré roads.

The country *westward* of the line Réthel—Rheims, was not equally secure. Although Soissons and Laon were garrisoned by troops of the Government-General, still the detachments sent to pacify the country were repeatedly disturbed from the directions of Rocroi, Vervins, and St. Quentin. Besides this, the fortress of La Fère, then still held by the enemy, projected far southward, and barred the Rheims-Laon-Compiègne line of railway, so necessary for the supplies of the north line of investment of Paris.

Such being the circumstances, the march as far as Rheims was effected on the broadest possible front, and almost as in times of peace—except that the precautions mentioned in the orders of the 5th November were observed; but after passing this town care had to be taken to ensure the rapid concentration of the Army, as well as its constant readiness for action.

The foregoing survey of the situation will have served to render the following more intelligible:

On the 7th November the Army reached the line Conflans—Briey, on the 8th the line Étain—Vaudoncourt, in the formation and strength already stated. Head-quarters marched with the VIIIth Army Corps. The latter was accompanied by a Saxon pontoon train, which had been attached to the Xth Army Corps during the investment of Metz, and was now being escorted to its own corps. On entering Étain at midday of the 8th, the Commander-in-Chief received news of the capitulation of Verdun; General Gayl's troops were to enter the place next day. Independently of the importance otherwise attaching to this event, it was particularly welcome, for it enabled those troops of the VIIIth Army Corps that were with General Gayl's corps to rejoin the Army immediately. It also now became possible to make a change that had been projected for some time, viz.: recalling the 65th Regiment to the VIIIth Army Corps, whilst the 60th Regiment was transferred in its stead to General Gayl's detachment, with which it afterwards passed over to the troops of the Government-General of Lorraine.

This brings us to an important change of organisation, orders for which had been issued at the King's Head-quarters some time ago, but only reached Head-quarters of the 1st Army by field-post on the evening of the 8th November. This communication was dated Versailles, 31st October; the following are its principal contents:

'Now that the capitulation of Metz has set the armies in front of this fortress free to undertake operations in the field, His Majesty the King commands that, in proportion as the 1st and IInd Armies advance, so shall troops of the Line of these armies relieve the Landwehr troops now immediately in face of the enemy, the latter troops to be henceforth employed in garrison and "Etappen" duty. This involves a change in the "Etappen" and garrison troops now attached to the armies and the Governments-General. The 1st Army will undertake the duty of carrying on the sieges of Mézières and Verdun, and will therefore provide for the relief of the Landwehr troops now engaged before those places; the Army will, it is true, for a time have only 1 battalion and 1 squadron of "Etappen" troops left, but these will probably suffice to garrison the chief "Etappen" station. It may be assumed that the lines of communication to the rear of the Army will be sufficiently safe during its march through the territory already occupied by the Governments-General of Lorraine and of Rheims.

(Signed)   'MOLTKE.'

Adjoined to these orders was a summary of all 'Etappen' and garrison troops, showing how they were now to be distributed between the four armies and the three Governments-General, and according to which there were to be attached—

			Battalions	Squadrons	Batteries
To the Government-General of Rheims		. . .	17	4	3
,,	,,	Lorraine . . .	20	6	2
,,	,,	Alsace . . .	23	9	2½
,,	Inspection-General of Etappen of the 1st Army		1[1]	1	
,,	,,	,, IInd ,, .	4	2	
,,	,,	,, IIIrd ,, .	16	9	2
,,	,,	,, Meuse ,, .	4	2	

It was then laid down as a general rule that such garrison artillery and pioneer companies as were employed in a siege should be at the disposal of whatever command was in the first case entrusted with the siege, but that, this once over, they must either be employed in a fresh siege, or else again placed under the direct orders of His Majesty's Head-quarters.

In addition to these orders, which, as we have seen, were received much after date, a letter from the Governor-General of Rheims, General Rosenberg-Gruszynski, arrived at Étain on the 8th, requesting that his 'Etappen' troops, then stationed in front of Mézières, might be relieved as soon as possible, to enable him to employ them solely on garrison and 'Etappen' duty, in accordance with the new instructions from Versailles. With regard to the state of affairs at Mézières, the letter mentioned that at this moment there was a corps of observation, consisting of 5 battalions, 3 squadrons, and 1 battery, under Colonel Kettler, in front of the fortress, with head-quarters at Boulzicourt; the siege artillery now there consisted of 8 heavy mortars, and 4 garrison artillery companies; 2 garrison companies, and 36 other siege guns were on their way thither.

These accounts reached the Commander-in-Chief at Étain from Versailles and Rheims, and gave him a clear insight into the situation of affairs; they showed what by-work was now

---

[1] The greater part of the battalions numbered 1,200 men each, 5th and 6th Companies having been formed. This was the case with the St. Wendel Battalion of the 30th Landwehr Regiment, the one left with the 1st Army. The squadron was one of the 6th Reserve Hussar Regiment.

required of his army. In addition to the sieges of Thionville and Montmédy, originally entrusted to the 1st Army, the latter had to undertake those of La Fère, Verdun, and Mézières also. General Zastrow was furnished with the necessary instructions with regard to Thionville and Montmédy; the arrangements already made for besieging Verdun were rendered unnecessary by the fall of the fortress, which now had to be garrisoned by troops of the Government-General of Lorraine. This set the whole of the VIIIth Army Corps free for further operations, but, as the sieges of La Fère and Mézières still had to be undertaken, it became necessary to detail troops of the Army of Operation for this purpose, so that the lowest force—2 Army Corps—with which, according to the original order, it was to reach the Oise, could not be kept up. The 4th Brigade was already detached to La Fère. The nearest force at hand for Mézières was the 1st Division, which had been on the march from Briey towards Réthel ever since the 4th November. It had the strength which the letter from Rheims pointed out as necessary for the siege of the fortress, for it might be assumed that all that had still to be done there was to continue siege-works already in progress, and that there, as well as at La Fère, all necessary siege matériel (guns and siege-artillery companies) was available. In consequence, the 1st Division was informed of the intelligence received from Rheims, and ordered to discontinue its march upon Réthel, and proceed to Boulzicourt, where it was to relieve the troops of the Government-General, and then undertake the siege of Mézières. The pontoon-train of the 1st Army Corps was also sent there to establish communication between the besieging troops on both banks of the Meuse.

A telegram from General Groeben, dated the 7th November, arrived at Étain: his reconnaissances had proved that no organised hostile free-corps existed in the Argonnes. The telegram was followed up by a letter giving the following details: The detachment had assembled on the 2nd November at Fresnes, and marched on the 3rd as far as the Meuse, on the

4th to eastward of Clermont ; officer patrols scoured the country up to the line Grand Pré—St. Ménéhould. Resistance had nowhere been met with ; from all enquiries it seemed, on the contrary, probable that all attacks made upon our troops up to the end of October had either been the acts of a band of vagabonds that infested the country even in times of peace, or had proceeded from the garrison of Montmédy. On the 6th General Groeben had marched in three columns to Neuvilly, Les Islettes, and St. Ménéhould, from which position he had searched the Forest of La Chalade on the 7th, and found a considerable quantity of buried arms, but no signs of any hostile bands. Considering the duty entrusted to him to be fulfilled, the General awaited the arrival of the army in the Argonnes district, as he had been ordered to do.

On the 9th November, the day Verdun surrendered, the 1st Army made a circuit round the north side of the fortress, and advanced as far as the Meuse, the VIIIth Army Corps occupying the line Consenvoye—Monthairon, with Head-quarters at the former place. The 1st Army Corps advanced with the 3rd Brigade and the Corps Artillery to Damvillers and neighbourhood, the 1st Division reached Beaumont. The right flank column of the latter had a trifling engagement with a reconnoitring detachment which came out of Montmédy.

The plateau west of the Moselle across which the left wing of the Army had been hitherto marching, was in general flat and open ; the country along the Meuse which it now entered, on the 9th, was more hilly. At a short distance from the left bank of the river rise the wooded heights of the Argonnes, in several parallel ranges of hills, filling the space between the rivers Meuse and Aisne. The woods are of beech and oak, with, for the most part, dense undergrowths, and were on the 11th November sprinkled with the first fall of snow. The roads crossing the mountain country are good, and, as is everywhere the case in France, macadamised, but lead mostly through long defiles, without cross-roads. The Argonnes, therefore, form an impediment well known in military history — that is to say, supposing forces to be at hand on the plains westward of the forest, ready to fall upon the heads of the columns when they debouch from the mountainous and wooded district. There was no chance of this during the march of the 1st Army, so that the beauties of the landscape, which were perceptible even in the month of November, could be fully enjoyed. On the 10th November the VIIIth Army Corps and Army Head-quarters reached the neighbourhood of Clermont and Varennes (well known from Louis XVI.'s ill-fated flight); the 3rd Brigade and Corps Artillery of the 1st Army Corps came to Dun on the Meuse, the 1st Division to Le Chêne, where it received the orders to march to Mézières. The division set off thither on the 11th November. On the same day the VIIIth Army Corps advanced to the west outlet of the Argonnes at St. Ménéhould and Vienne le Chateau, the 3rd Brigade, &c., to Grand Pré. Army Head-quarters moved to Vienne le Chateau. On the 12th November the Army halted in this position, after five days' uninterrupted and, for most of the troops, very heavy marching. Here the 3rd Cavalry Division rejoined the Army, and from this time forward took its post between both army corps. The infantry and artillery hitherto attached to the division now returned to the VIIIth Army Corps.

Whilst the Army was thus assembling at the west debouches of the Argonnes and recruiting its strength for further operations, Head-quarters at Vienne le Chateau were principally occupied in making the necessary arrangements for the siege of Mézières, General Moltke having placed the siege matériel and gunners originally intended to be employed against Verdun at the disposal of the 1st Army for the siege of the former fortress; the greater part of this matériel was, however, still on the road from Strasburg.[1]

[1] The siege of Verdun had been conducted with very insufficient matériel; for instance, the only available guns were the very inferior ones found in the conquered French fortresses. The forces in front of the place were also in the beginning barely sufficient to hold their ground against the hostile garrison; the latter, having been

Another telegram from Rheims brought the news that the siege matériel and gunners originally intended for the siege of Mézières had been meanwhile sent to Soissons, to be employed against La Fère, and that only eight French mortars were in front of Mézières. It now, therefore, became necessary to move the siege train at Verdun, and that still on its road thither, to Mézières. This could be done, partly by means of the main line of railway viâ Commercy, and partly by the Clermont-Rheims line, but preparations for opening traffic on the latter line had only just commenced, and the main line was so much taken up by other traffic, that it could not be solely relied upon for the purpose; attention was, therefore, turned to the land transport of the siege-train, and a correspondence was commenced with the respective Governments-General, and with General Zastrow, with regard to procuring the necessary 3,000 relay horses. Part of the garrison artillery companies at Verdun were handed over to General Zastrow to meet his requirements for the siege of Thionville.

During the days which now followed, the Army crossed the wide plains of Champagne. The VIIIth Army Corps, now complete, marched on the left, the 3rd Brigade and Corps Artillery of the 1st Army Corps on the right wing, the Cavalry Division in the centre, and in this formation the Army reached the line Suippe—Vouziers, on the 13th, Mourmelon—Attignies, on the 14th, and Rheims—Réthel, on the 15th November. The 1st Division had also halted on the 12th, and marched, with the greater part of its force, on the 13th, to the rear of the cantonments occupied by the troops of the Government-General on the left bank of the Meuse, in front of Mézières; whilst doing this the 41st

considerably reinforced, among others by escaped prisoners from Sédan, made repeated sorties, and even succeeded in spiking some guns. When Metz fell, it became possible to reinforce the corps before Verdun by troops of the 1st Army, but Prussian siege-artillery and, for the moment, even artillery ammunition were still wanting. In spite of this, the commandant of the fortress accepted the conditions offered by General Gayl, probably because he considered further defence to be hopeless, now that siege-artillery might be daily expected to arrive by the Commercy road. Had the siege continued, the operating part of the 1st Army would have been momentarily weakened, but it would not have been delayed in its advance.

Regiment had a slight engagement with a sortie detachment of the enemy. The 43rd Regiment, one squadron and one battery, crossed the Meuse at Donchéry. From this position the investment was completed on the 14th, on both banks of the river, the East district being in general occupied by the 2nd, the West district by the 1st Brigade; a special duty of the latter was to hold the passages over the river Sormonne and to watch the road to Rocroy. General Bentheim established his head-quarters at Boulzicourt. The former corps of investment under Colonel Kettler's orders returned to the Government-General of Rheims on the 14th.

General Manteuffel, with his Head-quarters staff, went already on the 14th from Suippe to Rheims, in order to place himself in direct communication with the Government-General respecting further arrangements: the latter will be better understood if we return for a moment to Metz.

The transport of prisoners from there had in the meantime been completed by the 10th, with the exception of the convalescent soldiers that were still at Metz; the troops under General Zastrow were thus set free for other service. In pursuance of the directions given him on the 6th, the General reported on the 11th that General Kameke would invest Thionville with 10 battalions, 6 squadrons, and 4 batteries of the 14th Division from the 13th on, but that the actual siege would not commence until the arrival of the siege-guns expected from the home fortresses, those as yet at Metz not being sufficient for the purpose. On the 15th, the General stated, a detachment of 5 battalions, 4 squadrons, and 1 battery would arrive in front of Montmédy, for the purpose of investing this fortress and watching Longwy. About the same time the Army Reserve, under General Senden, would be assembled at Briey, and ready to start. Ten battalions, 2 squadrons, and 4 batteries of the 13th Division would then still remain as garrison at Metz.

We have already heard how far the state of affairs in front of Mézières had changed in the meantime. The siege-train originally intended for the siege of this fortress had been sent to Soissons, to be used against La Fére. The speedy arrival of the Verdun siege-train was a thing not to be counted upon, for nobody could say what the result of the promised requisitions of horses would be. It was, however, ascertained at Rheims that there was reason to expect traffic to be opened on the Clermont-Rheims line of railway by the 20th; orders were therefore given to convey the siege-train by land transport alone from Verdun to Clermont and from thence per rail over Rheims to Boulzicourt. Experience had hitherto shown that a considerable time must elapse before this could be carried out; an actual besieging of Mézières was therefore for the present out of the question. Under such circumstances, all that could be immediately done was to protect the district occupied by our troops against any attack from Mézières, Rocroy, and Givet by paralysing the injurious influence of this fortress triangle. To effect this, it was not necessary completely to invest the first-named fortress, but merely to occupy a judiciously selected position with a corps of observation. General Senden's detachment, being weaker in infantry but stronger in cavalry, was better adapted to this service than the 1st Division, besides which, it was already a matter of regret that the latter should be absent from the 1st Army Corps during the coming operations. General Zastrow's report that General Senden's detachment was ready to start reached General Manteuffel at Suippe, whereupon the latter immediately telegraphed back to despatch the last-named detachment by way of Stenay and Sédan to Boulzicourt, where it was to arrive on the 22nd and relieve the 1st Division.

In consequence of the changes in the organisation of the Governments-General and the 'Etappen' service, as ordered at Versailles, the directions given to General Zastrow had to be modified in other respects also. The following orders were therefore, among others, sent to him on the 14th November from Rheims:

'1. The security of the country and in particular of the

"Etappen" roads is now entirely the business of the Governments-General, for which purpose the "Etappen" troops will be handed over to the latter as soon as they return from the transport of the prisoners.

'2. The detachment under General Schuler von Senden, hitherto intended to form the Army Reserve, is hereby placed under your Excellency's orders for the purpose of first investing and then besieging Mézières; I have yesterday already telegraphed orders for its march from Briey to Boulzicourt.

'3. In addition to the sieges of Thionville and Montmédy, I commission your Excellency to undertake that of Mézières also, bearing in mind the following considerations:—

'Your Excellency will first besiege Thionville and invest Montmédy, commencing operations against each place on the 20th and 15th of this month respectively, according to your yesterday's telegram. As soon as Thionville is taken and the siege-corps now there set free, the attack on Montmédy and Mézières will commence, unless, indeed, the situation of Montmédy should forbid a regular siege and make it preferable to starve the place out. At all events, when Thionville falls you will, inclusive of General Senden's troops, have a sufficient force to besiege both places at the same time, for it will then become the duty of the Government-General of Alsace to garrison the place, or else the two battalions of the 72nd Regiment[1] can be employed for this purpose. The siege-matériel and gunners already at your Excellency's disposal will suffice for Thionville.

'As affairs at Thionville and Montmédy for the moment more especially concern your Excellency, I shall myself make the necessary arrangements for conveying the siege-park from Verdun to the neighbourhood of Mézières. Even according to the most favourable calculation, three weeks will elapse before

[1] The 72nd Regiment belonged originally to the VIIIth Army Corps, but changed places with the 70th Regiment, and was at the first sent to Saarlouis. Its battalions were afterwards brought up singly from thence, and were for the greater part stationed in front of Thionville when Metz capitulated.

it can commence action there. Your Excellency will therefore instruct General Senden to carry out the investment of the fortress in the interim, with due regard to the number of his troops and the security of the siege-train as it arrives by degrees. The heavy pontoon-train of the 1st Army Corps will remain at Mézières at General Senden's disposal.

       (Signed)   'MANTEUFFEL.'

The view Army Head-quarters took of the state of affairs at Mézières, to which we have alluded above, is expressed in the following instructions, addressed in the first instance to General Bentheim, for the troops in front of Mézières during the period previous to the commencement of the siege of this fortress; they were dated Rheims the 15th November :

'The siege of the fortress of Mézières must not be commenced until means sufficient to ensure success have arrived and can be brought to bear upon it. *Until this is the case I forbid any half-measures, such as bombarding the town and the like, which only cause loss of life and destruction of property, without obtaining any military result.*

'Previously to the commencement of the siege, the corps in front of Mézières has a twofold duty to perform :

'1. To secure the right flank of the Army of Operation and its communications to the rear, within the sphere of the Government-General of Rheims, against any undertakings of the enemy proceeding from the fortress-triangle, Mézières—Givet—Rocroy.

'2. To protect the siege-park and other matériel as it successively arrives.

'Momentary circumstances and the features of the country will determine the details of the position to be taken up, but the future point of attack must be fixed at once, so as to be able to employ the interval in making all kinds of preparation—perhaps also in establishing the siege-park and the batteries, if this should be compatible with the present position of the detachment. I remark in this respect that of course the point which promises the most speedy success is the one to be selected, but that the choice of the south or east front of the fortress would be desirable, because the general military position would make it easier to base the Siege-Corps and protect the parks there than elsewhere.

'The position to be taken up *previous* to the commencement of the siege will be selected solely with reference to the two above-mentioned considerations, but not with a view to reducing the place by hunger; it will therefore not be necessary to extend the line of investment farther than the available force permits. All I expect is, investment on the south and observation on the north side towards Rocroy and Givet; expeditions may be undertaken in the latter direction, providing the main object be kept in view.

'The commander of the troops in front of Mézières will hand these instructions over to his successor if a change takes place in the command.

(Signed) 'MANTEUFFEL.'

These general instructions regarding the course of action to be followed against the Ardennes fortresses were deemed all the more necessary, because all possibility of Army Head-quarters exerting any direct influence on the conduct of the sieges must naturally cease by degrees, as the distance increased. These sieges were in fact conducted for the most part independently under the special direction of General Kameke. We shall, however, relate the events connected with them so far as they concerned the operations in the field, and are referred to in the different instructions and reports which continually passed to and fro.

With regard, lastly, to La Fère, a rumour had been promulgated that the place would capitulate. A detachment composed of troops of the Government-General of Rheims was despatched from Laon on the 13th November under Colonel Kahlden to reconnoitre the place, but found it garrisoned by 2,000 men, and armed with a numerous artillery. The recently appointed commander, Captain Planche of the Navy, showed himself determined to defend it. Interruptions in the railway traffic had delayed the transport of the 4th Brigade from Pont à Mousson, but on the 13th General Zglinitzki reported from Soissons that he would be in front of La Fère by the 15th. The siege-train, numbering 26 heavy guns, was to be brought up from Soissons by the 18th. We may add here already that La Fère was invested on both banks of the Oise on the 15th and 16th, in the face of a severe but harmless fire from the fortress, the 4th Brigade occupying in particular the villages of Charmes, Danizy, Travecy, Quessy and Fargniers. On the other hand, the arrival of the siege-train was delayed because the requisitioning of horses prescribed by the Government-General of Rheims was carried out very negligently.

On the 15th November, instructions from Versailles, dated the 9th November, arrived at Rheims, regulating the use of such lines of railway as were open as follows :

‘ *The* 1st *Army* will keep those it has hitherto used which run together at Saarbrücken and then continue to Metz, Frouard, Epernay, Rheims.

‘ *The Army of the Meuse* will also keep its present lines to Saarbrücken and from thence the above-mentioned lines in common with the 1st Army by way of Soissons to Paris.

‘ *The* IInd *Army* will alter its lines of communication so that they all converge to Neustadt and Weissenburg and then follow the lines Nancy—Frouard—Blesme—Chaumont and Nancy—Neufchateau — Chaumont. The traffic between Nancy and Neufchateau will be effected by means of land-transport.

‘ *The* IIIrd *Army* will keep its present lines, all traffic of the North-German Corps converging at Weissenburg, whilst that of the South German Corps will be conducted solely on the Kehl—Strassburg line as soon as this is opened, which may be expected very shortly.

‘ As all lines from Frouard run together on a tract which is under the direction of the Railway Commission at Nancy, the latter has been instructed to regulate and forward all trains laden with supplies for the army according to the following scale which corresponds to the strength of each army.

> For the Ist Army 3,
> ,, Army of the Meuse 3,
> ,, IInd Army 4,
> ,, IIIrd ,, $\begin{cases} 4 \text{ from Weissenburg,} \\ 2 \text{ ,, Kehl.} \end{cases}$

'These figures do not represent the number of trains to be sent forward daily, but give the ratio which must be adhered to as the average, not of the *daily* traffic but of that of a longer period, it is intended that additional assistance shall be given and a fair balance established by the Intendant-General of the Army when necessary.

(Signed) 'MOLTKE.'

This held forth a sure prospect to the Ist Army of being able to use, at least partially, the great main-line of railway for its supplies. Army Head-Quarters therefore determined to keep in addition to this line, only the south 'Etappen' line, Metz—Verdun—Rheims as its basis, and to give up the north line Grand Pré—Réthel. This lightened the task of guarding the 'Etappen' lines, the duty of the Government-General of Rheims; the latter was therefore informed of it and also of the measures taken with regard to Mézières.

Thus on the 15th November, the different parts of the Ist Army were in the following positions:

a. Troops under command of General Zastrow.

13th Division for the most part in Metz.

14th ,, ,, ,, before Thionville.

A detachment of both divisions (5 battalions, 4 squadrons, and 1 battery under Colonel Pannewitz) in front of Montmédy, 1 battalion and 2 squadrons of this detachment were at Longuion watching Longwy.

From Metz to Rheims. 35

General Schuler von Senden's Corps at Briey, with orders to relieve the 1st Division in front of Mézières.

b. The actual Army of Operation under General Manteuffel.

VIIIth Army Corps round about Rheims.

3rd Brigade and Corps Artillery of the 1st Army Corps at Réthel.

c. Detached troops.

4th Brigade in front of La Fère.

1st Division   ,,   Mézières.

As soon as it had wound up its affairs at Metz, the Inspection-General of 'Etappen' followed Head-Quarters to Rheims, where it remained for the present, in order to regulate the supplies of the Army, which had received a new basis in consequence of the recently published instructions respecting the use of the railways.

CHAPTER II.

From Rheims to Compiègne—The Army forms line on the Oise.

(NOVEMBER 16TH TO NOVEMBER 23RD.)

ON the 16th a day's halt was granted to the troops that had already reached the line Rheims—Réthel. Before the march of the army was continued, the following circumstances had to be duly considered :

We have already remarked in the preceding chapter that it would be necessary to keep the army in a greater state of readiness for action as soon as it entered the tract of country westward of Rheims and Réthel, where the sphere of influence of the Government-General of Rheims ceased at Laon and Soissons, the two extreme points garrisoned by its troops. It was therefore determined, with a view to shortening the breadth of front on which the army was to form along the Oise by one-half, not to extend the right as far as St. Quentin, but only to Guiscard, for so long as the 1st Division might still be absent. With regard to the hostile forces in these parts, information had been received that a north army was being organised under Bourbaki at Lille, with the intention, it was said, of relieving Mézières. Another army was said to be forming at Rouen under General Briand, for the purpose of advancing against the west front of the investment of Paris. Later accounts which came in up to the 15th November, spoke of troops assembling at Amiens, and gave the number of the forces in this neighbourhood as 25,000, of those at Rouen as 27,000, and those at Lille as 33,000.

The Army reaches the Oise. 37

We refrain from explaining more fully the conclusions which Head-Quarters of the Ist Army drew in the first instance from the foregoing considerations; they are expressed in the orders issued on the 16th, and in the instructions given to the 3rd Cavalry Division on the 18th November.

The orders of the 16th were as follows:

'The army will resume its advance to-morrow, and march daily for the next five days. The route already given to the VIIIth Army Corps will remain unchanged, the corps will therefore reach the neighbourhood of Compiègne on the 21st, and then push forward advanced guards on the roads to Montdidier and Beauvais.

'The 3rd Cavalry Division will march on the 19th to the neighbourhood of Coucy, on the 20th to the district between Villequier—Aumont and Guiscard, so as to place itself on the right flank of the army, which it is to cover until further orders. To effect this, it will be reinforced by the 8th Rifle Battalion, and a Horse Artillery Battery of the VIIIth Army Corps, both of which must join the division at Coucy by the latest. As soon as the Ist Rifle Battalion reaches Guiscard, it will also join the Cavalry Division. It will be the duty of the latter, after the 21st, to push reconnoissances from Guiscard in the directions of St. Quentin, Arras, and Amiens; not only for the purpose of covering the flank of the army, but also in order to obtain as accurate intelligence as possible regarding the strength, movements, and position of the French Army of the North, the bulk of which, according to the last accounts, is supposed to be between Lille and Rouen. Reports hereon are to be sent, not only to the commander of the cavalry division, but also straight to my head-quarters.

'Up to the 19th the 2nd Infantry Division will keep the route previously fixed for it, but will march on the 20th to St. Gabain (making a circuit south of the fortress of La Fère, now being besieged by the 4th Brigade), on the 21st to the region on this side of Noyon. On the 22nd an advanced guard will be pushed forward beyond Noyon, in the direction of Amiens.' (Here follow instructions fixing the boundaries between the districts to be occupied by each of the main sections of the army.)

'When the army has passed beyond the line Soissons—Laon, it will enter a region which has as yet been scarcely touched by our troops, I therefore recommend greater caution during the march, and increased watchfulness on the part of the outposts; at the same time, however, every possible care must be taken to spare the troops, and to avoid over-fatiguing them by unnecessary concentrations, or too crowded cantonments. Generals commanding army corps, and officers in command of troops, will arrange these matters according to their own judgment, each in his own respective district.

'It is important that generals commanding divisions and independent detachments keep up continual connection with each other, and communicate every occurrence and intelligence of importance, not only to their superior authorities, but also to each other. My previous orders respecting the disarmament of the country remain in force.

(Signed) 'MANTEUFFEL.'

In addition to the above, the 1st Division was ordered to send the 1st Rifle Battalion, immediately after receiving these orders, in six marches, by way of Laon to Guiscard, there to join the cavalry division. As soon as the 1st Division itself should have been relieved by General Senden, it was instructed to march on the 23rd over Marle to St. Quentin, and to reach the latter point on the 29th. So late an arrival of the 1st Division would, however, have hampered the operations; attention was, therefore, now already turned to the possibility of bringing it up from Boulzicourt by rail, over Rheims and Laon.

With the exception of the Rifle Battalion which marched, and the pontoon-train, which was left with General Senden, this railway transport was really effected. It is true, the six daily trains originally promised by the railway administration were reduced to four, and the whole division did not come into line until several days after the time originally fixed, but nevertheless its last detachments came up with the army sooner than its foremost troops would have done had they marched. Having thus briefly anticipated events, we shall presently see how important it was that the leading troops of the division were able to take part in the Battle of Amiens. They formed in some degree an equivalent for the absent 4th Brigade, which the want of teams for the conveyance of the siege-park in Soissons had so much delayed that it could not commence the siege of La Fère before the 25th.

The duties allotted to the cavalry by the orders of the 16th November were set forth more in detail in special instructions sent to General Groeben on the 18th, from Braisne, specifying them as:

' 1. The procuring of reliable information regarding position, strength, and movements of the enemy's troops in the northwest of France, so as to afford the Commander-in-Chief a sure basis on which to found further operations. It is important that the cavalry division push far on ahead of the army, screening its movements, and obtaining this information as soon as possible, because the army being still in the act of coming into line, it can yet be moved in any direction, according to the substance of the information received.

' 2. To hold the enemy's country in subjection by a display of troops, and by periodically occupying the more important points.

' 3. To deceive the enemy by showing flying columns of mixed arms in different parts.

' The simultaneous attainment of all three objects will not be effected by merely detaching small reconnoitring parties or officer patrols, even though they be pushed very far forwards. On the contrary, it will be necessary for this purpose to send out so-called flying columns possessing in themselves a certain degree of offensive and defensive strength. Riflemen will therefore decidedly be a necessary element in this formation ; and if the men are put on carts they will be able to follow the movements of the cavalry even on long marches, and will cover its retreat by occupying the defiles. Such columns can be accompanied by a few guns, which will materially assist in the cases 2 and 3. Flying columns pushed forward a day's march or more a-head of the main body of the division, in the directions of St. Quentin, Arras, Amiens and Montdidier, will, in their totality, represent a foremost échelon of the division, from which smaller reconnoitring parties and patrols are thrown forward. The latter will then be enabled to push all the further forwards and gain all the better information from having the flying columns to fall back upon.

'Immediately before and after the commencement of the campaign, the cavalry division gained great credit for the good intelligence respecting the enemy brought in by small officers' patrols; now, however, the case is different. At that time strength, organisation, and position of the enemy were in the main known, his outpost duty was deficient, the population still quiet. We may be perhaps now in face of a less important enemy, but of one whose organisation is new, and, therefore, for the most part unknown to us, and whom experience will have taught to rival us in vigilance. We are, at the same time, in a country in the act of rising up in arms, where we must expect to find the peasant one moment standing with folded arms before us, and the next changing to a franc-tireur behind us. The measure of detaching single officers and troopers miles distant, so advisable it is when judiciously employed, must in such a country be accompanied by particular precautions, in order not to risk them in vain.

'It has, it is true, lately happened that whole companies and squadrons even have been surprised and carried off, for instance, the "Etappen" stations at Stenay and other places; but in this respect also circumstances are now different. In order to plan, arrange, and execute a surprise, some time is required. Fixed posts, like "Etappen" stations, that have, as it were, settled down in their quarters, and probably do not perhaps keep up the necessary degree of watchfulness for weeks running, are more exposed to such surprises. These are much more difficult to put in practice against flying columns, that only remain for one night at the same place.

(Signed) 'MANTEUFFEL.'

Advancing on both banks of the Aisne, the army was between Breuil and Chateau Porcien (Head-Quarters Jonchéry) on the 17th, between Braisne and Sissonne on the 18th, and reached the following positions on the 19th : VIIIth Army Corps Soissons and neighbourhood, 3rd Brigade and corps artillery round about Laon. The cavalry division marched to Coucy, where it was joined by the 8th Rifle Battalion and a horse-artillery battery of the VIIIth Army Corps. Head-Quarters moved to Soissons. A telegram from General Zastrow arrived here with the news that the investment of Montmédy was effected, and that the 74th Regiment had had two successful encounters with the garrison of the fortress at Chausancy and Thonelle, in which the enemy had lost about 50 prisoners.

On the 19th the cavalry pushed forward 4 officer patrols beyond the Oise, 2 strong ones of 60 horses each over Compiègne and Noyon, and 2 smaller ones in the directions of Guiscard and Ham. The whole tract of country north of the line La Fère—Roye, was found free of the enemy as far as the latter place, but patrols that advanced still farther northwards, were fired at in Ham and in the village of Cugny, some 4½ miles further south, partly by men out of uniform. The presence of the enemy was further proved by an advance of about 6 companies and 4 guns from the direction of Ham against the west-front of the investment of La Fère, almost simultaneously with which a sortie was attempted from the fortress. General Zglinitzki repulsed both attacks with considerable loss to the enemy, capturing a number of prisoners and an ammunition-wagon. A series of slight engagements had also taken place in front of Mézières during the last few days, all of which ended in our favour, and with but trifling loss to us.

On the 20th November the 3rd Brigade marched from Laon to the neighbourhood of St. Gobain; the bulk of the VIIIth Army Corps was round Attichy, its advanced guards already occupied Compiègne to-day. The cavalry division marched upon Guiscard, and pushed forward flying columns to the north and west, which scoured the country about as far as St. Quentin, Ham, Nesle, and Roye. At Ham alone the presence of hostile 'Gardes Mobiles' was ascertained; nothing else was seen of the enemy.

In order to make clear the momentary state of affairs, and the measures that were in consequence taken preparatory to forming the army on the line of the Oise, we must turn back for one day. In the course of the 19th, when at Soissons, Army Head-Quarters received instructions from Versailles, respecting the coming task of the army; they were dated on the 18th, and contained the following:

'The command of the army is hereby informed that His Majesty the King, approving of the operations hitherto carried out, has pleased to command that the 1st Army continue its advance from the line Compiègne—Noyon, in the direction of Rouen. Whether or not, in so doing, the main forces of the army follow the Amiens road, will depend whether the considerable forces of the enemy, said to be assembling in that neighbourhood, remain there, or, as is most likely, retreat on the advance of the 1st Army. At all events Amiens is of itself sufficiently important a place to justify its being occupied, and held by a strong detachment in either case.

(Signed) 'MOLTKE.'

We have already seen that the army had up to this time advanced with such expedition that the broad expanse of country lying between the Moselle and the Oise (157½ miles, as the crow flies) had been crossed within a space of fourteen days. The general state of affairs had rendered this necessary, in order that the army might as speedily as possible take up a position from which it could effectively operate against any advance which the enemy might make upon the north line of the investment of Paris. Having reached the Oise, and gained possession of the passages over this river, the army was now in every way in a position to fulfil this defensive duty, and could even pursue offensive objects, as was proposed by the instructions of the 18th. However, as the attitude of the enemy did not demand immediate action on the part of the 1st Army, it was deemed not only advisable but also necessary to grant the troops a brief repose, for three reasons; firstly to refit after the fatiguing marches which had followed immediately upon the blockade- and guard-service at Metz,[1] secondly in order to be able to bring up as many of the absent detachments as possible for the approaching operations, and lastly, and chiefly, in order that the reconnaissances made by the cavalry division in the meantime might afford a sure guide to the next steps to be taken; Rouen being pointed out in the instructions as the main object in view, it was necessary that the detachment which made the detour over Amiens should be of sufficient strength to ensure the capture of this important place also.

It was in consideration of these circumstances that the following orders were issued at Attichy on the 30th:

'In the course of the next few days the army will close up on the line of the Oise, and will, if circumstances do not necessitate an earlier start, probably not resume its advance before the 24th. In continuation of my orders of the 16th, I desire that the interval be employed as follows:

'The VIIIth Army Corps having occupied Compiègne with an advanced guard to-day, will move its main body to the right

---

[1] Among many other things, we would remind our readers of the repair of the foot-clothing, which is so important and so necessary from time to time.

bank of the Oise to-morrow. The cavalry division, which has orders to advance to Guiscard to-day, will reconnoitre the country in front of the right wing, and on the right flank of the army by pushing columns far forwards. As a corresponding measure, the 1st Army Corps will take possession of the passages over the Oise at Noyon to-morrow. The transport of the 1st Division from Boulzicourt to Laon has commenced to-day, its leading troops will reach the latter place to-day; orders have been given to the division to march by échelons to Noyon, stopping on the road at Coucy for a night. The 1st Army Corps will then, according as it arrives, be distributed in the district north of the line Bessous—Blérancourt, extending its quarters as far to the right as necessary. As soon as the 1st Army Corps has taken up its quarters, the cavalry division will move its main body forwards into the triangle Roye—Nesle—Ham, and will above all things ascertain whether any considerable force of the enemy is at Amiens.

'The Saxon pontoon-train,[2] hitherto accompanying the VIIIth Army Corps, will be sent to Coucy, and be attached to the 1st Army Corps.

'Increased vigilance will be necessary on the part of the outposts as soon as the troops take up quarters on the right bank of the Oise. As long as no large bodies of hostile troops are proved to be in the neighbourhood, a continuous line of outposts will not be necessary, but a very lively system of patrols must be kept up on the roads leading towards Lille, Amiens, and Rouen, besides which, each separate cantonment will be answerable for its own security.

(Signed) 'MANTEUFFEL.'

In pursuance of these orders, the VIIIth Army Corps took up its quarters on both banks of the Oise, round about Compiègne on the 21st November; the leading troops of the 1st Army

---

[2] It had at this moment reached Soissons under escort of a battalion of the 28th Regiment.

Corps reached Noyon; the foremost échelon of the 1st Division (1st Regiment) had arrived at Laon the day before; General Groeben advanced from Guiscard to Ham, with a detachment of the cavalry division, and took possession of the town and of the old fortified castle without meeting any opposition. The enemy, 1,500 men and 2 guns, was said to have left per rail for Amiens the night before. The cavalry division then established the bulk of its forces at Guiscard, and further westwards in the direction of Nesle. Detachments, each composed of 1 company, a few squadrons, and 2 guns, were stationed at Ham and Roye, from whence they reconnoitred in the directions of St. Quentin, Péronne, Amiens, and Bréteuil.

On the 21st Army Head-Quarters moved from Attichy to Compiègne, where they were established in the Imperial Palace, in company with Head-Quarters of the VIIIth Army Corps.

The country between the Aisne and the Oise is covered for many miles by the dense forest of Compiègne, which is bounded on the east by the valley of Pierrefonds, with the spa of the same name, and an imperial castle, perched on a high rocky ledge, and rebuilt after the plan of a castle destroyed in the time of Richelieu. Between this remarkably picturesque spot and Compiègne reigns the deep solitude of the dark forest. This wood is intersected by broad avenues which cross a central hill, from the summit of which any one looking westwards beholds the imperial palace of Compiègne at his feet, and beyond it, on the other bank of the Oise, the ancient county of Picardy.

When the 1st Army reached Compiègne, it came in the immediate neighbourhood of the sphere of observation of the Army of the Meuse. The latter had already sent the following information to Attichy. The body of troops immediately adjoining the 1st Army was the Saxon Cavalry Division (General Count Lippe), with 3 battalions of infantry and 2 batteries; it was stationed at Chantilly, and had pushed forward strong detachments to Creil, Mouy, Beauvais, and Clermont; the division patrolled in the directions of Bréteuil and Montdidier, and kept up communication with the Guard Cavalry Brigade of Prince Albrecht junior, at Gisors on the Epte. The latter brigade, also reinforced by 3 battalions and 2 batteries, fronted towards Rouen. The last intelligence sent in from Beauvais spoke of the intention on the part of the enemy to advance eastwards from Rouen.

In answer to this communication the Commander-in-Chief of the Army of the Meuse was informed of the next steps the 1st Army intended to take, in accordance with the points of view stated above. At the same time, the co-operation of the detachments at Beauvais and Clermont was requested, as cover to the left flank of the 1st Army when it resumed its advance.

On the 22nd and 23rd November the army continued to take up its positions along the Oise in the intended manner. The VIIIth Army Corps moved its whole force, with the exception of the trains, to the right bank of the river on the 22nd, and took up quarters *à cheval* of the roads to Montdidier and Clermont, opening communication with the detachment of the Army of the Meuse in the latter direction. The 15th Division was on the right, the 16th on the left wing of the corps.

The 3rd Brigade and the corps artillery of the 1st Army Corps had reached its quarters on both banks of the Oise, in and round about Noyon, on the 22nd. On the 23rd the two foremost échelons of the 1st Division (1st Regiment, 1 battalion of the 43rd Regiment, 1 squadron, 1 battery, and a sanitary detachment), arrived from Laon. The corps artillery and the battalion of the 43rd Regiment remained on the left bank of the Oise, all other troops were moved to the right bank, the 3rd Brigade westward, the 1st Regiment eastward, of the Noyon— Guiscard, road.

Under the present circumstances General Manteuffel now handed over the command of the 1st Army Corps to General Bentheim, who had arrived at Laon on the 22nd.

On the 22nd and 23rd the following intelligence reached Compiègne from the different detachments of the army :

The Army reaches the Oise. 47

General Zglinitzki reported the arrival of part of the siege-train on the 23rd, and his intention to commence the bombardment of La Fère early on the 25th. General Zastrow telegraphed on the 22nd that 76 heavy guns had opened fire on Thionville. The enemy had returned the fire vigorously at first, but afterwards only feebly; fires were burning in the town since 3 P. M. Lastly, on the 22nd, General Senden reported the arrival of his detachment in front of Mézières.

We have already heard that the principal object of these detachments was to open the lines of railway commanded by the enemy's fortresses, especially the important Ardennes line, making them available for the supplies of the German armies. Submitting willingly to these higher considerations, still the commander-in-chief's constant aim was to confine this detaching of troops, as regarded time and numbers, within the absolutely necessary limits. The task now before the 1st Army held forth the prospect of many a serious struggle, for which the greatest possible co-operation of all forces was desirable. The opinion resulting from these considerations is expressed in the following letter, written by General Manteuffel to General Zastrow, on the 23rd November from Compiègne:

'The summary of our past operations sent to your Excellency yesterday will have shown that it is my intention that General Senden's detachment shall rejoin the army later, I request your Excellency also to turn your attention now already to this eventuality. I have ordered the division to establish itself in front of Mézières, and have placed it under your Excellency's command, in order that it may check any attempts which the enemy may make from his fortress-triangle, Mézières—Rocroy—Givet, to operate against our right flank during the period which will elapse before the siege of the first-named fortress can commence. In consideration of the small force of infantry at General Senden's disposal, and with the intention of simplifying his task at Mézières, I have given orders that the siege-train intended to be used against this fortress shall for the present only be conveyed from Verdun to Clermont, and not proceed to Boulzicourt until sufficient troops are assembled there to conduct the siege and protect the train.

'Your Excellency will fix the proper time for this last transport, and will give the necessary orders. It will probably not be feasible until Thionville falls. A division of the VIIth Army Corps will then become available for the siege of Mézières, because, according to the instructions of the 31st of last month, the Government-General of Alsace will then have to furnish the garrison of Thionville. In like manner the garrison of Montmédy will eventually have to be provided by the Government-General of Loraine. The garrison of Metz must, it is true, be given by the 1st Army, but I leave it to your Excellency's judgment whether it be not possible to induce the Government-General of Alsace to join in this duty. This would be decidedly advantageous to the Army.

'It has been necessary to detach troops during our past operations, and will still be so during those before us; I therefore request your Excellency continually to bear in mind that it will be desirable gradually to push forward all troops in rear of the army whenever circumstances permit it, and to make your dispositions accordingly. For this reason your Excellency will most particularly endeavour to place General Senden's division at my disposal as soon as possible.

(Signed)   'MANTEUFFEL.'

Such was, in the main, the situation of affairs when the campaign in Picardy commenced.

The effective strength of the 1st Army according to the states on the 21st November, was as follows:

	Infantry	Cavalry	Guns
1st Army Corps (including the troops in front of Mézières and La Fère)	19,148	1,084	84
VIIIth Army Corps	19,096	1,139	90
3rd Cavalry Division (not counting the troops attached to it)	—	2,210	6
Total	38,244	4,433	180

SECOND PERIOD.

OPERATIONS IN PICARDY AND NORMANDY UP TO THE TAKING OF ROUEN.

(NOVEMBER 24TH TO DECEMBER 6TH.)

CHAPTER III.

Advance upon Amiens—Reconnoitring Actions at Quesnel and Mézières— Advanced Guard Action at the Luce—Capitulation of Thionville.

(NOVEMBER 24TH TO NOVEMBER 26TH.)

THE general plan on which the operations during this period were based was laid down in the Versailles instructions of the 18th November, ordering the 1st Army to take both Rouen and Amiens, but it was left to the independent judgment of the commander-in-chief to decide whether it would be necessary to make the detour over the latter town with the bulk of the army, or whether a detachment would suffice to take possession of it. The position the army had taken up on the Oise—with its left wing extending beyond the direct road from Compiègne to Rouen—was one still adapted to *either measure.* The final decision on these points was to depend on what reports the cavalry might send in, General Groeben having advanced to Roye on the 23rd with the main body of his force, and pushed a mixed detachment further forward to Quesnel. The reconnaissances made on the 22nd had produced the following results: In one direction St. Quentin, in the other Bréteuil, had been reached without encountering resistance, small bodies of francs-tireurs only had been seen, and had fired at the patrols in the villages near Montdidier. Péronne was said to be garrisoned by 1,000 to 1,500 men. A squadron of the 14th Lancers, advancing on the road to Amiens, got as far as Beaucourt (almost half-way between Roye and Amiens), and pushed a patrol still farther on, beyond Domart up to the wood of Gentelles (6¾ miles from Amiens), bringing back the information that all statements of the inhabitants agreed as to Amiens and neighbourhood being occupied by 17,000 men of all arms. Bourbaki—respecting whose dismissal or non-dismissal from his command in the North contradictory reports were rife—was said to be there in person. In the main, these statements confirmed the earlier intelligence received regarding the organisation of considerable hostile forces, and, combined with the enemy's retreat from Ham towards Amiens, and with the eastward movement of the troops from Rouen, reported by the Army of the Meuse, made it appear probable that the advance of the 1st Army had induced the enemy to attempt to concentrate his main forces, hitherto at Lille, Amiens, and Rouen, on the centre of his line. To effect this, the enemy had command of the main line of railway connecting these three towns, to the protection of which line, especially of the tract between Rouen and Amiens, he had always devoted great attention. The hostile troops that had often been observed at Formerie[1] had evidently been stationed there for this purpose. These purely military reasons would in themselves have advocated a speedy march upon Amiens, in order to break through the centre of the enemy's forces supposed to be assembling there, and were still further supported by political reasons also, which influence more or less the decision

---

[1] The commander of the Saxon detachment at Clermont, General Krug, reported on the 23rd that Marseille, Grandvillers, and Formerie were occupied in force, Gournay but slightly; whereas on the 21st Prince Albrecht's Brigade had advanced as far as Andelys, and up to the line of the Andelle, without meeting any forces worth mentioning. A rumour communicated both by General Groeben and by the detachment at Clermont, to the effect that the enemy did not intend seriously to defend Amiens, but would fall back to Lille, was considered far less probable.

of generals operating independently. It had, namely, to be taken into consideration that the necessity of evacuating Orleans had decidedly raised the self-confidence of the French. A fortnight had elapsed since that event occurred without any decisive blow having been struck by the Germans. To judge from the remarks of the press, this seemed not to have been without influence on the state of feeling of the neutral powers; their future attitude might depend on the despatches sent by Mr. Odo Russell, who had just then arrived at Versailles.

The result of all these military and political considerations was the decision, formed on the afternoon of the 23rd, to march on Amiens *without* waiting until all the troops had reached the Oise. It is true General Manteuffel hoped to be able during his advance to bring up the still absent parts of the 1st Army Corps by degrees, so as to have them at hand when the expected general action ensued. The advance of the army was at the same time intended to afford the necessary support to the far-reaching reconnaissances of the cavalry division.

On the 23rd the commander-in-chief issued the following orders:

'The army will resume its march as follows: The VIIIth Army Corps will march to the line Ressons–Léglentière to-morrow, and will reach Montdidier and neighbourhood with the bulk of the corps on the 25th. A detachment with a strong force of cavalry will be sent towards Bréteuil by way of St. Just, it will patrol in the direction of Marseille, and keep up the communication with the troops of the Army of the Meuse stationed in Clermont and Beauvais, and also with the 3rd Cavalry Division in the direction of Poix and Amiens.

'On the 25th the 1st Army Corps will échelon all its available troops between Noyon and Roye. The latter place must be occupied, and will form, in general, the right wing of the army. The corps will make arrangements that such detachments as are still to the rear follow by way of Noyon as they come up, but will for the present still keep up the communication with the troops investing La Fère.

'The 3rd Cavalry Division will keep a garrison at Ham until further orders, so as to cover the right flank of the army, and will reconnoitre the country in the directions of St. Quentin and Péronne. Further, the division will immediately break up the lines of railway which radiate from Amiens. That leading to Arras, and eventually that leading to Abbeville also, are to be destroyed as thoroughly as possible; the others only so far as is necessary to deprive the enemy of the use of them, at the same time having an eye to the possibility of our working them ourselves later. The bulk of the 3rd Cavalry Division will advance on the 25th to Moreuil, in order to obtain continual intelligence of the enemy, and to cover the front and right flank of the army.

'The corps are recommended to leave their trains at a due distance to the rear, those of the 1st Army Corps as much as possible behind its left wing. My Head-Quarters move to Montdidier on the 25th.

(Signed) 'MANTEUFFEL.'

Before proceeding further we give the following brief description of the features of the country which the army was now about to enter, although, of course, they only became known as the operations proceeded.

The district between the Oise and the ocean, the Somme and the Epte—ancient Picardy—is a highly cultivated hilly country, crossed in all directions by good roads, and containing numerous towns, villages, and other localities. The woods mostly consist only of small patches. The sweeping undulations of the ground which intervene between the different streams, form in many cases broad open plateaus, easy to be overlooked. This is especially the case with the plateau of Sains and Dury, between the Noye and the Celle, in the immediate neighbourhood of Amiens, which town lies at the foot of the plateau, and is completely commanded by it. On the other hand, Picardy is intersected by numerous water-courses, which, from the nature of the adjoining country, bear the type of military positions. The most important one of these is the River Somme, which rises in the neighbourhood of St. Quentin. This river is for the most part accompanied by a broad tract of swampy meadow-land, and canalisation has divided it into several channels, which sweep in a bend southwards past Ham and Péronne, and then flow past Corbie and Amiens to the ocean. The tributary streams of the Somme which rise in the south, viz., the Avre, the Noye, and the Celle, are of the same character, but the heights which accompany them are in general steeper and wooded; they flow together in the neighbourhood of Amiens, so that the intervening country spreads out like a fan from this town. The Avre is joined by the Luce, which flows westwards from Rosières. These peculiarities of the country throw difficulties in the way of the combined action of different columns marching on Amiens from the south.

Whilst the main body of the army was marching on the 24th to the position it was to take up on the 25th—the line Roye-Bréteuil—the following events occurred with the 3rd Cavalry Division, which we left on its way from Roye to Quesnel on the 23rd. The detachment pushed forward to the latter place (14th Lancer Regiment, a company of rifles, and two guns under Colonel Lüderitz) came at 1.30 P.M. upon two companies of 'gardes mobiles,' that held Quesnel and a neighbouring copse. The rifle company opened fire in the front, whilst Major Strantz advanced with the lancers and the artillery on the enemy's right flank. The fire of our artillery caused the latter to quit the village in a quarter of an hour, upon which it was entered by the rifles. The lancers and artillery followed in pursuit until darkness set in. Taking advantage of several copses, the enemy retreated northwards to Caix, at the last in complete confusion, and with the loss of his baggage. Colonel Lüderitz pushed a squadron of the advanced guard and a small detachment of rifles forward from Quesnel as far as Hourges, in the direction of Amiens. Early on the morning of the 24th these troops were attacked by about 1,000 'gardes mobiles,' upon which Colonel Lüderitz advanced to their support to Mézières. The rifle company defended this village, inflicting considerable loss on the enemy, and did not evacuate it until three hostile battalions advanced to a concentric attack on it. In addition to these, the enemy then brought forward three other battalions north-eastward of the village, south of which several squadrons and four guns also became visible. Colonel Lüderitz, therefore, retreated fighting over Quesnel to Bouchoir, General Groeben having sent a detachment from Roye to the latter place, to cover his retreat. In the meantime the enemy broke off the fight on getting on a line with Beaucourt, and several of his detachments halted in this neighbourhood, but by the evening of the 24th General Groeben occupied this position with the troops he had assembled at Bouchoir. The losses of the cavalry division in these actions amounted to about 24 men. Information of these events reached Army Head-Quarters at Baugy on the evening of the 24th. Immediately afterwards a telegram arrived from Berlin, stating the enemy's troops then assembled in and round about Amiens to amount to 46,000 men, including 11,000 troops of the line, and 42 guns.

In the course of the night another telegram arrived from Metz announcing the capitulation of Thionville. The bombardment had lasted fifty-four hours, during which time the artillery of the besiegers fired 8,600 shots. When the first parallel was opened the fortress hoisted the white flag, at 11 A.M. of the 24th. By 12.30 P.M. a capitulation was signed on the basis of the Sedan conditions, by virtue of which, in addition to various other matériel, about 200 guns and 4,000 prisoners fell into our hands. The besieging troops had lost 24 men.

The 25th of November.

On this day the main body of the army reached the line Roye–Bréteuil, as appointed by the dispositions of the 23rd, but only the 3rd Brigade of the 1st Army Corps (6 battalions, 3 squadrons, and 2 batteries) had as yet arrived at Roye; 4 battalions, 2 squadrons, and 2 batteries of the 1st Division and the corps artillery had by this time come up with the army, but were still écheloned as far back as Noyon. The next échelon of the 1st Division consisted only of cavalry, artillery, and trains; the three last échelons which then followed contained infantry, but could not reach the Oise before the 25th, 26th, and 27th. General Bentheim had in the meantime joined the 1st Army Corps. On the 25th the bulk of the VIIIth Army Corps was in the neighbourhood of Montdidier, and further westwards. The 15th Division pushed its advanced guard over the Avre in the direction of Moreuil, the 16th Division was on the left wing of the corps, and had posted a strong detachment at Bréteuil.

On the 24th and 25th the army of the Meuse made the following changes in its position. The cavalry brigade of Prince Albrecht junior having to depart on other service, Count Lippe's division took its place on the line of the Epte, established its Head-Quarters at Gisors, and provided for the security of the army in the direction of Rouen. In place of the latter, the Guard Dragoon Brigade (Count Brandenburg junior) arrived at Clermont on the 25th, and was to move the greater part of the brigade to Beauvais on the 26th. At the same time that this communication arrived, intelligence was received that General Bourbaki was appointed to the command of a corps d'armée in the Army of the Loire, and was replaced *ad interim* in the north by General Farre.

Such was the situation, as far as it was known at Head-Quarters in Montdidier, up to the afternoon of the 25th. We have already mentioned that up to this time hopes had been entertained of being able to combine the bringing up of the still absent parts of the 1st Army Corps with the advance of the army upon Amiens. It was under this impression that the orders had been issued on the afternoon of the 25th. In the meantime, however, General Groeben's despatch from Quesnel arrived towards evening, reporting what the cavalry division had ascertained in the course of the day; this altered the position of affairs. According to his orders,[1] General Groeben had started early on the 25th from Bouchoir for Moreuil, but heard at Quesnel already that Moreuil and the wood in front of this village were held by the enemy in force. Patrols, sent forth in all directions, were also met by musketry fire; they ascertained, partly from information and partly by their own observation, that hostile troops accompanied by artillery were at Boves, Gentelles, Cachy, and Villers-Bretonneux, &c.; in the region, therefore, between the Luce and the Somme. They had also heard that numerous troops had been brought up to Amiens from Lille, Arras, and Boulogne; still further reinforcements were expected. General Groeben had pushed his advanced guard further forward, accompanying it himself, and had thereby become convinced that he would scarcely be able to hold his ground in face of such a force in the intricate country near Moreuil; he therefore stationed his main body at Quesnel, and his advanced guard on the ridge which stretches from Beaucourt to Fresnoy. The 1st Rifle Battalion arrived at Bouchoir, in the rear of his position.

Yesterday's and to-day's news afforded clear proof that an advance upon Amiens would not only be no wild-goose chase, but that it was even doubtful whether the forces of the 1st Army would be strong enough to cope with the enemy. On the one hand it seemed most desirable to wait until the whole 1st Army Corps was assembled, and even to bring up the troops from La Fère; on the other hand, every delay would necessarily be of advantage to the enemy. Were the latter left time to concentrate his forces at Amiens, he would perhaps, having command of the railway, reinforce his troops there to a far greater extent than the 1st Army, the resources of which were but limited, would be able to do. And then in that case we should lose

[1] Vide the orders of the 23rd.

not only all chance of taking the enemy by surprise,[1] but perhaps the initiative of action also, the advantage of which had been so strikingly demonstrated by the first period of the campaign.

The idea which led to quitting the line of the Oise before the concentration of the army was completed, led now also, if followed up consistently, to overrule these scruples, even though they were correct according to theory.

At such moments General Manteuffel was wont to ask the opinions of those persons especially in his confidence. The commanding general of the VIIIth Army Corps, General Goeben, was at the moment in Montdidier: he, as well as the chief of the staff of the army *ad interim*, unanimously pronounced themselves in favour of an immediate advance upon Amiens; from the above-mentioned reasons General Manteuffel therefore gave the following orders at 8.30 P.M. of the 25th:

'At 8 A.M. to-morrow the VIIIth Army Corps will advance with the 15th Division upon Ailly and with the left flank detachment at Bréteuil in the direction of the road-junction at Essertaux.

'At the same time the 1st Army Corps will push the 3rd Brigade with the divisional artillery and the 10th Dragoon Regiment to Quesnel, the Corps Artillery to Bouchoir; the 1st Division will provide an escort for the latter. All other available troops of the 1st Division will assemble to-morrow in and beyond Roye. General Groeben will take command of the right wing of the Army until General Bentheim arrives at Quesnel; the 3rd Cavalry Division will then be under the orders of the latter general. The present duty of the cavalry division will be to

---

[1] Even as late as the battle of Amiens we read French papers in which the 1st Army was said to have occupied an entrenched camp near Laon, and German papers likewise, complaining of the dilatory, slow movements of General Manteuffel. Such opinions, which at the time we heard of them had been already refuted by facts, were then a source of satisfaction to us, as they proved that the movements of the 1st Army had not prematurely transpired, and that surprise was an element which at that time really to a certain degree stood in our stead.

hold fast the enemy without pressing him, and to destroy the lines of railway in his flank and rear, as has been already ordered. The right flank detachment[1] of the division will move to Ham to-morrow, reconnoitre the country in the direction of Péronne and St. Quentin, and keep up the communication with the siege corps at La Fère.'

The 26th of November.

When the advance of the army took place on the 26th, the enemy was found to have fallen back before the vanguard of the VIIIth Army Corps, and had apparently already evacuated Moreuil and the country south of the Luce the evening before. The main body of the VIIIth Army Corps reached its appointed position, therefore, without opposition. The 16th Division came to Ailly, and had a detachment of 3 battalions and 2 squadrons at Essertaux. One brigade of the 15th Division marched to Moreuil and neighbourhood, the 30th Brigade was moved up to the Luce and occupied Haille, Thennes, and Domart. On pushing the line of outposts on beyond the stream, French riflemen and francs-tireurs offered resistance, and somewhat later the enemy advanced with 3 battalions from Gentelles and proceeded to attack Domart, but was repulsed on both wings with considerable loss, whereupon our outposts were established north of the Luce. Our losses amounted to 60 men. Head-Quarters of the VIIIth Army Corps went to Moreuil, those of the 1st Army to Plessier. The 3rd Brigade, the 1st Infantry Regiment and the Corps Artillery of the 1st Army Corps reached the neighbourhood of Quesnel and Arvillers; General Bentheim established his Head-Quarters at the latter place. These troops of the 1st Army Corps amounted to 9 battalions, 5 squadrons, and 11 batteries. Three battalions, 1 squadron, and 1 battery

---

[1] During the preceding days this detachment had been moving about in the neighbourhood of Ham, Nesle, and Chaulnes, changing its quarters continually, according to its instructions, and thereby covering the advance of the Cavalry Division beyond Roye, at the same time reconnoitring the country towards the Somme.

Action at the Luce.

under Lieutenant-Colonel Hüllesheim reached Roye to-day, the leading troops of the other échelons of the 1st Division, Noyon. The patrols sent forward to the Luce found Démuin and Ignaucourt unoccupied by the enemy at midday. As soon as intelligence reached Head-Quarters at Plessier that the 15th Division had possession of the line of the Luce, orders were despatched to the 1st Army Corps to push its outposts up to this stream also in the course of the day. In the afternoon the main body of the cavalry division moved to Rosières, on the right wing of the 1st Army Corps. The division was ordered to push reconnaissances to Braye and Corbie the same day, and to ascertain for certain whether the enemy had really destroyed the bridges over the Somme, as had been reported by the right flank detachment at Chaulnes and from other quarters. A strong officer's patrol had, namely, been sent on the 24th to the neighbourhood of Harbonnières, and on the 25th still further on to Sailly on the Somme, with orders to destroy the railway between Corbie and Albert. The patrol found the bridges at Sailly destroyed, with the exception of a few foot-bridges, over which the patrol passed in single file, and rode somewhat farther in the direction of Treux, but then turned back because the villages north of the Somme were occupied by hostile troops that tried to cut off its retreat. This attempt to cut the railway communication between Amiens and Arras had therefore failed. The retreat of the enemy's advanced detachments behind the Luce and the destruction of the bridges over the Somme led to the supposition that the enemy's principal position was on the other bank of the Somme, and that on this bank of the river he would confine himself to defending Amiens. It was therefore intended on the 27th to concentrate the 1st Army, in its present formation, so far forwards and to the left that only the joint course of the Noye and the Avre would separate the two wings, and on the 28th to carry out the real main attack upon Amiens. With this view the following orders were issued at 5 P.M. of the 26th:

'The VIIIth Army Corps will take ground to-morrow between

the Noye and the Celle with its advanced guard on the line Hébécourt–Sains–Fouencamps. Patrols will be sent forward towards Amiens, and the country in the direction of Poix and Marseille will be well watched.

'The 1st Army Corps will keep touch with the VIIIth Corps, and move the bulk of its troops up to the Luce, about to the line Thézy–Démuin. The cavalry division will remain under General Bentheim's command until further orders, and will be pushed forward between the Luce and the Somme in the direction of Amiens. It will direct its attention principally to the whole line of the Somme, the passages over which it will reconnoitre, and endeavour to obtain information regarding the enemy's forces on the other side of the river.

'The passages over the Noye and the Avre are also to be reconnoitred, those over the former river by the VIIIth, those over the latter by the 1st Army Corps, and are to be repaired, so as to ensure the means of communication between both Army Corps.

(Signed) 'MANTEUFFEL.'

The enemy had in the meantime moved his whole force to the south side of the Somme and even assumed the offensive between the Somme and the Luce in the direction of the latter river, so that the above-mentioned measures taken by the Prussian Head-Quarters, combined with the simultaneous advance of the enemy, brought about the battle of Amiens, and thus on the 27th that decisive result was attained, which had not been expected until the 28th.[1]

---

[1] We here give a brief summary of the enemy's situation as stated by General Faidherbe. On the 19th November, the command of the XXIInd Corps, then still in the process of organisation, had been transferred *ad interim* from General Bourbaki to General Farre. The forces at the time available, consisting of the brigades of General Lecointe and Colonels Derroja and Bessol, and the still incomplete brigade of Colonel Ritter, with 4 squadrons and 7 batteries (nominally 17,500 men strong), were assembled in all haste on the 24th at Amiens, when the news of General Manteuffel's advance arrived. They were here joined by the garrison of Amiens, 8,000 men, with 12 heavy guns under General Paulze d'Ivoy, and by 3 battalions which were brought

up from Lille and Arras to occupy the line of the Somme. Immediately before and during the battle two more heavy batteries arrived from Douai and Brest. Feeling that there was no chance of holding Amiens if the XXIInd Corps maintained an absolute defensive on the right bank of the Somme, General Farre determined to take post on the heights between the Avre and the Somme. His foremost line of defence began at the Avre, and then followed the line Gentelles–Cachy to the dominant heights at Villers-Bretonneux. On the 26th Colonel Bessol's Brigade was at Villers-Bretonneux, Colonel Derroja's at Boves, General Lecointe's between both. Early on the 27th General Paulze d'Ivoy was pushed forward beyond the entrenchments at Dury, and reinforced by the newly arrived batteries.

CHAPTER IV.

The Battle of Amiens.

(NOVEMBER 27TH.)

AT 9 A.M. of the 27th November, General Bentheim set off along the Amiens road with the troops assembled at Quesnel and Bouchoir, in order to take up his appointed position Thézy-Démuin; Lieutenant-Colonel Hüllesheim had started from Roye at 8. By 11 A.M. reports came in from the vanguard that the enemy was stationed at Gentelles, Cachy and Marcelcave, and had occupied the woods of Domart and Hangard, south of the latter village. Musketry fire was heard on the right flank, in the direction of Aubercourt, but nothing was to be seen of the enemy on either side of the Domart–Amiens high-road. This circumstance led the 1st Army Corps to deviate from its original line of march, and it was soon seriously engaged with the enemy on its north, in the direction of Cachy and Marcelcave. General Bentheim's right flank was supported by the cavalry division placed under his orders for the day. On the left wing of the Army the battle commenced by the VIIIth Army Corps advancing between the Noye and the Celle. This caused a kind of gap in the centre of the line, in the neighbourhood of Thennes, to which place the commander-in-chief and his staff had ridden that morning. The troops of the 1st Army Corps expected to arrive at this point had not come up, therefore the only available force here present consisted of the Head-Quarters escort (Major Koppelow's battalion of the 28th Regiment, and Captain

The Battle of Amiens.

Rudolphi's squadron of the 7th Hussars) which had accompanied the general from Plessier.

These circumstances which we have thus briefly premised, and the swampy valley of the Avre, prevented in general the co-operation of both wings of the army during the battle. The narrative of the day's events will therefore be clearer if we trace the course of the action on each separate wing successively.

1. Progress of the Battle on the Right Wing.

The advanced guard of the 1st Army Corps (6 battalions of the 3rd brigade, 3 squadrons, and 2 batteries) under General Pritzelwitz, which had occupied the passages over the Luce the evening before, reached the stream at 11 A.M. and pushed a vanguard beyond it over Domart and Hangard. The advanced guard itself then moved forward according to the following disposition:

'The 4th Regiment takes the left, the 44th the right wing, cavalry and artillery to be distributed on both wings; the 1st and Fusileer battalions of the 4th Regiment (extreme left) will keep their hold on the high-road and advance against the Bois de Domart, the 2nd Battalion against the west part of the Bois de Hangard which consists of two separate halves. The 44th Regiment is first to follow the latter battalion, and then to proceed in the direction of the east part of the Bois de Hangard.'

The main body (1st Regiment, 2 squadrons, 8 batteries) was ordered by General Bentheim to occupy the passages over the Luce from Hourges to Ignaucourt, but to plant its artillery at the junction of the Domart–Roye and Démuin–Morcuil roads.

These measures were in the main carried out. On the left wing the Bois de Domart was soon cleared of the enemy, whereupon the infantry turned towards Gentelles, and advanced with such rapidity that General Bentheim deemed it necessary, on account of the nature of the country, to arrest its progress, so that it might first await the effect produced by the fire of the divisional artillery. This measure agreed with the disposition of the leader of the advanced guard, who also intended the left wing to be slightly refused and to wait upon the advance of the right wing. The result of this halt was that a standing musketry fire ensued, which, jointly with the fire of the artillery, induced the enemy to quit Gentelles, leaving only a small detachment in part of the village, and to fall back with the remainder of his troops stationed there in an easterly direction upon the forces assembled at Cachy. The latter very soon advanced with several successive lines of skirmishers against the Bois de Hangard. After this wood had been cleared of the enemy, it was occupied by the 2nd Battalion of the 4th Regiment, the greater part of which was stationed in the northern projecting corner of the west half; the battalion succeeded in repulsing the attack. In the meantime the 44th Regiment (Major Dallmer) had entered the eastern portion of the Bois de Hangard. Leaving one battalion in the wood, Major Dallmer advanced with the two others against a redoubt between Villers-Bretonneux and Marcelcave; this redoubt, as well as some entrenchments thrown up to protect the railway, was occupied by the enemy in force. The 44th Regiment carried the redoubt, then established itself in it and maintained it. This spirited advance had a decisive influence on the fate of the day. It was, however, at the same time the cause that the considerable breadth of front which circumstances had imposed upon the Army Corps at the commencement of the action could now be no more reduced. In order at least somewhat to diminish it, General Bentheim ordered the left wing to be drawn nearer in the direction of Cachy. The observation of the Amiens–Domart road, upon which even now nothing was to be seen of the enemy, was left to the dragoons.

For some time after this the combat came to a standstill in the following positions: On the Prussian left wing were dragoons, on both sides of the high-road; 2 battalions of the 4th Regiment maintained a skirmishing fight against Cachy; 1 battalion

The Battle of Amiens.

of the regiment was engaged in the west part of the Bois de Hangard, where a fierce fight still raged. One battalion of the 44th Regiment was between both halves of this wood, the two others in the entrenchments at Villers, repulsing repeated attempts of the enemy to retake them. The artillery was engaged on both wings. The main body (3 battalions and the Corps Artillery) was still in its position south of the Luce. After midday, some time after the attack made by the enemy from Cachy against the Bois de Hangard had been repulsed, it almost seemed as if the action were drawing to an end: this was, however, not the case. On the contrary, the enemy renewed his attack from Cachy with increased vehemence, and suddenly brought forward several batteries (it is said 36 guns) between Cachy and Villers-Bretonneux, which seemed just to have arrived on the field. The principal force of this fire fell on the Bois de Hangard and the country behind it, almost up to the passage over the Luce at Démuin. General Bentheim now brought forward the whole of the Corps Artillery; 4 batteries east of the Bois de Hangard, the 2 Horse Artillery batteries north of Domart. This was of very good effect. The 4 batteries east of the Bois de Hangard, in company with 2 adjoining batteries of the 1st Division, effectually checked the advance of the enemy's infantry which had already gained some ground, and then, although mostly within range of the fire of the French infantry, they engaged the hostile batteries which for some time steadily maintained the combat. The ammunition both of infantry and artillery had to be replenished during the fight, and the battalions of the 44th hitherto posted in the wood had to join in the struggle. The sending of the two Horse Artillery batteries to the left wing was also a successful move. There, namely, the two battalions of the 44th Regiment having moved somewhat to the right, detachments of the enemy's infantry had again advanced to Gentelles, from whence they endeavoured to press upon the left wing of the 1st Army Corps, in company with fresh troops that had arrived from Amiens. In consequence, the 2 battalions were drawn nearer to the high-road, and the 2 batteries arrived just in time to check the enemy's advance at this spot. In this state the fight now continued for some time, viz.:

On the left wing 2 battalions and 4 batteries were engaged with the enemy in Gentelles and the reinforcements he had received from Amiens; 2 battalions carried on a fierce musketry fight at the Bois de Hangard, on their right 6 batteries were engaged with the enemy's artillery. Two battalions of the 44th Regiment were in the redoubt, the cavalry was stationed on both wings, somewhat refused. The 1st Regiment was at the Luce. About 3.30 P.M. Lieutenant-Colonel Hüllesheim came on the field and reported the approaching arrival of his échelon (3 battalions, 1 squadron, and 1 battery). General Bentheim desired him to occupy Domart and Thennes, and at the same time ordered the 1st Regiment to leave only one battalion at the Luce, and to advance with the two others eastward of the Bois de Hangard in support of the Corps Artillery which was still harassed by the enemy's infantry. The battalion of the 44th Regiment in the Bois de Hangard joined in this advance. This brought matters to a crisis. The enemy gave way and was followed by three Prussian battalions at 'pas de charge,' accompanied by the right wing batteries and the cavalry. Loud cheers burst forth along the whole Prussian line.

In the neighbourhood of Villers-Bretonneux 4 batteries of the Corps Artillery took up a position from which they shelled the retreating enemy; infantry, cavalry, and the divisional artillery continued to advance. Villers-Bretonneux was carried by storm, 9 officers and 320 men falling unwounded into our hands at this spot, besides 2 flags and about 800 wounded, mostly consisting of marine infantry, chasseurs-à-pied, men of the 43rd Regiment, some gardes mobiles and engineers. In the meantime night had fallen, and obscured the view of the situation. The enemy was retreating partly towards Amiens, covered by the village of Cachy, which he still held, and partly across the Somme, keeping hold of Corbie.

Whilst these events took place with the 1st Army Corps, the main body of the cavalry division had already marched from Rozières to Bayonvillers at 8 A.M.; its advanced guard, which had stopped at Fresnoy and Beaucourt yesterday, took the direction of Lamotte, somewhat farther left. Two squadrons were detached to reconnoitre the passages over the Somme between Corbie and Braye; patrols scoured the country towards Marcelcave, Villers-Bretonneux, and Corbie.

According to the reports which came in, considerable forces of the enemy were near Villers-Bretonneux, and both banks of the Somme were occupied. Cerisy was the only spot at which a patrol succeeded in crossing the river.

Another report stated that hostile infantry had been seen near Morcourt. This, coupled with the appearance of large bodies of the enemy at Abancourt, induced the division to front to the north. The advanced guard remained at Lamotte, the main body moved to Marcelcave. During this march, at about 1 P.M., heavy artillery fire was heard in the direction of Cachy, upon which General Groeben took up the connection with the troops fighting there, threw 7 companies of rifles into Marcelcave at 2.30 P.M., and advanced against Villers-Bretonneux, on the north side of the railway, with 10 guns and 12 squadrons. For nearly an hour the artillery of the division shelled the enemy's left flank batteries, and the swarms of French skirmishers that advanced against our right flank. The effect produced by the fire was apparently great. Somewhat later General Bentheim ordered the cavalry division to place itself on the right wing of the 3rd Brigade, at that moment advancing against Villers-Bretonneux to the south of the railway. General Groeben accompanied this movement as far as the Mont du Bois l'Abbé, and, when the action had completely died out, took up alarm-quarters in Marcelcave, Wiencourt, and Gillancourt. The 2 battalions of rifles were not engaged; shortly before the combat ended they were brought forward to the redoubt near Villers which had been taken by the 44th Regiment.

2. PROGRESS OF THE BATTLE ON THE LEFT WING.

We have already heard that the VIIIth Army Corps held the following positions on the evening of the 26th:

The 30th Brigade (General Strubberg) of the 15th Division (General Kummer) at the Luce, the 29th (Colonel Bock[1]) at Moreuil; the 16th Division (General Barnekow) at Ailly with a left flank detachment at Essertaux.

In consequence of the orders of the 26th, General Goeben made the following dispositions for the 27th:

The 15th Division was to march with one brigade to Fouencamp, with the other to Sains; the 16th Division to move its main body to Hébécourt and to push the left flank detachment to Plachy-Baconnel. Advanced guards were to march to St. Fuscien and Dury, and to reconnoitre the entrenchments said to have been thrown up by the enemy near the latter place.

At 10 A.M., whilst engaged in executing these movements, the 30th Brigade came upon the enemy, who occupied the woods on the left bank of the Noye at Fouencamp and Paraclet in force. The latter was first shelled by a battery which drove up between Dammartin and Fouencamp, and then vigorously attacked. By midday Paraclet was taken, and the enemy driven back in the direction of Boves.

In the meantime the 29th Brigade had reached Sains. The advanced guard was in the act of occupying St. Fuscien when it received orders to send a strong detachment in the direction of Boves to the assistance of the 30th Brigade, which, to judge by the heavy artillery fire heard there, was seriously engaged.

---

[1] At the commencement of the campaign Colonel Bock was on the Staff of General Obernitz with the Würtemberg Division, and took command of the 29th Brigade at Rheims. He led the brigade in a brilliant manner during the whole of the campaign in the North, but died in the spring of 1871, immediately after his return home.

Colonel Bock led 14 companies and 2 batteries partly over the farmhouse Le Cambos and partly along the dell farther to the right. The effect was very great. The infantry of both brigades stormed the castle-hill [1] of Boves and Boves itself; General Strubberg's Brigade then took St. Nicolas also by storm. Heavy columns of French infantry, with 2 batteries, part of which came from Gentelles, attempted to regain the lost ground, but soon retreated in haste towards Amiens upon being effectively shelled by our artillery. Railway trains, no doubt full of infantry, tried to come forward from Amiens, but were compelled to turn back by the fire of our batteries, whilst a heavy battery of the enemy fired at our troops without producing any effect.

The fire was now only kept up against the wood of Gentelles in which there was a strong force of the enemy, and died out when twilight set in. The 15th Division established itself for the night in the localities it had conquered. It had inflicted considerable loss on the enemy and had taken about 400 prisoners.

The course of this day's events on the extreme left wing, 16th Division, was as follows:

Early in the day the division found some advanced posts of the enemy at Sauflieu which fell back hastily upon Hébécourt; here, however, an obstinate struggle ensued. Several battalions of French chasseurs had ensconced themselves in and at the sides of the village, a copse farther to the rear was occupied in force, and the inhabitants also took part in the fight. The 32nd Brigade (General Beyer von Karger), assisted by the fire of the batteries, attacked the enemy vigorously. Village and wood were carried after much bloodshed, as under the circumstances but little quarter was given. Two squadrons of the 9th Hussars found an opportunity of charging and cutting down a few companies of chasseurs.

The Division now pressed on beyond Dury to reconnoitre the

---

[1] A height near Boves, with the ruins of an ancient castle on its summit.

country, and found itself in face of a strongly-fortified position on the other side of the village, consisting of carefully-constructed entrenched batteries connected by rifle-pits. The troops advancing against it were met by a sharp fire of musketry, and after a short time by the fire of artillery also. The batteries of the division took up a position in front of the entrenchment and were reinforced by two Horse Artillery batteries of the Corps Artillery, which Lieut.-Col. Borkenhagen led forward to within range of the enemy's infantry fire. Two companies of the 70th Regiment carried a cemetery only 300 paces in front of the enemy's works at the point of the bayonet and entrenched themselves in it. Even this, however, did not silence the artillery in the enemy's works, in face of which the division settled itself for the night, keeping Dury and the cemetery occupied.

3. Events in the Centre of the Line of Battle.

When General Manteuffel rode on beyond Thennes with his staff in the course of the forenoon, the successful progress of the action of the VIIIth Army Corps was distinctly perceptible, but it was not so easy to obtain an insight into the course of events on the right wing. Officers of the staff were despatched in all directions to procure information and to make arrangements for whatever mutual assistance of both wings might become necessary. The right wing seemed particularly in need of support. Shortly after midday General Manteuffel sent a request to General Goeben to assist the right wing if possible by pushing forward beyond Fouencamp in the direction of Gentelles. An answer was returned that the whole of the VIIIth Army Corps was already engaged, and for the moment incapable of detaching any troops. It therefore became necessary to let both wings continue the struggle independently of each other. The want of troops in the centre of the line suggested, however, the idea that the enemy might take advantage of this circumstance and, advancing from the wood of Gentelles, gain possession of the passage over the Luce at Thennes. He would thus, at least for a time, have broken the connection between the two halves of the army. It seemed necessary at all events to show some troops here also, in order to hide this state of affairs from the enemy. Accompanied by his whole staff, and sending forward hussar patrols in all directions, General Manteuffel therefore ascended the plateau north of the Luce. He kept his station here from midday upon a conspicuous height between the two high-roads leading to Amiens, and opposite to the wood of Gentelles. In order still further to conceal the weakness of the centre, the battalion of the 28th Regiment was now also brought forward, and stationed in a neighbouring dell. A slow skirmishing fire was sustained with the enemy in the Gentelles wood, the latter returning the fire at first only feebly, but afterwards with much vigour. The fire took effect among the Commander-in-Chief's staff, Major Koppelow was wounded. Late in the afternoon, when the enemy began to press upon the left wing of the 3rd Brigade, the general was in some danger of being cut off from the bridge at Thennes, and of being forced back upon the almost impassable Avre. He therefore withdrew shortly before twilight set in to the windmill hill south of Thennes, followed by his escort, the infantry of which occupied the passage over the Luce, whilst the hussars held their ground on the other side of the stream for some time, though often pressed by the enemy.

It was known at Head-Quarters that the left wing of the army was in possession of Fouencamp and Boves, but uncertainty still prevailed as to the fate of the day on the right wing. At 5 P.M., therefore, General Manteuffel despatched orders from the above-mentioned height at Thennes to the 1st Army Corps, leaving it to the option of its commanding general to take up the originally intended position at the Luce, in connection with the VIIIth Army Corps, either to-day or to-morrow. The cavalry division was also again placed at General Bentheim's disposal. It was thought that circumstances might occur to render Moreuil an important point as connecting link between both wings. The VIIIth Army Corps was therefore desired to provide a garrison for it. Head-Quarters staff was in the act of despatching these orders, when a report came in from General Zglinitzki, stating La Fère to have capitulated the same day.[1] Orders were telegraphed to this general to march to Noyon immediately, with at least 3 battalions, 1 squadron, and 1 battery. As soon as the artillery and musketry fire had subsided on all sides, the Commander-in-Chief rode to Moreuil, and took up his quarters in the Château of the Legitimist Count du Plessis, an extensive and ancient brick building, magnificently fitted up. In the course of the night further reports arrived here, showing the victorious issue of the battle; the full extent of the advantage gained was, however, not evident until next day. As far as the VIIIth Army Corps was concerned, there had from the beginning been no doubt on this subject, but still the enemy had in this quarter a strong support in his entrenched position north of Dury. On the other hand the position of the weak 1st Army Corps had at times been critical, but had changed for the better towards evening, and had ended with the complete defeat and the retreat, almost indeed the flight, of the enemy, whom darkness alone saved from total rout.

The loss of the 1st Army in the Battle of Amiens amounted in dead and wounded to—

VIIIth Army Corps	24 officers,		430 men	
1st	,,	42 ,,	739	,,
Cavalry Division		0 ,,	15	,,
Total[2]		66 ,,	1184	,,

[1] This telegram and other reports could only be read with difficulty, by the help of lucifer matches lighted under shelter of the windmill, for the night was wet and windy.

[2] Among the killed were Captain May of the 44th Regiment, well known as a military writer,* and Lieut. Prince Hatzfeld of the 9th Hussars; among the wounded

* Captain May was the author of 'Military Retrospections,' a work which made some sensation shortly after the campaign of 1866.

besides 20 men missing who were taken prisoners in Gentelles, but fell into our hands again on the capitulation of the citadel of Amiens.

We will close this chapter with a few remarks on the want of a reserve at the disposal of the Commander-in-Chief during the battle. The reason was that, each corps having its own distinct line of march, it was not deemed expedient, weak as the army was, to disturb the organisation of the corps and weaken them still further by setting apart a permanent reserve *before* the day of battle. The battle of Amiens was the result of an encounter; a general action had not been expected to take place on the 27th. We have heard how the Head-Quarters escort was made use of to supply the deficiency, and that it sufficed to fill the gap in the centre of the line, and to dispute the ground there. It must remain an unsettled question what results might or might not have been attained if an actual reserve had been at hand at this spot. We do not wish to draw *general* conclusions from this, but still believe that in this *special* case the troops were employed to more advantage and with better effect on the wings of the line. The narrative of the course of events proves that the detailing of a reserve from the right wing might have placed the fate of the day in that quarter in jeopardy.

Major Dallmer, leader of the 44th Regiment, and Lieutenant-Colonel Borkenhagen of the Artillery, the latter of whom died of his wounds soon afterwards. General Faidherbe states the losses of the French Army of the North in the Battle of Amiens to have been 266 killed, 1,117 wounded, 1,000 missing, and numerous gardes mobiles disbanded.

CHAPTER V.

Capitulation of La Fère—Occupation of Amiens: surrender of the Citadel—Formation of the 1st Army preparatory to its march on Rouen—German Administration established in the Department ' de la Somme'—State of affairs of the VIIth Army Corps.

(NOVEMBER 27TH TO NOVEMBER 30TH.)

WE now turn to La Fère, the capitulation of which place became known on the battle-field of Amiens in the course of the afternoon of the 27th. The siege-park having arrived, the building of batteries was accomplished undisturbedly in the course of the night between the 24th and 25th. Early on the 25th, 7 batteries placed on both sides of the village of Danizy, commenced the bombardment. In the course of the day fires already became visible in the town. The enemy, at first probably taken by surprise, returned the fire from all fronts of the fortress; but by midday already some guns on the north-east front seemed to be dismounted, and to all appearance the fires in the town could not be quenched. On the 26th a fog hid the enemy's artillery from view; it was therefore only possible to continue the bombardment of the town. Nevertheless, at midday already a flag of truce appeared. Negotiations commenced immediately, and were brought to a conclusion next morning. The conditions granted were in the main those of the capitulations of Sedan and Metz. The fortress surrendered at midday. The want of cellars and shell-proof buildings had been the cause of this speedy result. The garrison—78 officers, 2,234 men—was escorted to Laon as prisoners of war. This success was achieved by the 4th Brigade with a loss of 7 men killed and wounded during the whole period of investment and siege. The trophies consisted of 113 cannon, 5,000 muskets, and considerable matériel of war.

In consequence of the orders sent from the battle-field of Amiens, General Zglinitzki despatched his troops to Noyon on the 28th, and arrived there on the 29th, with 5 battalions, 1 squadron, and 1 battery. One battalion and the siege-artillery companies remained for the present at La Fère. The Government-General of Rheims refused to furnish a garrison for the place, therefore General Senden was instructed to send a battalion of his detachment there. On the 30th November the battalion of the 81st detailed to this duty, relieved the battalion of the 4th Brigade at La Fère, whereupon the latter followed the army. Major Mackeldey, of the 81st Regiment, took the duties of commandant of La Fère, the previous commandant, Colonel Bartsch, commanding the siege-artillery, having, together with the siege-train and the greater part of the siege-artillery companies, been called to the siege of Paris by supreme orders from Versailles.

28th November.

The full extent of the advantage gained on the day of Amiens, and particularly the plight in which the enemy was in consequence of his defeat, were far from being recognised on the evening of the 27th. The enemy's retreat in front of our right wing between the Luce and the Somme was not yet proved for certain. At the request of the Commander-in-Chief, General Goeben had come to Moreuil to confer regarding the state of affairs at the left wing. It was his opinion that to attack the entrenchments on the plateau of Dury in front would cost a very heavy loss, without affording the certainty of success. To hurl the army headlong against these entrenchments and the almost impassable Somme, would have been an inexcusable act; corresponding orders were therefore issued from Moreuil, at 11.30 P.M. of the 27th.

First of all the Commander-in-Chief thanked the troops for the bravery displayed by them in the battle, and then gave the following preliminary orders for the 28th:

'The Ist Army Corps to keep its hold of the positions it had conquered, and cause reconnaissances to be made by the cavalry division between the Luce and the Somme; at the same time also to occupy the line of the Luce, according to orders previously given. The VIIIth Army Corps to establish itself on the ground it had gained, fronting Amiens, and to hold a division in readiness to come to the assistance of the Ist Army Corps, in case the latter should still be engaged with the enemy between the Avre and the Somme. In like manner the Ist Army Corps to be prepared to assist the VIIIth.'

It was the Commander-in-Chief's intention to wait in this position for the arrival of the still absent parts of the Ist Army Corps, and then to push forward in whichever direction it should seem easiest completely to dislodge the enemy. Late at night, however, Lieutenant-Colonel Burg, Chief of the Staff of the Ist Army Corps, arrived as bearer of the news of complete victory on the right wing. It was therefore probable that the enemy had already been dislodged in this quarter, as an immediate result of the battle.

On the morning of the 28th the Ist Army Corps took up the appointed positions on the Luce, establishing its advanced guard north, and its main body south of the stream. General Bentheim's Head-Quarters moved to Mézières. The troops of the Ist Division that were on the march from Noyon closed up by degrees, and the cavalry division went to Villers-Bretonneux and neighbourhood.

The very first advance of the patrols showed that Cachy and Gentelles were evacuated by the enemy. All the neighbouring villages were full of French wounded, arms and baggage. Other patrols that reconnoitred the Somme, found the bridges destroyed in many places (the sound of the explosions had been heard during the night); considerable bodies of troops were even beyond Sailly, retreating northwards, and Corbie was also said to be evacuated. In consequence of these reports, which came in in the course of the forenoon, General Manteuffel ordered the immediate advance of the cavalry division in pursuit of the enemy, for which purpose the bridge-train of the 1st Army Corps was placed at its disposal.

On the right wing the victory was more effectually followed up, and more important results were obtained. Detachments of the 16th Division, which were pushed forward beyond the Celle, had broken up the Amiens-Rouen line of railway and telegraph. The reopening of the enemy's fire from the entrenchments in front of Dury was looked forward to at daybreak, but did not take place. On the contrary, patrols advancing beyond Dury found that the enemy had evacuated these works, abandoning guns and ammunition-wagons. They were immediately taken possession of by the 40th Regiment, which now pushed its outposts up to the first houses of Amiens, without encountering any fire. As soon as this was reported, General Goeben pushed the 16th Division forward to Amiens, and entered the ancient capital of Picardy at midday, at the head of the 40th Regiment and 2 batteries. The town lies at the north front of the often-mentioned plateau between the Avre and the Celle, on the south bank of the Somme. It has broad and handsome streets and squares, and about 70,000 inhabitants. On the north bank of the river, close to the houses of the town, lies the citadel, a rambling old fort, built on the bastion system, and commanding the open country on the right bank of the Somme to a considerable distance. Although the scarps of the ditches were in a somewhat neglected state, still the north front of the citadel was perfectly storm-free, and well provided with heavy guns. On entering Amiens, our troops ascertained that the enemy was in full retreat northwards. This retreat had been decided on in a council of war held at Amiens at 1 A.M., and had been commenced immediately afterwards. In consequence, the national guards entrusted with the defence of the entrenchments at Dury had refused to perform this duty, and had even, as was said, broken their muskets. On the other hand, a few hundred men had remained behind in the citadel under the command of an energetic officer, who refused to surrender the fort, but as yet attempted no hostilities. He was allowed time till the next morning to consider.

The 15th Division remained for the day in its positions at Boves, Fouencamps, St. Fuscien, and Sains.

Intelligence of these events reached Moreuil at midday, and rendered the situation perfectly clear. During the night all we knew was that we had gained a victory ; the unresisting evacuation of so important a town and so strong a position showed to what a degree the morale of the enemy's troops must also have suffered from the battle. The first impulse to the pursuit of the enemy had, as we have seen, been given by the Commander-in-Chief, when the first news of the enemy's retreat arrived. The question now was to turn the victory to account *strategically*, i.e., to decide on the future operations. This decision was taken in the course of the same afternoon, and was based on the following considerations :

The occupation of Amiens, ordered by the Versailles instructions of the 18th November, was, with the exception of the citadel, now effected. According to these instructions the main object of the operations still was Rouen, and General Briand's army assembled there. These higher orders were also perfectly in harmony with the general military situation, for at that time it was by no means proved for certain in which hostile mass lay the enemy's chief power of resistance, whether in General Farre's (afterwards General Faidherbe's) army at Amiens, or in that of General Briand at Rouen. According to all accounts hitherto received, the *greatest* danger menacing the investment of Paris seemed to lurk at Rouen. This opinion was still further confirmed by symptoms of an intention on the part of the enemy to assume the offensive which were observed in that quarter. Thus, for instance, a detachment of all arms belonging to Count

The March to Rouen decided on.

Lippe's cavalry division was surprised at Etrepagny (only 9 miles west of Gisors) on the night of the 29th November. If, therefore, the operations of the 1st Army were pushed further northwards, this army would lose all capability of protecting the investment of Paris against any undertaking proceeding from Rouen. The advance of the army in that direction would soon have been checked by the girdle of French fortresses which afforded the beaten army of the North a sure place of refuge, for the 1st Army had no siege matériel at its disposal, and so many necessary detachments had already been made that it was impossible to post troops before Arras, Lille, Cambrai, Valenciennes, or Douai, &c. also, without depriving the army of all power of operating in the field.

The main idea which had given rise to the operations against Amiens was to disturb the organisation of the enemy's armies. In order to follow up this idea it became a necessity, consistent both with the instructions of the 18th November, and with the general military situation, not to allow the army to be enticed to follow the enemy and entangle itself among the northern fortresses, thereby leaving the enemy in Normandy free scope, but rather now to turn against the latter. *The march to Rouen was therefore decided on.* It was intended to turn the position of affairs at Amiens to as much advantage as possible during the brief period that must necessarily elapse before the army could be formed for its new operations. But all undertakings in this quarter became a secondary consideration as soon as the expedition to Rouen was determined on as the main object in view. Such measures of *minor importance* were, in addition to the pursuit of the enemy as already ordered, the display of a large force at Amiens, for the sake of the moral effect, which always did us good service with our foes, and the establishment of a permanent garrison at Amiens by gaining possession of the citadel. It was intended to act purely on the defensive on the line of the Somme, but to secure and watch the river, so as to be able to offer timely resistance in case the enemy, now thrown back northwards, should again assume the offensive.

The following orders and events were the results of these considerations and determinations. First of all the following orders were given on the afternoon of the 28th :

'The 3rd Brigade with 2 field-batteries will march to Amiens to-morrow and will occupy the town. The commander of the Brigade (at the time Colonel Busse) will for the present undertake the duties of commandant of the town. The remainder of the Ist Army will move to the Moreuil–Ailly–Conty road, preparatory to marching upon Rouen ; its leading troops will reach Essertaux to-morrow. General Zglinitzki's Brigade, now on the road from La Fère, will follow by way of Montdidier.

'The VIIIth Army Corps will form échelons on the Amiens–Poix–Forges road and south of it, so that its leading troops are on a line with Creuse to-morrow. It will so time its march that the Moreuil–Essertaux road is left free for the Ist Army Corps by 10 A.M.

'The 3rd Cavalry Division will send the two rifle battalions and the Horse Artillery battery of the VIIIth Corps back to their respective corps, and will hand over one cavalry regiment to each corps until further orders. The two remaining cavalry regiments and one Horse Artillery battery, together with the 3rd Brigade, will form a combined detachment under the command of General Groeben. The duty of this detachment will be to *garrison Amiens, cover the rear and flank of the army operating upon Rouen against the enemy's forces in the north, and in particular to protect the Amiens–La Fère–Laon railway from any hostile undertakings.*

' Army Head-Quarters will move to-morrow to Amiens.'

(Here follow instructions regulating the boundaries of the different cantonments.)

(Signed) 'MANTEUFFEL.'

This movement was not a wheel of the whole Army to the left, but a facing to the left of each individual Army Corps, so that the VIIIth Army Corps, as the one farthest north, now formed the right wing of the army. This saved much unnecessary marching, and facilitated the closing up of General Zglinitzki's brigade, which could now rejoin its corps by marching diagonally by the Montdidier road.

29th and 30th November.

Whilst the army was employed in marching to the above-mentioned positions, the concentration of the whole of the 1st Division was effected and General Manteuffel moved his Head-Quarters to Amiens. On approaching the town musketry and artillery fire was heard within it. The citadel, namely, persisted in refusing to surrender when the respite granted to it expired. In consequence, the soldiers of the 16th Division, quartered in the neighbouring houses, began firing on the Frenchmen who showed themselves on the ramparts.[1] The fire, however, soon ceased because friend and foe both wished to spare the town as much as possible. To all outward appearance the fire produced no result, but in reality this was not the case, for the brave commandant, Captain Vogel, lost his life, a circumstance of which we did not become aware until the next morning.

The importance of the citadel, securing as it did the possession of the town itself, was too evident not to justify an attempt to carry it by assault. On the evening of the 28th, General Manteuffel had therefore already ordered all the heavy field batteries, supported by detachments of infantry and cavalry, to take up positions on the north bank of the Somme. In default of siege artillery, it was hoped that the overwhelming number of field guns would compel the citadel to surrender. It was not intended that this should delay the march of the army to Normandy. If necessary, the batteries were to overtake their respective corps by forced marching. The passage of the

---

[1] Some especially daring individuals are said even to have attempted to scale the fort, but were baffled by the steepness of the ramparts.

guns to the north bank of the river caused some momentary difficulty. According to the reports previously sent in from the right wing, all the bridges in the neighbourhood seemed to have been destroyed by the enemy, and the bridge at Amiens lay under the guns of the citadel. A careful reconnaissance made by Major Fahland of the engineers showed, however, that only the bridges at Sailly, Corbie, and Daouars were impracticable, and that those at Bray and La Motte Brebière (between Daouars and Corbie) were untouched. Nevertheless, with the assistance of the pontoon-trains, bridges were thrown over the river at Longpré[1] below Amiens in the course of the night of the 29th. The batteries crossed here, and by daybreak of the 30th 66 guns were placed in a semicircle around the citadel, ready to open fire. General Schwartz of the Artillery directed the whole undertaking. The defence of the citadel was, however, paralysed by the death of its commandant; the white flag was hoisted as soon as the Prussian batteries were in position, and by 8 A.M. a capitulation was signed on the basis of that of Sedan. In the course of the forenoon the citadel surrendered and was occupied by Prussian troops. More than 30 guns, 11 officers, and 400 men[2] fell into our hands. The sum total of the trophies won by the battle of Amiens, was 2 flags, above 40 guns, and more than 2,000 prisoners, including 800 wounded. Besides, considerable matériel of war was found in Amiens, and 7 locomotive engines with 100 railway carriages were captured. These did good service later.

The question may perhaps suggest itself here why the Amiens victory was not followed up still further, as General Manteuffel's instructions both before and after the battle had repeatedly denoted the intention of doing so. In this case, however, we must bear in mind the circumstances which most particularly

---

[1] There are two villages of this name below Amiens, one in the immediate neighbourhood of the town, and one some fifteen miles lower down the river: the former of these is the point in question.

[2] The latter, mostly sons of inhabitants of Amiens, were afterwards liberated by permission of his Majesty as equivalent for a contribution paid by the town.

Formation of the Army.

favoured the enemy's retreat, viz.: the imperfect acquaintance with the state of affairs on the evening of the battle-day and the difficulty of crossing the river Somme. The former circumstance deterred those immediately engaged with the enemy from carrying the pursuit into the night, whilst the latter only admitted of the cavalry reconnaissances being pushed up to the bank of the river, where they had to turn back on account of the broken bridges[1]—officers' patrols now hastened forward in the directions of Albert, Doullens, Abbeville, and on the intermediate roads, but saw nothing more of the enemy. They only heard that he had retreated in all directions, in some cases in good order, in others in great confusion and without arms. According to accounts which came in from the north at the same time, the bulk of the enemy's army had retreated 'en déroute complète' in the direction of Arras.

When the Commander-in-Chief started for Rouen he gave General Groeben special instructions respecting the duties of the detachment placed under his orders, which consisted of—

The 3rd Infantry Brigade (4th and 44th Regiments, Colonel Busse, later General Memerty).

General Mirus's Cavalry Brigade (7th and 14th Lancer Regiments).

Two field batteries of the 1st and a Horse Artillery battery of the VIIIth Corps; in the whole 6 battalions, 8 squadrons, 18 guns, besides 1 company of pioneers and 1 siege-artillery company brought up from La Fère to garrison the citadel.

The substance of the instructions mentioned above was as follows:

'When the army commences its march to Rouen, General Groeben's duty will be:

---

[1] Our victories in the French war seldom admitted of an immediate pursuit of the enemy, because, generally speaking, the latter held his last defensive positions with great tenacity until darkness set in. In the second period of the campaign the shortness of the days was very much in his favour. The retreat was then effected under cover of the long nights, and by the help of the railways the necessary start was gained before daybreak.

'1. To cover the march of the army.

'2. To occupy the position at Amiens and hold it against attacks of the enemy.

'3. To cover the Amiens–La Fère line of railway.

'4. To deceive the enemy now retreating after the battle of Amiens as to his own (General Groeben's) strength and movements.

'The measures best adapted to attain these objects are in the main identical. Amiens must be provided with a permanent garrison, but detachments pushed far forwards will also prove the surest means for securing this place. I therefore desire that General Groeben keep his troops as much on the move as possible, not assembling them at any one point unless operations of the enemy oblige him to do so.

'The enemy whom we have beaten at Amiens has retreated in haste and in disorder, and will at least require some time to reorganize and refit his troops before he will again be capable of any operations of importance. This interval of time will be employed by the army in carrying out the expedition against Rouen; by General Groeben in throwing impediments of all kinds in the way of any concentration of the enemy beyond the Somme. For this purpose the Amiens–Arras and La Fère–Cambrai lines of railway and telegraph must be destroyed at a point at least two days' march distant from their termination, therefore beyond Albert and St. Quentin. Both these latter towns and other suitable localities are to be alternately and temporarily garrisoned by flying columns. Similar measures will be taken with regard to the Abbeville railway. Péronne must be watched, and I look forward to receiving a report whether and by what means it may be possible to gain possession of the place.[1] General Groeben's task is therefore one of an

---

[1] During the march to Rouen, on the 3rd December, a report arrived from General Groeben. Major Heinichen, with 2 squadrons of the 7th Lancers (formerly detached

essentially defensive character, but one requiring at the same time a considerable amount of activity and initiative. The security of the operations of the army makes it of the utmost importance, and I particularly insist that no leader of troops at any time should lose sight of this point of view, and that all strive to overcome difficulties in order to further our joint purpose. The garrison of the citadel will be a firm *point d'appui*, and will enable the detachment to employ the greater part of its forces *farther forwards*, because in case of eventualities it will suffice to hold the town in subjection.'

The prefect whom Gambetta had installed in the Somme department fled from Amiens when the French troops quitted the town. No co-operation in the civil administration of the departments east of the Oise was to be expected on the part of the Government-General of Rheims, for the latter had already refused to provide a garrison for La Fère, in which the supreme command of the army acquiesced. The task of arranging all matters, especially those connected with the civil administration of the newly conquered districts, lay, therefore, for the time being, on Head-Quarters of the 1st Army; this made the want of 'Etappen' troops very palpable. The Inspection-General of 'Etappen,' accompanied by its small escort, had meanwhile followed the army from Rheims to Compiègne, and was now ordered to come to Amiens, where it arrived on the 3rd December. The Commissary-General of the Army, Sulzer, was appointed by General Manteuffel prefect of the Somme department *ad interim*, with Amiens as seat of government, and a proclamation was issued acquainting the inhabitants of the town with this measure. The official relations between the préfec-

---

to Ham), had reconnoitred Péronne on the 30th, and summoned the place to surrender, but in vain. It was garrisoned by about 3,000 'gardes mobiles.' Major Heinichen was of opinion that the fortress, being completely overlooked on the south-east side from Doingt, could not withstand a serious bombardment. It was, in consequence, left to General Groeben's judgment to make a slight attempt on Péronne, but one that would not compel us to besiege the place.

ture, General Groeben's command, and the Inspection-General of 'Etappen,' were regulated by instructions addressed to each of these authorities and drawn up in the same terms.

They were as follows:

'Whilst the army continues its operations towards the Seine, the regular course of civil administration has been re-established in the department of the Somme, but, it being necessary to guard this department against the enemy, it at the same time still remains within the sphere of the military operations. As long as this exceptional state of things continues, the official relations between the different authorities will be regulated in the following manner:

'In all cases in which it would cause too much delay to wait for my orders, General Groeben, with his Head-Quarters at Amiens, will act as my representative as Governor-General of that district occupied by the 1st Army which lies westward of the Government-General of Rheims. In accordance with the instructions given him to provide for the security of this district against attacks from the north, he will in particular guard the La Fère–Amiens railway and the important point Noyon, as a protection to the railway and our hospitals established there.

'The Inspection-General of "Etappen," which still has 6 companies and 1 squadron at its disposal, will keep open the communication between Amiens and the army, and on all accounts occupy and secure the Amiens–Rouen railway.

'The Préfecture of the Somme will direct its efforts to opening the latter line and the Amiens–La Fère line as soon as possible, and will call up the 3rd Field-Railway Detachment from Laon for this purpose. The repair of the bridge at La Fère will prevent direct railway communication in rear of the army for some time to come; in the meantime the rolling stock found at Amiens will serve to open traffic on part of the Amiens–Rouen line, and to shorten the communication of Amiens with Compiègne by way of Noyon. It will be useful for many

State of Affairs of the VIIth Army Corps.

purposes, for instance for the post, for the transport of prisoners, sick, etc.[1]

'All these authorities are requested to communicate with each other and concert the best means for carrying out these orders.

(Signed) 'MANTEUFFEL.'

We still have to cast a brief retrospective glance at the events which had meanwhile occurred at the part of the army under the command of General Zastrow.

General Senden's detachment still kept its position in front of Mézières, and was but little molested by the enemy. It watched the triangle of fortresses and scoured the country with flying columns towards Rocroy and in other directions. This gave rise to several successful encounters with the enemy, at Rimogne, at Harci on the 1st December, etc. General Senden was now specially recommended to keep a good look-out westwards, as it was very possible that the Army of the North, after effecting its retreat upon Arras, might make some attempt against the corps of observation. When Thionville fell it was General Zastrow's intention to reinforce General Senden's detachment by degrees, and to proceed to Sténay himself in the beginning of December, so as to be nearer to the approaching siege of Montmédy. On the 27th November, however, a telegram arrived at Metz from Versailles, ordering the 13th Division and the Corps-Artillery—therefore the greater part of the VIIth Army Corps—to start for Chatillon-sur-Seine immediately. The object of this measure was to cover the extensive tract of country which intervened between the theatre of operations of the IInd Army and that of General Werder. The part of the VIIth Corps which marched thither ceased to form part of the 1st Army; the 14th Division

---

[1] We must remark here that Versailles Head-Quarters had some time before ordered these lines to be repaired, so as to be able to employ them for the use of the army. The situation of the line from La Fère to Amiens was certainly a very exposed one, but it was, nevertheless, the only one which could be put to any use as long as the bridge over the Oise, which the enemy had destroyed at Creil, was not repaired. As soon as a provisional bridge was constructed here, the 1st Army was able to shift its line of communication to the rear to a safer line, viz. Rouen–Amiens–Creil.

and General Senden's detachment were all of General Zastrow's troops that remained with it. It now became General Loewenfeld's business to provide garrisons for Metz and Thionville and to watch Longwy. The troops available for this purpose were: the 72nd Regiment, 12 Landwehr Battalions, the 1st Reserve Dragoon Regiment and 3 batteries of General Kummer's former Division. This detachment was placed under the direct orders of the Versailles Head-Quarters. The direction of the sieges along the Ardennes railway was now undertaken by General Kameke, who had already begun to move the siege-train from Thionville to Montmédy. Now that the troops of the 13th Division, hitherto employed in front of the latter fortress, were withdrawn, the whole of the 14th Division had to proceed there. This rendered it impossible to reinforce General Senden's corps as was intended; therefore a *simultaneous* attack on Montmédy and Mézières, for which preparations had already been made, was now no longer feasible, because General Manteuffel still insisted on the instructions he gave in Jouy and in Rheims, forbidding any active siege to be commenced without a force sufficient to guarantee success, being strictly carried out. General Senden's detachment was now placed under General Kameke's orders.

This was the general state of affairs in the north when the operations commenced in Normandy.

CHAPTER VI.

Advance to Normandy—Action at Buchy—The 1st Army enters Rouen.

(DECEMBER 1ST TO DECEMBER 6TH.)

THE troops available for the coming operations were : the VIIIth Army Corps, together with the 8th Cuirassier Regiment of the Cavalry Division, the 1st Army Corps, less the 3rd Brigade, which remained at Amiens, but including 5 battalions which were coming up from La Fère by way of Montdidier, and the 5th Lancer Regiment of the Cavalry Division. In addition to these troops, a telegram from Versailles placed the Guard Dragoon Brigade, then at Beauvais,[1] at the disposal of the 1st Army during its operations against the Seine. The Saxon pontoon-train was also to remain with the army during this period. The whole force consisted of 43 battalions (at that time numbering scarcely 30,000 men), 31 squadrons, 168 guns. The Army of the Meuse promised that Count Lippe's Cavalry Division, then at Gisors, should co-operate with the army in the direction of Fleury.

Intelligence derived from various quarters stated the strength of the enemy at Rouen and neighbourhood to be about 44,000 men, 11,000 of which were troops of the line, with 94 guns, mostly of heavy calibre. Patrols sent out by the Beauvais detachment had discovered several French battalions, some

---

[1] One battalion of the 2nd Regiment of Guards and 1 battery were attached to the brigade. The battalion was now withdrawn to rejoin the troops investing Paris, and 1 squadron remained behind at Chantilly, so that only 7 squadrons and 1 battery took part in the operations against Rouen.

squadrons of hussars, and a body of francs-tireurs to be at Fromerie and along the line of the Epte as far down as Gournay. They were supported by a considerable force. Grandvillers was also still occupied by hostile infantry and cavalry on the 10th December.

Meanwhile the Prussian Army Corps had carried out the orders given to them, and were distributed along the routes appointed for each. The heads of their columns were as far forward as Creuse and Essertaux. On the 1st of December, the first frosty day, the march westwards was commenced.

In the first instance the Commander-in-Chief made his dispositions for the march of the army as far as the line of the Epte. It was known that this river was held by the enemy; the leading troops of both corps were to reach it on the 3rd December. The VIIIth Army Corps marched principally by the road which leads through Poix and Fromerie by the side of the railway. The 1st Army Corps advanced by way of Ccnty, and gradually moved on to the south road Bréteuil–Rouen. It was rejoined by the 4th Brigade on the 2nd December. The boundary between the quarters of the two corps lay about halfway between both roads. Army Head-Quarters went to Conty on the 1st and to Grandvillers on the 2nd December. On the 3rd the advanced guards of both corps reached the Epte at Forges and Gournay without meeting the enemy, the latter having retreated westwards; his last troops only left the Epte the preceding night. The 1st Army Corps had opened communication with the Guard Dragoon Brigade at Beauvais. By order of the Commander-in-Chief, this brigade joined the march of the 1st Army Corps and closed up to the Epte—somewhat south of Gournay—on the 3rd December. An infantry brigade, 1 cavalry regiment, and 2 batteries of the VIIIth and 1 cavalry regiment of the 1st Army Corps were set apart as general reserve of the army in the battle which was expected in front of Rouen. These troops were still to form part of their respective corps, but were from the 3rd of December on to be moved towards the centre of the army, so as to be at the disposal of the Commander-in-Chief at any moment.

The formation of the 1st Army was in the first instance as follows :

Right Wing.—VIIIth Army Corps (3 brigades of infantry, 2 regiments of cavalry, 13 batteries) on and north of the direct road from Amiens to Rouen. The leading troops of the corps at Forges, Head-Quarters in Gaillefontaine.

Left Wing.—1st Army Corps (3 brigades of infantry, 2 regiments of cavalry, 12 batteries) on the Bréteuil–Rouen road ; leading troops of the corps at Gournay, and the Guard Dragoon Brigade at the Epte south of this place. Head-Quarters La Chapelle, near Songeons.

Army Reserve in the centre.—General Strubberg's Brigade, 8th Cuirassier Regiment, and 2 batteries at Pommereux, southeast of Forges, the 5th Lancer Regiment at Bazancourt, six and three-quarter miles west of Songeons.

Head-Quarters of the army in Songeons.

December 4th.

On the 3rd of December, the following orders were given at Songeons :

'The 1st Army Corps will march to-morrow to La Haye and Lyons la Forêt, the VIIIth to Buchy, the Army Reserve to Argeuil. Taking Gournay and Forges as their starting points, the 1st Army Corps will leave the former place at 8.30 A.M., the VIIIth the latter at 9 A.M. In Gournay a squadron of the 1st Guard Dragoons will join Head-Quarters as my escort. General Brandenburg will march with the remainder of his squadrons and the battery to La Ferté (between Forges and Argeuil) at daybreak and report there to General Goeben. From to-morrow on the 1st Army Corps will keep up the communication with Count Lippe's detachment in the direction of Etrepagny and Fleury.'

The following instructions for the commanding generals, showing the future intentions of the Commander-in-Chief, were subjoined to these orders:

'It is my intention to move the army so far in the direction of Rouen to-morrow, that reconnaissances can be pushed forward next day up to the town and the enemy's position, which we may expect to find in that neighbourhood. The rest of the army will remain in the positions it takes up on the 5th. These latter must be chosen by the Army Corps with some regard to their defensive capabilities, in case the enemy assume the offensive, an event which is not impossible.

'If the Ist Army Corps should wish to occupy the line of the Andelle to-morrow already, and if this can be done without bringing on a serious engagement, I have no objection to the foremost troops of the corps being pushed so far forwards. The Dragoon Brigade attached to the VIIIth Army Corps will enable the latter to cover the right flank of the army without detaching infantry far in this direction, and at the same time to push reconnaissances round the enemy's flank in the apparently open country north of Rouen. The enemy's railway communication with Dieppe and Havre may be destroyed.

(Signed) 'MANTEUFFEL.'

These orders were communicated to Count Lippe by the Ist Army Corps.

The river Epte rises at Forges and flows southward past Gournay and Gisors to the Seine, discharging itself into the latter at Vernon. Where the lines of march of the Ist Army crossed the river, it forms the boundary between the ancient provinces of Picardy and Normandy, now termed 'Département de la Somme' and 'de la Seine-Inférieure.' Immediately beyond Gournay the landscape changes from the table-land and the mostly open plains of Picardy to the hilly and intricate country of Normandy, which greatly resembles the east part of Holstein. The pasture grounds, fenced in with hedgerows, abound with large herds of cattle that seek and find ample nourishment in the meadows until late in the autumn and winter. Here, as well as in Picardy, numerous seats of the ancient nobility are seen, often most picturesquely situated and in extent and style truly deserving of the name of 'château,' an appellation of which the French are well known to be very prodigal.

The enemy gave up the line of the Epte without a struggle. But more than a day's march beyond the front of the 1st Army Corps ran another stream, the Andelle, which also springs from the watershed at Forges and flows through a pleasant meadow valley, bordered by wooded slopes, past Fleury to the Seine. Extensive woods cover the country between the Epte and the Andelle, confining the view considerably. The Gournay–Rouen high-road crosses the mountains in many windings, which increase the distance between the two towns materially. To the west of the Andelle the country becomes less intricate and more open. Broad table-lands, intersected by deep-sunken ravines, spread out towards the Seine, in most cases sweeping close up to this river, and then descending to its edge in steep and precipitate slopes. At a spot where the valley widens out, surrounded and overlooked by the neighbouring hills like an amphitheatre, traversed and divided into two unequal halves by the broad Seine, lies the ancient capital of Normandy, Rouen, with more than 100,000 inhabitants—an especially imposing and picturesque sight.

The army marched on the 4th December according to the above-mentioned orders. The 1st Army Corps entered the country we have just described by the Gournay road; its leading troops did not get as far as La Haye, but stopped, with permission of Army Head-Quarters, at La Feuillie. The outposts that were pushed forward towards the Andelle found Vascoeil occupied by the enemy, and a patrol was fired on by hostile infantry in the wood of Lyons la Forêt. A reconnoitring detachment sent forward by Count Lippe (3 companies, 4 squadrons, 3 guns) also encountered the enemy in front of Ecouis and fell back to Le Thil for the night, intending to open communication with the 1st Army Corps next morning by way of Lilly. Intelligence was received that Les Andelys was also occupied by the enemy. At midday of the 4th the Army Reserve reached the neighbourhood of Argeuil, where Army Head-Quarters soon afterwards also arrived and were quartered in the castle of the Marquis Castelbajac. At the same time the first information arrived of the events which had occurred at the right wing, followed up in the course of the afternoon and the ensuing night by still further reports, bringing the following news :

On the morning of the 4th, General Goeben had marched in three columns of brigades, each composed of all arms, viz., on the left, General Kummer, with the 29th Brigade, on the Forges high-road; in the centre General Barnekow, with the 32nd Brigade, by Sommery upon Buchy ; on the right, Colonel Mettler, with the 31st Brigade, by the circuitous route over Neufchatel to St. Martin.

At Manquencay already the left wing column met a hostile detachment of 6 battalions with a battery; the latter was planted on the heights of Forgettes. General Kummer gave orders to attack the enemy, who was immediately routed, and retreated in the direction of Bose-Bordel, leaving his wounded and one dismounted gun behind him. An attempt which the enemy made to hold a second position at Rozeron likewise ended in his speedy retreat after a brief fire.

As General Kummer's appointed route led southward from Forgettes, he did not pursue the enemy any farther. The pursuit was, however, taken up by General Barnekow's column, which was marching on the Sommery road, and was continued as far as Mesnil Godderoy, but without overtaking the enemy. About 40 unwounded prisoners had been taken.

When the right wing column debouched from St. Martin about midday, it came upon about 6 French battalions, which withdrew in a south-westerly direction to Elteville ; but Colonel Mettler pressed them hard and succeeded in cutting off part of the detachment, taking 8 officers and 227 men prisoners.

Actions at Buchy. 95

A flank detachment of the 31st Brigade (2 battalions, 1 squadron, and a battery under Major Elern) took a still more westerly route, and at 4 P.M. came upon a detachment of about 1,200 of the enemy at Bosc le Hard. The latter was driven from its position after a fight of an hour, with a loss of 100 prisoners, and, being forced to retreat in a north-westerly direction, was unable to fall back upon Rouen. The 16th Division then went into cantonments along the two lines of railway which join near Bosc le Hard. General Goeben established his headquarters at Buchy. The trophies of the day consisted of 1 gun and about 400 prisoners who were sent next day to Argeuil. Our loss was very trifling.

December the 5th.

In consequence of the reports on the combats at Buchy, the 1st Army Corps was ordered to push forward to the Andelle on the 5th, and to be ready for a general advance of the army towards the Seine next day. In all other respects the previous orders, commanding reconnaissances on a large scale, were to be carried out, the Gournay-Rouen road to mark the boundary between the reconnoitring sphere of the 1st and VIIIth Army Corps, whilst General Lippe was to reconnoitre in the direction of Fleury and Les Andelys.

In order to give support to the reconnaissances made by his corps in face of the forces displayed by the enemy, General Goeben moved the 16th Division early on the 5th as far forward as St. André (five miles west of Buchy), and stationed the 29th Brigade at St. Germain in support of it. A right flank detachment was to endeavour to push on to the junction of the Dieppe and Havre railways at Malaunay. General Goeben guided the reconnaissance in person. He met with no further resistance, and as early as 11 A.M. sent in a report from Quincampoix (six and three-quarter miles from Rouen) announcing the evident retreat of the enemy and his own intention to enter Rouen the same day. The 1st Army Corps had some trifling engagements in which several prisoners were captured, and advanced to the

Andelle, occupying the line of this river and pushing outposts and reconnaissances still farther forwards. The main body of the corps stopped between La Haye and Lyons la Forêt; the commanding general established his head-quarters at La Feuillie.[1] Communication was opened with the VIIIth Army Corps and Count Lippe's Cavalry Division, and information obtained that the enemy occupied an entrenched position in front of the corps extending from the north of Montmain to the high-road; other accounts at the same time declared the enemy to have already evacuated Rouen.

These various reports reached Argeuil in the course of the afternoon, and caused the following orders to be despatched to General Bentheim at 7 P.M.:

'The 1st Army Corps will push forward its advanced guard to-morrow towards the line Puits de l'Aine–Montmain. Should this line be defended by the enemy, the advanced guard will front towards it, but without engaging in any serious action. Under cover of this position the main body will march against the line Tourville–Les Andelys, in order to drive whatever troops the enemy may still have in this quarter into the Seine. Count Lippe is requested to co-operate with this movement on the left wing. If the Montmain position be already evacuated, the advanced guard will march direct upon Rouen, keeping in connection with that wing of the main body which marches on Tourville. The Army Reserve will march from Argeuil upon Epreville between the Andelle and Rouen. All these movements are to commence at 7 A.M. to-morrow, because time is of the utmost importance in following up the advantage we have already gained. I shall go to Rouen to-morrow by way of Epreville.

(Signed) 'MANTEUFFEL.'

---

[1] The battalion that was following the army from La Fère reached Beauvais to-day, having been sent to this town to punish the inhabitants for insults offered to the German surgeons who remained after the departure of the previous garrison. Besides this, Count Lippe had also sent a mixed detachment there on the 4th.

General Goeben was informed of these orders and requested, in case he should already have entered Rouen, to take measures for pursuing whatever troops of the enemy might have retreated to Dieppe and Havre on the right bank of the Seine, early the next morning.

The enemy, however, escaped the effects of these measures by a hasty retreat. General Goeben, too, met with no further resistance beyond Quincampoix and entered Rouen with two brigades at 4 P.M. of the 5th. Only a slight skirmish with the last troops of General Briand's army took place here. Eight heavy guns were found in some entrenchments in front of Rouen, which the enemy had just abandoned. First of all it was ascertained that intelligence of the issue of the combats at Buchy had reached Rouen on the evening of the 4th, it was brought there partly by the beaten troops themselves. In consequence of this news, the enemy's army—said to have been from 35,000 to 40,000 men strong—had retreated, for the most part in the direction of Havre. The latter part of this intelligence was from the very beginning considered highly improbable, because the enemy had still been in front of the 1st Army Corps and Count Lippe's detachment *above* Rouen up to the 5th. It was very soon proved that the retreat had been effected on *both* banks of the Seine in all directions and principally by railway. After crossing the bridges over the Seine, the enemy had blown some of them up; part of his troops had dispersed. We are not acquainted with the state of the enemy's army, nor with the motives which guided General Briand's actions at the time of our advance upon Rouen, but according to all appearances, the enemy seems to have been completely taken by surprise by our march. The fact of its having been possible to remain so long in ignorance of the approach of an army of more than 30,000 men may perhaps be partly accounted for by the want of cavalry, but, above all, by the French national character, which is so prone to self-deception. This was shown by the newspapers which we found still circulating when we entered Rouen. According to them, the 1st Army was supposed to be in full retreat southwards, either in consequence of a defeat at Amiens or of reverses sustained by the army investing Paris. The troops that had been seen at the Epte were looked upon as mere éclaireurs, or detachments covering the flank of the army. Even during the first few days of our presence in Rouen, at a time when the issue of the battles in front of Paris, at Villiers, and Champigny must for some time past have no longer been any secret, a joyous excitement pervaded the crowds sauntering about the quays of the town, in consequence of a telegram distributed among them:

'Paris débloqué. Général Ducrot occupe la Marne.'

Be that as it may, up to the very last moment the town reckoned upon an energetic defence. This seems to have been intended by General Briand also on the 4th. As soon, however, as his troops that had been dispersed by General Goeben reached the town, he received the impression of being surrounded on all sides on the right bank of the Seine, and therefore determined early on the 5th to retreat. The painful excitement which this produced in the town is shown by the following placard affixed to the walls by the civil authorities of Rouen on the 5th of December:

'Hier nous faisions appel pour la défense de la ville à votre dévouement patriotique. L'autorité militaire promettait une énergique défense.

'Ce matin, à quatre heures, le général Briand nous confirmait cette détermination, et la garde nationale, au son de la générale, s'assemblait sous les armes.

'A cinq heures, le général Briand prevenait le Maire qu'il jugeait toute défense impossible en face de forces trop imposantes, et qu'il donnait l'ordre de battre en retraite. Un des adjoints, accompagné de plusieurs officiers de notre garde nationale, est allé lui demander ce matin encore ses dernières résolutions. Le général a persisté dans sa décision ; il a quitté la ville avec toutes les troupes placées sous ses ordres.

'Dans cette cruelle extrémité, il importait de vous faire connaître la part de responsabilité qui incombe à chacun.

'D'autres et pénibles devoirs vont naître : nous nous efforcerons de n'y pas faillir.'

Although it cannot exactly be said that the 1st Army was numerically superior, still we are of opinion that, in consideration of the above-mentioned features of the country, General Briand acted correctly in not defending Rouen itself after not having been able to hold his outlying positions.

We shall again refer hereafter to the peculiarities of the country, as they were of importance to the 1st Army also.

December the 6th.

As a natural consequence of the state of affairs, the 1st Army Corps saw nothing whatever of the enemy on the right bank of the Seine when it advanced on the 6th of December. The 1st Brigade, which took the direct road to Rouen, captured six heavy guns without carriages in some abandoned entrenchments at Darnetal. Still more guns, on the whole twenty-nine, were found in the course of the following days, besides a quantity of ammunition and other matériel of war. Early in the afternoon, General Manteuffel entered Rouen and announced to the inhabitants by a proclamation, that he appointed the military Judge-Advocate Cramer of the 1st Army Corps Prefect *ad interim* of the department de la Seine inférieure. As had already been the case in Amiens, the new Prefect in Rouen exerted himself also to the utmost to fulfil his difficult task. All that he could at the utmost reckon upon was the passive assistance of such subordinate French authorities and officials as had not quitted their posts, and of these only so far as the German civil authority could have military support. It was naturally not intended to interfere with the different branches of the civil administration, but it was desired to give the German occupation a permanent character by placing a German official at the head of the administration. This would at the same time serve the purpose of settling all necessary military demands, as, for instance, the unavoidable requisitions, by spreading the burden of them over the neighbouring country, as mildly and justly as possible and with due consideration to the feelings and interests of the inhabitants. With this view, Prefect Cramer even edited a German official newspaper, which published the German official accounts of the events of the war, in order to counteract the French press system, so calculated to nourish illusions. The military measures that were taken during the first few days after we entered Rouen, with a view to holding the country in subjection and pursuing the enemy in the directions of Dieppe, Havre, Pont Audemer, Bernay, Evreux, and Vernon, also served at the same time to strengthen the German civil authority. They, however, belong to the next period of operations.

On the 3rd December, General Sperling re-joined the army and resumed his duties as chief of the staff.[1]

We will now cast a brief retrospective glance on the results obtained in the first and second periods of operation. In execution of the instructions given at Versailles on the 23rd October and 18th November, the Army marched from Metz over Amiens to Rouen in the interval between the 7th November and the 6th December. The distance, as the crow flies, exceeded 260 miles. It was done in scarcely thirty days, therefore, including a day of battle, at a rate of nine miles a day. If we take into consideration the vast difference in length between the straight line and the actual line of march, and also the additional lateral deviations made by the troops quartered in cantonments distant from the direct line of march, we shall find that

---

[1] Although but imperfectly recovered from a serious illness, the General could no longer bear to remain absent from duties to which he was heart and soul attached. He fulfilled these duties until the end of the campaign in the North, although often obliged to overcome the most severe headache by his mental energy. This, however, brought on incurable disease, under which the General succumbed on the 1st May 1872. We state this as a tribute to the memory of our departed friend and comrade in the war.

Summary of results obtained.

this wonderful performance of the troops was still farther increased by at least fifty per cent.

The trophies in guns and prisoners taken by the army during this period amounted in the lowest round numbers to:

	Guns.	Prisoners.
Thionville	193	4,000
La Fère	113	2,300
Battle and citadel of Amiens	40	1,200
Actions at Buchy and taking of Rouen	30	400
Divers trifling actions	—	100
Sum total	376	8,000

The principal advantage gained by the foregoing operations lay, however, in the subsequent effects of the timely blow struck at Amiens, and the surprise of Rouen following so immediately upon the former. Both hostile armies, in the north and the north-west, which, had their operations continued unchecked and their junction been effected, might have seriously compromised the north and west investment of Paris, were by these means driven back in divergent directions, and to a considerable distance from the metropolis. This *offensive* task of the 1st Army was now at an end. The task of the army now became one of a more *defensive* nature. We shall narrate the measures taken, as well as the motives on which they were based, and the higher instructions which called them forth, in the next section of this book. We will only premise the remark that the general and the particular circumstances of the war demanded for this defensive task also a high degree of activity, so that the so-called winter quarters of olden times were as unattainable now as before. The frost which first set in mildly on the 1st of December daily increased in intensity from the moment we entered Rouen. On the following days there was a heavy fall of snow, with alternate frost and thaw. This had a most injurious influence on the state of the roads.

THIRD PERIOD.

OPERATIONS ON THE SEINE AND THE SOMME, FROM THE ENTRANCE INTO ROUEN TO THE BATTLE OF THE HALLUE.

(DECEMBER 6TH TO DECEMBER 24TH.)

CHAPTER VII.

Military position of the 1st Army in December, in general and in particular—State of affairs at Rouen—Operations of flying columns on both banks of the Seine.

(DECEMBER 7TH TO DECEMBER 11TH.)

BEFORE we describe the operations of this period, it will be necessary to call to mind the course which the war in France had taken since the end of November. If we take into consideration the main objects in view at that time, and not the mere local distribution of the German armies, and group them accordingly, we obtain the following picture of the situation.

For some time past Paris had formed the centre of attraction for both belligerent parties. The ultimate fate of the war depended on the question of conquering or maintaining the metropolis. Here, therefore, the operations of the French were of an essentially defensive, those of the Germans of an offensive nature. But, by reason of peculiar circumstances, Paris could not at that time be attacked, but had to be subdued by hunger. This compelled the German forces assembled there (IIIrd Army and Army of the Meuse), to maintain in general a defensive attitude. The point in question was, to deter the enemy inside the town from breaking through the 'iron circle' and to prevent

General Military Position.

his receiving any supplies from outside until forced by hunger to lay down his arms.

We have said that the fate of the war depended on Paris, therefore all other operations bore relation to this main object.

The fresh forces which France placed in the field naturally strove to raise the siege of Paris, the Ist and IInd German Armies opposed to them desired to frustrate this attempt, and to protect the investment of Paris against any attack from outside. Here, therefore, the principal object on the part of the French was the offensive, on the part of the Germans the defensive. To bring this defensive to a successful ending required, however, constant activity, and very often offensive operations. Besides, the Army of Investment on the one, and the two armies in the field on the other hand, had to hold themselves in continued readiness to afford each other mutual support. This produced the peculiar state of circumstances that the communication with the home country (for supplies and back transport) was kept up by the one main line common to all German forces, over Chalons and Frouard, whereas, as far as the operations were concerned, the armies in the heart of the enemy's country were based upon each other. Thus we, though on the so-called 'inner line,' could not turn this advantage to full account, because of the deficient working capabilities of the lines of railway in our hands, whilst our adversaries, though operating on the 'outer line,' had the command of an extensive net-work of railways, capable of a considerable amount of traffic.

The third great group of the German forces, comprising the troops in the north and east of France, was far less directly concerned in the struggle around Paris. It served to protect the existing lines of communication with the home country, and to open new ones. The troops of this group were:

1. The troops of the Governments-General, distributed over the whole of the territory occupied by us.

2. The 14th Division and General Senden's corps in front of the Ardennes fortresses.

3. The remainder of the VIIth Army Corps in the neighbourhood of Chatillon sur Seine and Auxerre.

4. The troops under General Werder's command, some occupied in besieging those Alsace fortresses that had not yet surrendered, others in covering these sieges &c. against the Franco-Garibaldian forces in the south-east of France. It is known that the latter by degrees assumed such dangerous proportions, that towards the end of the campaign this part of the theatre of war became at times one of the decisive centres of action. It was to meet this occasion that the ' South Army ' was formed.

After this cursory survey of the general state of affairs, we now turn to the *special task* of the second of these groups, that one to which the Ist[1] and IInd Armies belonged. Previous to the arrival of the former at the Oise, and of the latter at the Loire, the Army of Investment had been obliged to provide for its own security on its outer front. The detachments of the Army of the Meuse, of which we have already made mention, had sufficed for this purpose in the north, but for some time past it had become necessary to detach considerable bodies of troops to the south and the south west. When the enemy commenced his successful operations against Orleans, these troops were combined in a new command under the Grand Duke of Mecklenburgh-Schwerin. Towards the end of November the IInd Army reached the district between Paris and the Loire, and, for the sake of unity of command, the Grand Duke's troops were also placed under Prince Frederick Charles's orders. The latter then had at his disposal about 5 Army Corps and 4 cavalry divisions, viz., IIIrd, IXth, and Xth Prussian, and Ist Bavarian Army Corps, 17th and 22nd Infantry, and 1st, 2nd, 4th, and 6th Cavalry Divisions. The theatre of operations of this whole force lay in the south and south-west ; that of the Ist Army, which consisted in the beginning of 2 Army Corps and 1 Cavalry Division of 4 regiments, in the north-west of Paris. The 5th

---

[1] Somewhat later 2 Guard Cavalry Brigades, and General Senden's combined detachment by degrees joined the Army.

General Military Position. 105

Cavalry Division, stationed in the neighbourhood of Dreux and Evreux, operated between both armies; it was based on the west front of the Army of Investment, and at times supported by it. When the battle of Amiens and the taking of Rouen had completed the task more immediately before the Ist Army, the second battle of Orleans, which lasted several days, had been fought, and the grand sortie from Paris repulsed in the battles of Villers and Champigny. The enemy's forces were defeated at all points, and in part dispersed. Operations had for a time come to an end.

The question now at issue was, how the Ist and IInd Armies were to follow up the success they had achieved, and secure the advantages gained as firmly as possible, and in harmony with the new tasks now before them. The guiding motives of both armies were essentially the same. The more French territory they occupied, the more they deprived the enemy of men and other means of resistance. At the same time the starting points from which the enemy set forth in his attempts to raise the siege of Paris would be thereby forced farther and farther away from the capital. But, if the possibility of mutual support between the Army of Investment and the armies in the field was to be maintained, then our operations must not be pushed beyond a certain distance. There lay the bounds of the attainable. These points of view were laid down in the instructions which came somewhat later from the King's Head-Quarters, both as a general principle, and for each of the Field Armies in particular.

After this general survey, let us now return to the Ist Army. New instructions were expected from Versailles, but even before they arrived there was no doubt at Army Head-Quarters with regard to the points of view we have just enunciated. The measures which were taken immediately after the occupation of Rouen, were therefore perfectly in accordance with the opinions prevailing at the King's Head-Quarters. It was fully appreciated that the task now before the Ist Army was to maintain its hold of the country between the Seine and the Somme, together with the two important flank positions Rouen and Amiens, so as to be able to concentrate the bulk of the army at any time, and at any spot within this region which the situation might require. In the first place, however, the enemy must be pursued on the main lines of his retreat, even beyond the Seine, in order to prevent any fresh accumulation of troops, and their approach to the Norman capital. The *peculiar circumstances at Rouen* would in themselves have required this to be done.

Rouen is completely overlooked by the neighbouring heights on the right bank of the Seine. This situation of the town may well have been one of the reasons which induced General Briand to abstain from defending the town itself. These local considerations became of still greater weight now that *we* had to hold a *hostile* town of more than 100,000 inhabitants, among whom were 30,000 unemployed workmen. Even now already this mass of easily excited human beings crowded to the quays with ill-disguised hopes whenever a gun or cannon-shot was heard in the neighbourhood, and might have proved an absolute danger if our troops had been obliged to pass the town on a *retreat.*

The locality on the left bank of the Seine was equally unfavourable for defensive purposes. On this side the country in the immediate neighbourhood of the town is, certainly, more level, but exceedingly intricate. Here also, the same as on the north side, a labyrinth of detached buildings and gardens extend far beyond the faubourgs of the town. It would be difficult to discern the approach of an enemy if favoured by the inhabitants, and his approach would be remarked all the later because it would be screened by the extensive forests further off the town. The nearest of these woods—at La Grande Couronne—almost entirely covers the peninsula which the Seine forms there, and at the northern extremity of which Rouen is situated. South of this wood lies the large town of Elbeuf, with its numerous working class population, a very hot-bed of commotion, and therefore an object which must be watched.

State of Affairs at Rouen.

The intricacy of the whole country on the left bank of the Seine increases towards the south and south-west. Hedgerows, so characteristic of Normandy, are only found here and there on the right bank of the Seine, but abound on the left bank. By reason of this peculiarity of the country, connected operations of large bodies of troops were attended with great difficulty, cavalry and artillery, the two arms in which we were superior to the enemy, could be made but little use of. On the other hand, the locality was favourable to single combat, and to Guerilla warfare. Under the existing circumstances, therefore, it was more to the advantage of the French than of us. This was the case in the whole tract of country as far as the Rille, a river which rises in the south, and flows past Beaumont, Brionne, Pont d'Audemer to the Seine. Its nearest point to Rouen is two days' march off, and this stream forms the first important line of defence against troops operating in a south-westerly direction.

Soon after entering Rouen, the Commander-in-Chief commissioned General Schwartz of the Artillery, and General Biehler of the Engineers, to reconnoitre the country round about Rouen in detail, with especial regard to the defensive capabilities of the town itself, and the military situation at the time being. These reconnaissances produced the following results:

The faubourgs and rows of houses which stretch far out into the surrounding country would make it necessary to take up a line of defence far from the town, the length of which line would then amount to $12\frac{3}{4}$ miles. To make this position tenable, 15 redoubts would have to be thrown up, the troops necessary to defend it would amount to 25 battalions and 90 guns, inclusive of a general reserve, therefore 1 whole Army Corps. But even then the defence would still have remained weak. On the right bank several deep ravines reach high up on to the plateau, and would render it difficult for one part of the line to assist the other, added to which, the troops in this position would be separated by the Seine. This broad stream is under tidal influence at Rouen, so that there are no solid bridges *below* the town. The three bridges at Rouen itself (town bridge, suspension bridge, railway bridge), had been left intact by the enemy on his hasty retreat. The bridges at Pont d'Audemer and Manoir, higher up the river, were also uninjured, but those at Les Andelys and Courcelles had been destroyed by the enemy.

Thus, in the very first instance, the reconnaissances of both these generals confirmed the opinion that had been previously derived from a cursory survey of the country. An *immediate* defence of the town was impossible without placing the troops employed for the purpose in a position of great danger. At the same time the field operations of the army would be compromised if 1 whole Army Corps were to be permanently detained here.

It was therefore determined to secure the possession of this important town by keeping a great part of the troops available for this purpose at some distance from the place. If at any time they should be forced to retreat, they were on no account to pass through the inimically disposed town. The special dispositions for carrying out these measures will be given in the following chapters.

The despatch announcing the occupation of Rouen reached Versailles on the 6th December, and orders were sent from thence to pursue the enemy in the first instance in the direction of Hâvre. We have heard what orders the Commander-in-Chief had already given in this respect. In consequence of them General Goeben had pushed the Guard Dragoon Brigade to beyond Mormonne, to scour the country farther westwards. By this and by other reconnaissances it was ascertained on the 7th that the enemy's retreat had not been solely effected on the right bank of the Seine, as the first accounts had led to surmise. On the contrary, it was now said that the troops which had passed Yvetot in this direction had consisted principally of large bodies of 'gardes mobiles,' and the country to the north of Rouen was found in general free from the enemy. Everywhere

Operations on both banks of the Seine. 109

the national guards had given up their arms to the civic authorities, and the inhabitants were friendly disposed. The actual retreat of the enemy seemed to have taken place on the left bank, and principally by railway, to Pont Audemer and Bernay, rear-guards following along the roads.

In consequence of this intelligence, the following orders were given on the 7th December:

'Mixed columns of brigades will be pushed forward to Vernon and Evreux by the 1st, and over Pont Audemer and Bernay, as well as on the right bank of the Seine towards Hâvre, by the VIIIth Army Corps, for the purpose of pursuing the enemy, disarming the country, occupying important open towns for a time, and crushing all opposition. I expect that these expeditions will procure information respecting districts in which any considerable number of hostile troops may be forming.

'All columns will establish relay stations to Rouen, in order to be able to report progress often and to receive orders in proper time, in case their destination should have to be changed.

'These movements will commence early to-morrow morning, it is desirable that they should be executed quickly and with energy. Head-Quarters of the Army and of the VIIIth Army Corps will remain in Rouen[1] and those of the 1st Army Corps will also be moved there.

(Signed) 'MANTEUFFEL.'

In addition to this, the Commander-in-Chief had on the 6th already ordered an expedition to be made to the sea-coast, in order to stop all communication by land between the enemy's forces in the north and those in Normandy, and to prevent their uniting for a joint offensive. The troops detailed for this expedition (8th Cuirassier Regiment, 5th Lancer Regiment,

---

[1] During the first days of the occupation, Major Sachs, of the 70th Regiment, held the office of Commandant of Rouen; he was succeeded by Colonel Jungé of the Artillery of the 1st Army Corps, who fulfilled this important and often very arduous task during the whole of the ensuing period of operations. This position became one of great difficulty whenever offensive operations made it necessary to withdraw almost the whole garrison of this large and excitable town.

2 Battalions and 1 Horse Artillery Battery of the VIIIth Army Corps) were to meet at Cleres (a day's march north of Rouen) under command of General Dohna on the 7th. The General received orders to march to Dieppe, disarming the country on his road, and thoroughly to destroy the coast line of telegraph. The expedition was to be finished within six or eight days, and was to establish relays at Rouen, in order to be able to be employed in any other direction which the situation might demand.

General Lippe had followed the march of the 1st Army Corps on its left flank on the 6th, and taken up his quarters in Ecouis, he now returned to Gisors and undertook the task of watching the Seine above Les Andelys.

We will now follow the operations of the separate detachments, beginning at the left wing.

The 4th combined Brigade of the 1st Army Corps (6 battalions, 3 squadrons, 2 batteries, under command of General Pritzelwitz) crossed the Seine on a bridge thrown over the river at Les Andelys, and then pushed on to Vernon, where hostile troops were said to be assembled. During this march the detachment only came upon about 60 men, who asserted that they were national guards summoned to Vernon. They had uniforms and ammunition with them and were therefore carried off as prisoners of war.

Another detachment of the same Army Corps (5 battalions, 3 squadrons, 2 batteries, under Colonel Massow of the 1st Regiment) crossed the Seine at Pont de l'Arche, advanced on several different roads and reached the neighbourhood of Louviers on the 8th. A quantity of arms were found in the villages and destroyed, and it was ascertained that detachments of hostile infantry and cavalry with some cannons had passed by here and gone on farther in a southerly direction. Colonel Massow entered Evreux on the 9th, but finding a detachment of the 5th Cavalry Division under Colonel Trotha there, which had arrived the day before from Dreux, he at first went into cantonments north of the town. On the 10th December the 5th

Operations on both banks of the Seine. 111

Cavalry Division marched to Chartres and Colonel Trotha withdrew southwards to St. André, whereupon Evreux was occupied by Colonel Massow's detachment. The information obtained respecting the enemy was, that 12,000 to 14,000 men, principally 'gardes mobiles,' with 9 guns were said to have left here by the railway and to have gone over Conflans to Cherbourg.

The VIIIth Army Corps pushed forward the 29th combined Brigade (Colonel Bock) on the left bank of the Seine. After a march of nine hours, and much impeded by the snow, this Brigade reached Bourgachard as early as the 8th, and sent the heads of the cavalry on as far forwards as Pont d'Audemer. There also numerous arms were destroyed, the telegraph lines leading westward were cut, and somewhat later the railway was broken up at the junction near Montfort on the Rille. On the 9th the detachment went to Pont Audemer, the advanced guard to Toutainville. Coinciding accounts proved beyond all doubt that the bulk of the enemy's forces, 20,000 to 25,000 men, had retreated to Honfleur and had there crossed to the right bank of the Seine. Hussar patrols of Colonel Bock's Brigade rode on to Honfleur and Benzeville; they were fired at from both places, apparently by the last francs-tireurs that had not yet been ferried over the river.

On the right bank of the Seine General Goeben had despatched 2 battalions and 1 battery of the 16th Division to join the Guard Dragoon Brigade at Pavilly. Thus reinforced, General Brandenburg reached Pavilly on the 8th, Bolbec on the 9th, and then sent forward cavalry patrols on the two principal roads leading to Hâvre, viz.: over St. Romain and Montivilliers. At Gaineville the road was found to be barricaded and defended by French infantry; the farmhouses and small copses between Montivilliers and Harfleur were likewise occupied. All bridges over the small streams that flow into the Seine were destroyed. The information obtained here corroborated Colonel Bock's report, and showed that 25,000 of the enemy had retreated on the left bank of the Seine and had embarked on 18 ocean steamers between Cherbourg, Honfleur and Hâvre. The line Gaineville—Montivilliers being occupied in force showed the enemy's wish to cover his passage over the river. Hâvre was ascertained to be fortified on the land side; the statements as to the number of troops assembled there varied between 25,000 and 50,000 men. On the 10th, General Brandenburg advanced still farther to Angerville and caused Hâvre to be again reconnoitred on the 11th. The neighbourhood of Gaineville was occupied by the enemy as before, and was impassable; another patrol, however, succeeded in reaching the market-place of Montivilliers and saw French Infantry retreating southwards. The enemy was ascertained to have occupied a position on the Rouelle between Harfleur and Bléville, and evidently intended to make his first stand there. A squadron that was sent northwards to Criquetot and Gonneville discovered a body of, it was said, 2,000 men to be in that neighbourhood.

On the extreme right wing General Dohna's detachment, the destination of which was Dieppe, assembled at Cleres on the 7th December, marched on the 8th to Omonville and took possession of the sea port of Dieppe without any opposition on the 9th. About 1,500 muskets were destroyed here, 25 guns that were found in the strand-batteries were spiked. The coast line of telegraph was interrupted by cutting the wires and removing part of the apparatus. After having carried out the orders given to him, General Dohna marched on the 10th to Auffay.

The object gained by these operations was the subjection of a broad tract of country on both banks of the Seine, on the right bank up to the sea-coast,[1] Hâvre excepted, on the left as far as the Rille; this made the permanent occupation of Rouen possible. It is a fact that from this time forth the Investment of Paris was no more disturbed from the north or the north-west. On the other hand, we had not been able to inflict any further loss on General Briand's army during its retreat. Not even by

[1] This movement induced the French government to declare its own ports, Dieppe, Fécamp, etc., in a state of blockade.

the swiftest marching is it possible to overtake an enemy, who, as was here the case, avoids a decisive combat by retreating at the very first contact of the foremost troops, especially when this retreat is an eccentric one and accompanied by a partial disbanding of the troops.[1]

The general position of the bulk of those forces of the Ist Army engaged in the operations at the Seine on the 10th December was as follows:

About 3 brigades of the VIIIth and 1 of the Ist Army Corps at Rouen and neighbourhood; 1 brigade of the Ist Army Corps at Evreux, another at Vernon; one of the VIIIth Corps at Pont Audemer with orders to return along the Rille by way of Bernay; one brigade of cavalry to the west of Bolbec, fronting Hâvre, another one at Auffay on its way back from Dieppe, both of the latter reinforced by some battalions of the VIIIth Army Corps.

[1] The national guard and many of the garde mobile disbanded and returned to their homes. The pursuing troops often caught the men in the act of exchanging their uniforms for plain clothes.

CHAPTER VIII.

Arrangements made for forming the 1st Army in two groups, at the Seine and the Somme, and first steps taken to carry them out—Actions at the Rille—Reconnaissances in the direction of Havre.

(DECEMBER 9TH TO DECEMBER 14TH.)

ON the 9th of December Head-Quarters in Rouen received written instructions from the Supreme Command of the forces, dated Versailles, December 7th, of which the following were the chief contents:

'With respect to further operations of the 1st Army, His Majesty has deigned to command, that Rouen is to be occupied and that the left bank of the Seine is to be watched from thence. The chief forces of the 1st Army are to be employed in continuing the offensive against the enemy's troops that still hold the field in the north-west of France, and His Majesty considers that it is first of all necessary to pursue those troops of General Briand that have retreated towards Hâvre. It is left to the commander-in-chief to decide whether Hâvre can be taken by a *coup-de-main*.

'It is His Majesty's desire that the 1st Army shall on no account undertake any enterprise that will cost a loss of time; on the contrary, the object always to be borne in mind is, to disperse whatever hostile forces still appear in the field, which, however, does not forbid a renewal of the operations against the troops beaten at Amiens, supposing them again to advance from their gathering points at Arras, etc., etc.

(Signed) 'MOLTKE.'

Preparations on the Seine and the Somme.

In the meantime the following intelligence had been received with respect to the Army of the North which had been defeated at Amiens. The strength of this army was at first estimated at 45,000, afterwards at only 30,000 men.[1] It was said to have retreated over Doullens and Albert to Arras, and to have arrived there in the beginning of December, much shaken. All available troops at Lille were also pushed forward to Arras. Another account, which was confirmed on the 11th of December, said that the Army of the North was distributed over the region Frévent, St. Pol, Hesden, and Doullens. Further information was also received, stating that the 'levée en masse' had been proclaimed in the north, and that preparations were being made for striking a great blow in the direction of Paris. Similar reports were also sent by General Goeben.

After receiving the above-mentioned instructions, the commander-in-chief determined to distribute his army in a manner that would be the most likely to facilitate operations on the 'inner line between the Seine and the Somme, and to enable it to form quickly to the front in either of these main directions.'

For this purpose the army was to be formed in two principal groups, viz.: the 1st Army Corps and the Guard Dragoon Brigade, under General Bentheim, at the Seine; the VIIIth Army Corps and the 3rd Cavalry Division, under General Goeben, at the Somme.[2] At that time it was still intended that the 3rd Brigade should rejoin the 1st Army Corps at Rouen, as soon as the VIIIth Corps arrived at Amiens. We anticipate coming events by remarking that this intention was not carried out, because the French Army of the North, under General Faidherbe, very soon became the centre of attraction, and this compelled us to act more on the defensive at the Seine.

From the very first it was of the utmost importance to open

---

[1] The latter figure agrees in the main with General Faidherbe's statement in his History of the Army of the North.

[2] Appendix No. 2 contains the order of battle of the 1st and VIIIth Army Corps, on the 9th December.

traffic on the *Rouen—Amiens railway*. This line would enable us to move at least infantry quickly from one wing to the other, and thereby to multiply the action of these troops, in which, in comparison with the masses of the enemy, we were most deficient. The work of repairing the line had commenced on the 9th of December, and the intermediate stations, Poix, Fromerie, Forge, and Buchy, were garrisoned by General Malottki's 'Etappen' companies. The locomotive engines and railway cars found at Amiens and Rouen, though many of them were damaged and in need of repair, must afford the means of organizing traffic for the aforesaid purpose, there being no chance of being able to bring up other materials of transport from the rear. The repairs of the *Laon—Amiens railway* were certainly by this time drawing to an end, but this line was too exposed to the north to afford any certainty of *permanently safe* traffic on it. It was therefore decided to transfer the communication of the army to the rear on to the Creil—Amiens railway. A temporary bridge over the Oise[1] being in the course of construction, the time for opening traffic on this line was likewise drawing near. General Manteuffel gave orders to occupy and guard the Amiens—St. Just tract of this line; from Clermont on it was guarded by the Army of the Meuse.

On the 9th of December the commander-in-chief gave the following orders to the commanding generals:

'The tasks now before the 1st Army will be to keep possession of Rouen and Amiens, watch the left bank of the Seine, keep up the communication with the 5th Cavalry Division at Dreux, cover the north front of the Investment of Paris, and, if the enemy's Army of the North or General Briand's army should again assume the offensive, to defeat them for a second time.

'My orders therefore are:

'To General Goeben is given the task of holding Amiens and

---

[1] Vide note to Chapter V.

Instructions to the 1st and VIIIth Army Corps. 117

covering the north line of Investment of Paris. General Bentheim will hold Rouen, watch the left bank of the Seine, and keep up the communication with the 5th Cavalry Division and with General Lippe at Gisors. On his march to Amiens General Goeben will reconnoitre Hâvre with the bulk of his force, and ascertain whether it be possible or not to take the place by a *coup-de-main*. If this should not appear feasible, the General will not engage in any serious or tedious undertaking against the town, but will then march along the sea-coast to Amiens. General Dohna's detachment will be under General Goeben's orders, the Guard Dragoon Brigade under those of General Bentheim at Rouen. If the enemy advance from Hâvre or the south against Rouen, General Bentheim will, in consideration of the state of things there—not await the attack in the town, but will go out to meet the enemy and defeat him. To effect this it will be necessary to keep the bulk of the forces together, and flying columns must be sent far into the districts south of the Seine and in the direction of Hâvre, so as to keep a firm hold of the country as far as the line Pont Andemer, Bernay, Evreux. The latter town is of especial importance, because of the communication with the 5th Cavalry Division. Care must be taken to destroy all railways that are of use to the enemy beyond Pont Audemer, Bernay, and Evreux. On the other hand we shall open traffic on the Amiens—Rouen line in a few days, which will facilitate the concentration of our army that may perhaps become necessary.

'Both army corps will commence their movements early to-morrow morning. The commanding generals will arrange by mutual agreement the relief of the troops of the VIIIth Army Corps still on the left bank of the Seine, so that no crossing of the different marching columns may occur. As the troops proceed on their march they will disarm the inhabitants as before, and when not in face of the enemy, will march on a broad front for the purpose.

(Signed) 'MANTEUFFEL.'

In consequence of these army orders, the two army corps planned and executed the following movements between the 10th and the 14th of December:

General Bentheim brought up the combined 4th Brigade of General Pritzelwitz from Vernon to Rouen, where it arrived on the 13th. On the 14th the brigade pushed a mixed detachment (3 battalions, 3 squadrons, 2 batteries) to the region Caudebec on the Seine, Yvetot and Pavilly, to watch Hâvre when the troops of the VIIIth Army Corps left this part of the country. The other battalions of this and the greater part of the 1st Brigade remained for the present in Rouen. The corps artillery, with a guard of 2 battalions, was quartered in the precincts of the town south-eastward of it.

The task of watching the left bank of the Seine was given to Colonel Massow's combined brigade. We have already heard that this brigade had been at Evreux since the 9th; it was now ordered to detach part of the brigade to watch the Rille, and to march with its main body to Elbeuf and Bouille, where it was to hold itself in readiness to act either on the right or the left bank of the Seine.

Colonel Massow set off from Evreux on the 11th, and reached Le Neubourg with the main body. The detachment sent to watch the Rille under command of Colonel Legat marched farther to the left upon Beaumont, where the head of the vanguard was fired at. Colonel Legat proceeded to attack the town, but the enemy had in the meantime withdrawn in the direction of Serquigny. A squadron of dragoons advancing eastward of Beaumont charged and broke up a line of infantry that was still crossing the open plain, but was compelled to desist from farther pursuit on account of the fire from the villages of Bray and Tilleul-Othon, which were occupied by the enemy. The squadron lost 1 officer, 7 men, and 10 horses. Hostile 'gardes mobiles' were reported to be in Bernay and Serquigny. The railway, which had been already made impracticable at Couches, was now broken up at Beaumont also. On continuing his

Action at Serquigny.

march on the 12th December, Colonel Legat again encountered opposition at Serquigny. The enemy, about three companies, tried to gain possession of the bridge at this place, but was repulsed with loss. It was ascertained here that the French troops which had in the first instance retreated to Lisieux (said to consist of 12,000 'gardes mobiles' and 10 guns) had advanced again to Bernay. And, in truth, our pioneers, that were occupied in destroying the railway at Serquigny, and the infantry stationed there to cover their work, were attacked by three hostile battalions coming from the direction of Bernay at 1.30 P.M. of the 13th. A short but sharp fire ensued, which ended in the enemy retreating with considerable loss after about an hour's fight. The destruction of the railway at the junction was then successfully effected, and Brionne occupied by 4 P.M. We lost 1 officer and 14 men. On the evening of the 14th, orders arrived from General Bentheim, in consequence of which Colonel Massow's whole detachment drew nearer to the Seine in the course of the following days, and was écheloned along the Brionne—Rouen road, between St. Denis and La Bouille, with small detachments stationed at Elbeuf and Pont de l'Arche. The object of this movement was to tempt the enemy to cross the Rille at Bernay, upon which General Bentheim would have advanced against him with superior numbers, without being obliged to go too far away from Rouen.

While these events were occurring at the 1st Army Corps the VIIIth executed the following movements; the 29th Brigade (Colonel Bock) had been ordered not to return from Pont Audemer to Rouen along the Rille, but by the most direct route. On the 12th the brigade reached Rouen, on the 13th La Feuillée, taking, therefore, the south road to Amiens by way of Gournay; General Kummer and the 30th Brigade (General Strubberg) followed the north road, and were at Forges on the 13th.

General Goeben entrusted the reconnaissance of Hâvre, which the VIIIth Corps was ordered to make, to the 16th Division.

With the exception of the battalions with the detachments of Generals Brandenburg and Dohna, this division was concentrated at Rouen. It started on the 10th December, under the personal guidance of General Goeben, by way of Maromme, and its leading troops reached the neighbourhood of Angerville and St. Romain on the 11th. General Goeben's head-quarters were at Bolbec. We have already heard the result of the reconnaissances made by General Brandenburg in this quarter. General Goeben also came to the conclusion that the enemy intended to defend Hâvre, and had occupied the line Harfleur—Montivilliers for this purpose. The consequence of attacking this line, even supposing the attack to succeed, would be that we should be obliged to follow it up by attacking Hâvre also. Were we to break off our operations against Hâvre after having attacked the outermost line of its defences, it would most certainly be construed by our adversaries into a moral victory on their side. In accordance with his instructions, which prohibited any undertaking against Hâvre that would *cause a loss of time*, General Goeben therefore determined to confine his operations in this quarter to a mere reconnaissance. On the 12th he moved his head-quarters to Fauville, and pushed his troops by degrees to the right up to the line Cany—Yvetot, which they reached on the 13th. The Guard Dragoon Brigade was also despatched to Yvetot and there placed under General Bentheim's command. General Goeben reached Dieppe and the district south of this town on the 14th with the 16th Division, and was joined there by the detachment of General Dohna. It was now General Goeben's intention, in conformity with the army orders of the 9th December, to continue his march to the Somme in two main columns, the one marching in the direction of Abbeville, the other to Amiens.

On the 14th of December, the position of the troops of the 1st Army in Normandy was as follows:

1st Army Corps.—2nd Combined Brigade (Colonel Massow) on the left bank of the Seine, between Brionne and Elbeuf, fronting towards the Rille. Half of the combined 4th Brigade (General

Zglinitzki) and the Guard Dragoon Brigade (General Brandenburg) were on the right bank of the Seine in the neighbourhood of Pavilly, Duclair, and Yvetot, fronting towards Hâvre. Corps head-quarters, with $1\frac{1}{2}$ brigades and the corps artillery, in and near Rouen, where army head-quarters also were.

VIIIth Army Corps.—29th Brigade at La Feuillée; 30th Brigade at Forges, where General Kummer also was; 16th Division, General Dohna's detachment, and corps head-quarters at Dieppe and south of this town. The corps artillery, accompanied by a guard of two battalions, at Victor l'Abbaye (east of Totes). All these troops fronted towards the Somme and were marching in the same direction. Before we follow their movements any further, we must relate the events which took place at the Somme and in front of the Ardennes fortresses during the first half of the month of December.

CHAPTER IX.

Events at the Somme and in front of the Ardennes fortresses, during the first half of December—Surprise of Ham—Faidherbe's advance upon La Fère—Capitulation of Montmédy.

WE begin this chapter with a short summary of the events which occurred in front of the Ardennes fortresses.

The reconnaissances which the commander-in-chief had ordered to be made at *Mézières* had proved the south front to be the most favourable point of attack, not only because the attack would be more safely based on this side, but also from local and tactical reasons. General Senden's Corps still remained in its position south of the fortress and in the same observant attitude as before. No encounter had taken place there, save some trifling skirmishes with francs-tireurs. The task assigned to the detachment had been made easier by sending the small French siege-train to Sedan, which obviated the necessity of guarding it.

The fortress of *Montmédy* had been closely invested since the 7th December by 10 battalions and 2 squadrons. A small detachment kept up the communication with General Senden by way of Sedan. Two battalions, 2 squadrons, and 1 battery still watched Longwy, but were expecting to be relieved by General Senden's troops. The construction of batteries in front of Montmédy began on the 8th, but was much delayed by a fall of snow and by glazed ice; the transport of the siege-train from Thionville lasted some days longer. Here also General Kameke had decided to attack the south front. He intended to commence operations by an energetic bombardment of the place, but at the same time made every preparation for a regular siege, in case the bombardment should not have the desired effect. The fire was opened on the 12th December. A dense fog made it impossible to mark the shots and correct the range, but in spite of this impediment, the fortress capitulated on the 14th. Sixty-five guns fell into our hands, 2,500 men became prisoners of war.

We now turn to the events at the Somme.

The details of General Goeben's force, of the instructions given to him, and of the mutual relations between the three highest military and civil authorities at Amiens, have been stated in Chapter V.

Whilst the army was pursuing its operations on the Seine, General Goeben was engaged in completing the provisioning of the citadel of Amiens, and putting it in a position to make a stout resistance, according to his instructions. For this purpose, among other things, he brought up from La Fère 4 rifled French cannon and other artillery material, of which there was a deficiency at Amiens. Occupation was provided for the unemployed workmen by levelling, at the expense of the town, the entrenchments thrown up by the French at Dury. Small detachments of 1 company and 1 squadron each scoured the country and disarmed the population north of the Somme, whilst other detachments carried out the orders given by army headquarters for the destruction of the railways. The latter had been already partially broken up by the enemy during his retreat to the north, but our troops now completed the work of destruction, in order to throw as many impediments as possible in the way of any advance that our adversaries might attempt. Thus, up to the 3rd December, three railway-bridges were blown up between Arras and Albert, and the Abbeville line of railway was broken up. French infantry was seen on the ramparts of the last-named small fortress, but Doullens and its citadel were found to be unoccupied, neither was anything to be seen of the enemy in the direction of Arras. On the other hand, a fresh reconnaissance of Péronne showed that the enemy occupied the neighbouring villages on both banks of the Somme, and had begun to entrench himself in them. General Goeben, therefore, very judiciously refrained from attempting a *coup-de-main* against the fortress. From English newspapers and other private information, the General came to the conclusion that the French Army of the north intended again to assume the offensive from Arras over Péronne.

This was the state of affairs at Amiens on the 6th of December.

On the 3rd December, a strong detachment (2 battalions, 2 squadrons, and 2 guns) under Major Bock, of the 44th Regiment, started on an expedition from Amiens to St. Quentin, and reached Ham on the 4th. Major Bock continued his march to St. Quentin next day, and his foragers were met there by a shower of stones and several gun shots; at the same time a large crowd of people flocked together and tried to keep the detachment from entering the town; they also wounded a lancer of one of the patrols. Two shells thrown into the main street sufficed, however, to clear it, and the detachment then entered the town without further opposition. On the 6th, the railway bridges at St. Quentin and at Essigny-le-Petit, 4 miles further north, were blown up with complete success. Major Bock commenced his march back to Ham on the 7th, and left this town on the 8th, reaching Amiens on the 9th by way of Roye. The renewed spirit of resistance which had been first perceived at St. Quentin, was shown at different other places in the course of the following days (7th and 8th December). French chasseurs appeared at Marieux (between Doullens and Albert), and attempts were made by the enemy to repair the bridge which had been destroyed at Beaucourt, on the Albert—Arras line of railway. The French workmen fled, however, leaving their tools behind them, on the approach of the Prussian patrols. Consequently, General Goeben despatched 1 battalion, 1 squadron, and 2 guns to

Surprise of Ham.

Albert on the 9th December. This detachment succeeded in completely blowing up the stone railway-bridge north of Avelay by means of a mine containing three hundredweight of powder.

Another reconnaissance over Doullens towards Arras was made by Captain Le Fort with a squadron of the 7th Lancers on the 10th and 11th of December. On the 10th the squadron reached the country south of Doullens, and disarmed this town next morning without opposition. A sub-division of lancers that was pushed still further forward toward Arras was fired at by infantry from the skirts of the wood on this side of Beaumetz, and brought back word that Beaumetz was occupied by 1,000 'gardes mobiles' and numerous francs-tireurs. The squadron regained its cantonments near Amiens on the evening of the 11th.

A still stronger proof that the spirit of enterprise was reviving on the part of the enemy, was given by *the surprise of Ham*, which took place on the 9th December. Ever since the 7th of this month, a party of the 3rd Field-Railway Division had been stationed there, under cover of a detachment of infantry from La Fère, for the purpose of repairing the tract of railway between Laon and Amiens. Probably with the connivance of the inhabitants, a hostile battalion of 'gardes mobiles,' with cavalry and 2 guns, suddenly entered Ham from Péronne at 6 P.M. of the 9th. The greater part of the small Prussian detachment, which numbered at the most 180 men, though taken completely by surprise and surrounded, succeeded in taking refuge in the castle, but the fire of the enemy's cannon soon compelled them to capitulate. Only a few officers and men escaped to Péronne.

Intelligence of this surprise reached Amiens on the 10th, and was telegraphed the same day to Rouen, from whence an answer was returned desiring General Goeben to organize an expedition against Ham immediately. In consequence, and because it was possible that the Prussian detachment at Ham might still hold out in the castle, General Goeben sent off

Operations on the Seine and the Somme.

Captain Luckowitz, with 1 battalion, 1 squadron, and 4 guns, to its relief on the evening of the 10th. On the 12th, as these troops were marching from Ercheux, over Esmery-Hallon, upon Ham, they were met by a severe fire in front and flank in the neighbourhood of Eppeville (5¾ miles west of Ham). At the same time other hostile detachments prepared to turn their flank. Under these circumstances Captain Luckowitz fell back upon Roye, sustaining a rear-guard fight with the enemy, and intending to reach Amiens on the 13th. When news of these events reached General Manteuffel, which it did at mid-day of the 13th, orders were sent to General Goeben to re-take Ham, and to ascertain, by means of a reconnaissance pushed beyond Péronne, whether the enemy's expedition to Ham had merely proceeded from this isolated fortress, or whether we had in this case to deal with the van-guard of a hostile army again on the advance. The following information, received on the 13th, strengthened the latter impression.

In consequence of the news of the events at Ham, Major Mackeldey (commandant of La Fère) pushed forward a company along the railway on the afternoon of the 11th to reconnoitre in that direction. On reaching Mennessis (junction of the St. Quentin and Amiens lines of railway) the company was already met by the enemy's fire, and retreated to La Fère after a skirmish that was carried on in the dark, bringing back a few prisoners of the 17th French Rifle Battalion. In the meantime the Governor-General of Rheims[1] had despatched 1 battalion and 1 battery to La Fère, and from them General Rosenberg learnt on the 12th that the enemy was only 4½ miles from La Fère, with 1 regiment of infantry, 1 battalion of rifles, and artillery. The Rheims troops, therefore, remained at La Fère to reinforce the garrison, and Colonel Krohn, being the senior officer, took the post of commandant of the fortress for the time. The very same day the telegraph wires between La Fère and

[1] Lieutenant-General von Rosenberg Gruszynski.

Rheims were cut by the enemy, who occupied the villages on the right bank of the Oise, west and north of the fortress, Travecy, Fargniers, etc.

This news reached Versailles on the 12th, upon which the Army of the Meuse was ordered to push troops forward over Soissons. General Senden was also instructed to answer any demand for troops which the Governor-General of Rheims might make; and, on the 13th, a battalion of the 19th Regiment and a battery left Boulzicourt for Soissons per rail. General Goeben was also called upon to act correspondingly. Added to this, the following written instructions were sent to headquarters of the 1st Army on the 13th of December:

'It is not intended at the present moment that the occupation of the whole of the north-west of France should be permanently maintained. On the contrary, all that is for the moment necessary is to disperse whatever hostile troops may be gathering in the field, and in particular to oppose any attempt the enemy may make to raise the investment of Paris or to disturb our lines of communication. His Majesty the King, therefore, commands that the 1st Army shall move the bulk of its forces in the direction of Beauvais. Rouen must still remain occupied by an adequate force, and mixed detachments will continue to watch the left bank of the Seine from this town.

'The concentration of the greater part of the 1st Army at Beauvais will enable it to render timely assistance either to Rouen or Amiens, and also to assume the offensive energetically against any hostile corps which may break forth from the girdle of fortresses at the Belgian frontier.

'The duty now most immediately before the 1st Army will, therefore, be to cover the rear of the Army of the Meuse; at the same time there will be no objection to the bulk of the army again advancing from Beauvais to Amiens as soon as the present situation of affairs shall have cleared up.

(Signed) 'MOLTKE.'

CHAPTER X.

Concentration of the greater part of the 1st Army in the direction of Amiens.

(DECEMBER 13TH TO DECEMBER 22ND.)

THE accounts received at Rouen of the occurrences at Ham and La Fère did not show any immediate intention on the part of the enemy to attack Amiens, but rather led to expect the commencement of operations against Paris and against the communications of the 1st Army.

This was General Goeben's opinion also. The following observations, made by his detachments in the course of the 13th of December, and reported from Amiens to Rouen on the 14th, tended to confirm this opinion.

It was ascertained by a reconnaissance made from Albert in the direction of Bapaume, that 10,000 of the enemy, coming from Arras, had passed Bapaume the night before (between the 12th and 13th), and that the latter town was occupied by 1,500 men. The same day (13th December) a reconnaissance made by Major Heinichen approached Péronne from the west, and led to an encounter at Fouancourt (between Chaulnes and Bray) in which we had the advantage. The village, occupied by a few hundred French infantry soldiers, was taken at mid-day after an obstinate resistance, whereupon the enemy retreated to Péronne under cover of a dense fog. The villages in the direction of Péronne were occupied in force. Hostile troops were said to be assembling at Péronne, Ham, and St. Quentin : it was stated that 15,000 were already at Ham and St. Quentin, and 5,000 more at Péronne, together with 2 batteries recently arrived from Arras. Major Heinichen's detachment withdrew to La Motte in the course of the 13th.

Another reconnaissance, made on the same day from Amiens in the direction of Abbeville, obtained proof that the enemy had not yet repaired the damage done to the railway at Longpré and Eaucourt, but was met by a sharp skirmishing fire at Liercourt. The garrison of Abbeville was said to have been reinforced during the last few days by about 2,000 or 3,000 'gardes mobiles' and marine infantry from Boulogne.

The principal movement of the enemy seemed, therefore, to proceed from Arras and to be directed against Paris, passing by Bapaume, Péronne, and Ham, as well as by the roads further to the east (Cambrai, St. Quentin, etc.).

The forces of the 1st Army nearest at hand to counteract this movement effectively consisted of General Groeben's troops in the neighbourhood of Amiens and the 15th Division (General Kummer), the brigades of which were at the moment at Forges and La Feuillée.

The following will show the manner in which these troops were disposed of by head-quarters at Rouen on the afternoon of the 13th, immediately after the arrival of the news from La Fère.

We have already mentioned, towards the close of the preceding chapter, that orders were sent to *General Groeben* at mid-day of the 13th to re-take Ham. The general telegraphed back that because of the number of detachments now absent from Amiens, he should not be able to have his troops assembled and rested, ready to start on this expedition, before the 16th. The commander-in-chief agreed to this, and added that when the expedition started sufficient troops were to be left at Amiens to secure possession of the place, and that communication was to be opened with the 15th Division, which might be expected to reach the neighbourhood of Montdidier by the 17th or 18th.

General Groeben then reported that it would endanger the

safety of Amiens if he despatched more than 2 battalions, 4 squadrons, and 1 battery on this expedition, and that a detachment of this strength would reach Roye on the 17th.

The orders sent to *General Kummer* also on the afternoon of the 13th, desired him to concentrate his division at Montdidier as quickly as was possible without compromising the fitness for action of the troops. After reaching this point he was, jointly with General Groeben, to arrest any further advance of the enemy or to operate against his flank and rear. Pending General Goeben's arrival from Dieppe, General Kummer would have the command of his own and of General Groeben's troops.

Pursuant to these orders, on the 14th General Kummer reported as follows : He would reach the country between Formerie and Grandvilliers with the 30th Brigade to-day ; Crêvecœur on the 15th ; Bréteuil on the 16th, and Montdidier on the 17th. The marches lately made by the 29th Brigade had been fatiguing ; the brigade would therefore halt on the 14th at La Feuillie, march on the 15th to Gournay, on the 16th to Marseille, on the 17th to Bréteuil, and join the 30th Brigade at Montdidier on the 18th.

The result of the orders sent to Generals Groeben and Kummer on the afternoon of the 13th, and of the reports made by them was, that by the 18th, 15 battalions, 2 regiments of cavalry, and 5 batteries would be available in first line, either to fall on the enemy's expected line of march on Paris from Roye, Montdidier, and Bréteuil, or to continue their advance to the Somme.

We now still have to account for the other troops of the 1st Army. With regard to them, it was known at head-quarters that *General Goeben* intended to reach Abbeville from Dieppe on the 17th December. His corps artillery was to march by the high-road over Forges and Poix, and to reach the neighbourhood of Amiens on the 18th. Thus, by the 19th, General Goeben would also be ready to take part in any further operations on the other bank of the Somme.

General Lippe had reported on the 11th that he had received orders from the commander-in-chief of the Army of the Meuse to march to Beauvais, and that he would post strong detachments at Gisors and Clermont. In consequence, however, of the events at La Fère, the greater part of his troops moved to Compiègne on the 15th. We have already mentioned that the Army of the Meuse had sent another detachment (1 regiment of infantry, 1 squadron, and 1 battery) per rail to Soissons. On all sides, therefore, preparations were being made to check any further advance of the enemy upon Paris, or to fall on his flank and rear.

In the meantime, the Versailles instructions of the 13th (*vide* preceding chapter) arrived at Rouen on the 14th of December. Pursuant to them General Manteuffel despatched the following orders to Generals Goeben, Bentheim, and Groeben on the same day. These orders commenced with a summary of the intelligence received regarding the enemy, and the duties which the army now had to perform, and then contained the following directions:

'1. General Groeben will leave 3 battalions of the 3rd Brigade, both batteries attached to this brigade, and a regiment of cavalry at Amiens, and will set off for Roye on the 16th with the remaining battalions, the regiments of the 3rd Cavalry Division,[1] which must now be re-called, and the horse-artillery batteries. At Roye he will receive further orders from General Goeben.

'2. The 15th Division will continue its march to Montdidier.

'3. The 16th Division will not march to Amiens, but straight to Beauvais, and will report by what time it will be there.

'4. General Bentheim's task remains unchanged. He will still keep the Guard Dragoon Brigade.

'5. General Mirus[2] will remain as commandant at Amiens, and will take command of the detachment which stops there.

(Signed) 'MANTEUFFEL.'

[1] General Dohna's detachment.
[2] The first commandant of Amiens was Colonel Busse, who returned to the 1st Army Corps to take command of the 2nd Brigade when General Memerty arrived at Amiens.

The measures already taken by Generals Goeben and Kummer were nowise modified by these orders. All that was changed was that the troops marching under General Goeben's immediate guidance were directed to march on Beauvais, in pursuance of the Versailles instructions.

General Goeben received these orders in Dieppe on the night between the 14th and 15th. In consequence, he left Dieppe on the 16th by the Neufchatel road. The head of his force (16th Division and corps artillery) was to reach the neighbourhood of Beauvais on the 18th.

General Kummer reached Bréteuil with his leading brigade on the 16th, and then determined so to expedite his march that by the 18th the 30th Brigade should occupy Roye, and the 29th be between this town and Montdidier.

General Lippe's main body was, as we have already stated, moved to Compiègne on the 13th. By order of the Army of the Meuse he now also pushed the detachments left at Gisors and Beauvais more to the east: the former went on the 16th to Beauvais, the latter to Clermont. From Clermont communication was to be opened with Compiègne and with the detachment of the 1st Army at Amiens; at the same time measures were to be taken towards co-operating with the latter troops.

In consequence of General Lippe's division having thus moved to the right, the *1st Army Corps*, the left wing of which had hitherto been at Elbeuf, received orders on the 17th to occupy Gisors and to keep up the communication with Beauvais from this place. Besides this, the following changes had taken place in the general position of the 1st Army Corps since the 14th of December.

We have read in Chapter VIII. that General Bentheim had withdrawn his troops from the Rille with the intention of dealing a heavy blow on the enemy in case the latter should advance by way of Bernay. For this purpose, on the 15th, he concentrated (Colonel Massow's detachment included) 11 battalions, 4 squadrons, and 8 batteries between Elbeuf, Grande Couronne, and La

Bouille, and moved his own head-quarters to Elbeuf. General Pritzelwitz commanded the troops on the right bank of the Seine, and had under his orders, General Zglinitzki, with 3 battalions, 4 squadrons, and 2 batteries on the line Duclair—Barentin, facing Havre; and, on the right of the former, General Brandenburg, with 1 battalion, 5 squadrons, and 2 batteries. The latter held the line Pavilly—Cleres, from whence he watched the country in the direction of Dieppe. On the 14th the enemy's outposts were discovered half-way between Harfleur and St. Romain. A war steamer anchored at Caudebec, from which troops disembarked and fired on our patrols with musketry and artillery. On the 15th all had again disappeared, and nothing was to be seen of the enemy, even beyond Caudebec, Yvetot, and Yerville. On the 17th, however, our outposts at Duclair were again disturbed by the enemy's gunboats.

On the 16th General Bentheim advanced with the 1st Division on the left bank of the Seine: his main body reached Bourgtheroulde, the advanced guard St. Denis des Monts. Patrols that were sent forward to the Rille found Montfort unoccupied and the country farther south free from the enemy; but the heights on the left bank of the Rille beyond Brionne were occupied in force. The expectation which General Bentheim entertained of being able to strike a decisive blow in the country *between* the Seine and the Rille was therefore not realized this time. The accounts which came in from the right bank of the Seine made it appear injudicious to move stil farther from Rouen. Besides this, the action of both cavalry and artillery was much cramped by the increasing intricacy of the country. General Bentheim, therefore, determined to withdraw his troops to Rouen. He sent them there on the 17th, and established his line of defence on the left bank between Grande Couronne and Pont de l'Arche. Colonel Massow remained in this position with 1 regiment of infantry, 1 squadron, and 1 battery. On the 19th an 'Etappen' detachment (2 companies and 1 squadron) destined to occupy Gisors set off; under its escort the horse-artillery battery of General Brandenburg's Brigade returned to the Army of the Meuse. The Guard Dragoon Brigade itself remained with the 1st Army, and one squadron which had been hitherto stationed at Chantilly returned to the brigade by way of Gournay. We now leave the troops at the Seine in these positions and *return to the events in the east.*

No further advance of the enemy beyond La Fère had taken place in this quarter. It must remain undecided whether the counter-measures taken by the German troops had induced the French to abandon their purpose, or whether the whole movement had only been intended as a diversion to arrest our operations in Normandy; or, lastly, whether it was perhaps only meant to mask some other plan. According to the book written by General Faidherbe, who had in the meantime taken command of the French Army of the North, the French leaders had become convinced that La Fère could not be taken by a *coup de main,* and had therefore on the 14th already made up their minds to march upon Amiens. Be this as it may, with the exception of the trifling success obtained at Ham, the enemy derived no advantage from this La Fère expedition. The enemy's march upon Amiens did not follow close upon this diversion; therefore, by prematurely drawing our attention to the danger threatening from the north, it gave us time to make arrangements calculated to meet any eventualities.[1]

The accounts which reached Rouen immediately after the 14th did not at first throw a clear light on our adversary's intentions. It was reported from La Fère that the whole neighbourhood was evacuated by the enemy on the 14th. The French troops (5,000 men, with 18 guns), who had taken up a position opposite to the west front of the fortress on the 12th, had withdrawn

---

[1] We take this opportunity of correcting an opinion expressed by General Faidherbe, viz., that the return of the VIIIth Army Corps from Normandy had been decided on in consequence of the events at Ham and La Fère. To refute this we only need point to the army order issued on the 9th December, *previous* to the surprise of Ham. *Vide* Chapter VIII.

in two columns on the 13th—with one column, it was said, over Moy ; with the other, over Chauny in the direction of Noyon. Further reports came in on the 15th, stating the re-organised Army of the North to be marching in three columns, with a force of about 36,000 men, upon Abbeville and Amiens. It was said that another 20,000 men were at Lens, north of Arras, that a considerable force was assembling at St. Omer, and that the *levée en masse* ordered by Gambetta was progressing with undeniable success.

The same day reports reached Rouen from the reconnaissances ordered on the 13th, and pushed on the 14th from Albert to the rear of Péronne. One of the patrols sent in this direction came upon a line of French skirmishers at Le Sars, on the Albert—Bapaume road; another one reached the Bapaume—Péronne road without opposition. Both agreed in confirming the previous reports that troops of the enemy were marching southwards from Arras and Cambrai. They said that the columns which came from Arras were conveyed by railway as far as Achiet-le-Grand, a point north of the spot at which the rails were broken up near Avelay, and then marched by way of Bapaume to Péronne. Major Troschke, commander of a detachment stationed at Domart on the Luce, had also sent patrols to Roye on the 14th. The town was found to be occupied by the enemy, mostly only cavalry, but large bivouac-fires were seen south of the place.

When all these reports were compared at Rouen, the impression they produced was that the enemy was still occupied in concentrating his forces behind the Somme, under cover of Péronne. Whether the enemy's troops at Roye had the importance of an advanced-guard pushed forward in this direction, or whether this move was also nothing more than a mere diversion, was not clear. On the 15th or 16th of December it was equally unknown which direction the enemy's coming operations might take.

Towards the evening of the 16th, the German prefect of

Amiens arrived at Head-Quarters in Rouen with a letter from General Groeben. This letter showed that, according to the view he took of the situation, the general had deemed it advisable to leave only 2 companies of infantry, with the garrison artillerymen and pioneers in the citadel, and to march with the whole remaining force early on the 16th to join the 15th Division at Montdidier. This proved that the army orders of the 14th were not yet in the hands of the general when he took this step. In consequence of the departure of the troops, the Inspection-General of 'Etappen' and the German civil authorities established at Amiens had also quitted the town. The former had gone with the military chest to Conty, the latter had come to Rouen by rail.

The instructions given to General Groeben did not certainly set aside the possibility of Amiens being momentarily given up. But, from moral and political reasons, Head-Quarters of the army set great store on maintaining the German occupation of Amiens as long as possible. Amiens was therefore not to be defended to the utmost, nor were the troops to be sacrificed for this purpose, but it was not wished to make any alterations in the state of affairs there without cogent military reasons. Without such reasons existing, the departure of all troops from Amiens southwards might easily, at least in the eyes of our adversaries, appear like an involuntary evacuation of the place, caused by the *general* state of affairs. We know how apt the French were to draw conclusions of this kind, and how easily they were, under such circumstances, excited and morally buoyed up.

The Commander-in-Chief, therefore, deemed it necessary to restore the momentary position of affairs at Amiens to its former state, and this, if possible, before Amiens should be occupied by hostile troops. If necessary, it was to be effected by force of arms.

The case was so urgent that two mounted orderly officers were despatched from Rouen on the evening of the 16th with

Amiens evacuated.

escorts. One rode straight to Bréteuil (61 miles in a direct line), the other went per rail to Forges and then rode to Bréteuil. Both arrived here almost at the same time (7.30 A.M. of the 17th), and reported to General Kummer, who, as we have heard, had the command of the troops in this quarter, pending General Goeben's arrival. The letters brought by both officers contained the following instructions:

General Mirus was to start immediately to re-occupy Amiens, either with 3 battalions, or, if General Kummer thought necessary, with the whole infantry of the 3rd Brigade, as well as with 1 cavalry regiment and 2 batteries. General Groeben now resumed command of the cavalry division. As soon as the 2 regiments returned from General Dohna's detachment the division was to be formed as at the commencement of the war.

The 17th, 18th, and 19th of December.

The accounts which had reached Rouen from all quarters up to the forenoon of the 17th confirmed the retreat of the enemy to the Somme. The French detachment in Roye had also been withdrawn, but the enemy still continued to make expeditions south of the Somme. On the 15th our hospital at Quesnel was carried off by a French squadron. It was also proved for certain that considerable forces of the enemy were still marching from the north to the neighbourhood of Péronne.

General Manteuffel's original intention had been to move his Head-Quarters to Beauvais, in consequence of the Versailles instructions of the 14th. But now that all accounts and recent events showed that the Somme department was becoming the most important scene of action, the Commander-in-Chief determined to go there himself. Before leaving Rouen he telegraphed to General Moltke on the forenoon of the 17th, as follows:

'According to Your Excellency's instructions the position at Beauvais was to have been occupied, in order to cover the north investment of Paris, and, in case of eventualities, to push forward to Rouen or Amiens. The latter is now the most pressing. I therefore shall not let the 16th Division march to Beauvais, but shall assemble the bulk of my army on the line Bréteuil—Montdidier, whereby the troops will be spared a détour and will be more at hand for Amiens or for assuming the offensive northwards.'

At mid-day the Commander-in-Chief and his staff, escorted by Captain Plötz's squadron of the 1st Guard Dragoons, rode away from Rouen and established Head-Quarters at Le Héron.[1] From here the following orders were issued on the afternoon of the 17th, in accordance with the aforesaid telegram:

'According to the intelligence received in the course of yesterday and to-day, the enemy has not continued his march in the direction of Paris; he has, on the contrary, left the neighbourhood of Laon, La Fère, and Roye, and withdrawn behind the Somme by way of Ham.. He seems now to be drawing reinforcements from Arras and organising his troops in the neighbourhood of Péronne. Before the 1st Army undertakes any further operations, it must first be concentrated; my orders therefore are as follow: The 15th Division will form in and north of Montdidier, will wait there until the whole VIIIth Army Corps is assembled, and will open communication with General Lippe's detachment in Compiègne. Partial engagements with the enemy are to be avoided. The 16th Division will discontinue its march in the direction of Beauvais, and move from its present quarters in that of Bréteuil and Conty.' (The orders given to the 3rd Infantry Brigade and the 3rd Cavalry Brigade on the evening of the 16th remained unchanged.)

Towards evening of the 18th, General Manteuffel reached Marseille after a ride of $31\frac{1}{2}$ miles; on the 19th he was at Bréteuil. Official reports and other news, of which part awaited

---

[1] A chateau in the valley of the Andelle, near to the Rouen—Gournay road, belonging to the Pommereux family.

him there and part came in after his arrival, showed the state of affairs up to the 19th December to be as follows :

1. *General Groeben's detachment* had reached Ailly on the 16th, and pursued its march to Montdidier on the 17th. The main body of the 15th Division arrived here the same day. General Kummer had meanwhile received the orders of the Commander-in-Chief, commanding Amiens to be immediately re-occupied. He now gave the following orders : ' General Mirus will start for Amiens by way of Ailly early on the 18th, with 5 battalions, 4 squadrons, and 2 batteries, and must arrive there without fail the same day. If necessary, he must enter the town by force of arms. He will then push forward reconnaissances to the north of Amiens.'

These orders were carried out. General Mirus entered without opposition on the 18th.

The inhabitants of Amiens had in the meantime remained tolerably quiet. The French authorities had themselves issued placards, exhorting the population to behave with quiet and prudence, and especially insisting on the hospitals left in the town being respected.[1] All that happened was that a few hundred workmen assembled before the citadel, apparently with hostile intentions, but a few musket shots sufficed to disperse them. The commandant of the citadel, Captain Hubert, had announced that he would bombard the town if any attempt were made against the citadel : this seems to have made a great impression. On the afternoon of the 17th, troops of the enemy, headed by a squadron, were seen towards the east, moving in the direction of Pont les Metz. The commandant fired six shells at them, whereupon they withdrew. At mid-day of the 18th, movements of the enemy were again reported. This time they were on the Poullainville and Rainneville roads. The citadel fired five shells in this direction, and the enemy re-

---

[1] In consideration of this praiseworthy conduct on the part of the inhabitants, the commander-in-chief remitted a contribution which had been imposed upon the town by the commandant of the citadel.

treated northwards. In the course of the forenoon a patrol, which had been sent to Longeau (a village south of Amiens), had been fired at there by hostile troops. Thus, though no soldier of the enemy set foot in the town, still it was very evident that it had been the enemy's intention to gain possession of the place, and that he had been very near doing so.[1]

After entering the town, General Mirus sent out reconnoitring parties in all directions. The German prefect resumed his functions.

2. *15th Division.*—The advanced-guard of the 30th Brigade, under the command of Colonel Loe, occupied Roye on the afternoon of the 17th, and opened communications with the Saxon 18th Lancer regiment. This regiment belonged to a detachment (2 battalions, 17th and 18th Regiments of Lancers, and 1 battery) which had been pushed forward from Compiègne, under command of General Krug, by General Lippe's Cavalry Division. It had reached Noyon and Roye on the 17th, and had sent detachments of cavalry farther on to Ham and Nesle. These detachments and Colonel Loe's patrols brought back the news that forces of the enemy had marched from Nesle to Chaulnes on the 15th and 16th of December, and that the troops that had evacuated Roye had also gone to Chaulnes. A battalion of 'Chasseurs-á-pied' and some companies of 'gardes mobiles' had left Chaulnes early on the 17th and marched in the direction of Amiens. One of Colonel Loe's patrols had been fired at by these troops at Chaulnes. It was now the general opinion that the French Army of the North was marching along the Somme upon Amiens. On receiving these reports, General Kummer pushed forward the 30th Brigade on the 18th from Montdidier to the neighbourhood of Davenescourt on the Avre; the 29th Brigade reached Montdidier on the same day. No further movements of the enemy were, however, perceived on this side

[1] According to General Faidherbe's book, Generals Faidherbe and Farre reconnoitred the town in person from the high ground in front of the Faubourg Noyon on the 18th.

of the Somme; therefore General Kummer remained in his position between Montdidier and the Avre during the 19th, to await the arrival of the remainder of the VIIIth Army Corps, as General Manteuffel's orders desired. It was at first intended that the 3rd Cavalry Division, less the 7th Lancers which were with General Mirus, should assemble at Montdidier; but in consequence of the news received of the enemy, the division was also moved more to the north. On the 19th it stood in the neighbourhood of Arvillers, Bouchoir, Le Quesnel, and Hangest. One battalion and half a squadron of the 30th Brigade were at Roye.

3. *General Goeben* quitted his original line of march on Beauvais and turned to the left on the 18th. On the 19th he reached the neighbourhood of Conty with the 16th Division, and Bréteuil with the corps artillery. His Head-Quarters were at Ailly.

The *Inspection-General of 'Etappen*,' with its small escort, had been at Conty since the 16th. Early on the 18th strong bands of franc-tireurs and 'gardes mobiles' advanced from Poix; General Malotki was therefore obliged to fall back to Bréteuil. The very next day, however, the advance of the 16th Division compelled the enemy to retreat from Poix in the direction of Abbeville. Thus, upon the whole, the VIIIth Army Corps was within the square, Conty—Moreuil—Montdidier—Bréteuil, on the 19th of December. Detachments were pushed forward on both wings, viz., the 3rd Cavalry Division at Quesnel, General Mirus at Amiens, a small detachment at Roye. Head-Quarters of the army and the Inspection-General of 'Etappen' were in Bréteuil.

4. The forces which the enemy was evidently assembling behind the Somme were undoubtedly numerically superior to those of the 1st Army, which had besides to maintain its position at Rouen. It was, therefore, General Manteuffel's wish that the 14th Division should join the Army, and that Mézières should only be *watched* by General Senden's detachment, which had a smaller force of infantry. When Montmédy fell he made this

wish known at Head-Quarters at Versailles ; but after due consideration, the latter decided that the 14th Division, the foremost troops of which reached Boulzicourt on the 19th, should proceed with the *siege* of Mézières. However, on the very same day, *General Senden's detachment* set off to rejoin the 1st Army. The route for the detachment was fixed at Versailles: it was to march by way of Marle, reach St. Quentin on the 25th of December, and be joined by its absent detachment at Laon.

5. In addition to this, another Guard Cavalry Brigade (Guard Hussar and 2nd Guard Lancer regiments and 1 Horse Artillery battery) was put together under the command of Prince Albrecht, Junior, and placed at the disposal of the 1st Army. It was to reach Beauvais on the 22nd of December.[1]

6. Besides the official reports regarding the enemy which we have already mentioned, the following important news reached Bréteuil on the 19th.

A telegram arrived from Versailles stating that Faidherbe had concentrated part of the French Army of the North on the 16th at St. Quentin, and that the last mobilized troops having joined the army from Lille, he now had 62,000 men in the field.

According to other accounts, the enemy's forces opposed to the 1st Army Corps at Havre were estimated at 40,000 men.

Before reaching Bréteuil the Commander-in-Chief had already had a personal interview with General Goeben at Crêvecœur, between Marseille and Bréteuil, the result of which was that it was considered advisable to move the VIIIth Army Corps nearer to Amiens. The state of affairs which we have described above, and with which the Commander-in-Chief became acquainted on arriving at Bréteuil, especially the reports sent in by the 15th Division, showing the enemy to be moving his forces westward, tended to confirm this opinion.

[1] It was intended to reinforce the 1st Army still further by again giving it 8 mobilized Landwehr battalions for garrison and 'Etappen' service. The approaching arrival of these troops by way of La Fère was already notified, but the measure was for the time not carried into effect. On the contrary, the 8 battalions were sent to the south of Alsace, where circumstances demanded an increased display of troops.

Reconnaissance North of Amiens.

As all the troops operating against the Somme had been placed under General Goeben's orders, the Commander-in-Chief requested him to reinforce the garrison of Amiens by a brigade next day, and to move all his other troops nearer to the Somme if his opinion on the state of affairs should make it appear necessary.

The 20th and 21st of December.

General Goeben consequently caused the following movements to be effected on the *20th of December*:

The 16th Division moved the 32nd Brigade to Amiens, the 31st to Sains and Boves. The 15th Division advanced to the Luce, posted one brigade at Démuin, the other at Rosières, and pushed forward patrols to the Somme. The corps artillery went to Ailly, Moreuil, and the intermediate villages. The 3rd Cavalry Division marched to Chaulnes and Lihons, and reconnoitred the country to the north and east.

Generals Manteuffel and Goeben transferred their Head-Quarters to Amiens on the 20th. The same day General Ruville, recently appointed commandant of Amiens by his Majesty the King, arrived there. Count Lehndorff-Steinort was installed as Prefect of the Somme department, the previous prefect resuming his duties as Intendant of the Army. Herr von Pfuel was appointed Prefect of Rouen.

Whilst the VIIIth Army Corps was thus approaching Amiens and the Somme, General Mirus despatched a reconnoitring party, under Major Bock (1 battalion of the 44th Regiment, a detachment of cavalry, and 2 guns), on the road to Albert. As far as the country was commanded by the citadel the detachment met with no opposition. As soon, however, as it approached the woods southward of Allonville, in the neighbourhood of Querrieux, it was attacked on all sides by very superior numbers, and obliged to retreat to Amiens, closely pursued by the enemy, and with a loss of 50 men killed and wounded, besides a few missing. Though the detachment had not been able to get up to the enemy's main position, still it might well be assumed that the bulk of his forces was in the region between the Somme and the Hallue.

On the right bank of the former river the line of the enemy's outposts was now pushed forward to within three miles of the citadel of Amiens. As this made it appear probable that the enemy would soon assume the offensive, it became of the utmost importance to watch the passages over the Somme with great attention. General Mirus occupied the faubourgs St. Pierre and St. Maurice right and left of the citadel, the town bridge, and the bridge at La Motte. The observation of the Somme below Amiens was undertaken by the 16th Division; that of this river above the mouth of the Hallue, by the 15th Division and the 3rd Cavalry Division.

The following were the results of the reconnaissances which were made in the course of the *21st of December*:

The enemy had troops at Corbie. He held the whole line of the Somme from Bray to Corbie, and had destroyed all large bridges along this tract; wherever smaller bridges led over the stream, at mills or sluices of the canals, he had pushed outposts over on to the opposite bank. From Péronne several detachments were also posted on the left bank of the Somme. In the direction of Albert the enemy's line of outposts was westward of the woods of Querrieux and Allonville, in face of our outposts. On the road farther to the west, leading to Doullens and Abbeville, there was nothing to be seen of the enemy.

The vicinity of the enemy's army, from all quarters unanimously stated to number 60,000 men, left scarcely any doubt as to its being his intention to re-take Amiens. Orders were therefore sent to General Goeben on the afternoon of the 21st to concentrate his troops round Amiens next day. The 15th Division and 3rd Cavalry Division were to be pushed to the left, and due steps taken to mask this movement.

The 22nd of December.

These movements were executed on the 22nd of December. The army now stood in a concentrated position in and round Amiens, on the left bank of the Somme, viz.:

General Mirus's detachment in Amiens; the 16th Division there also, and in the villages south-west of the town; the 15th Division in Camons, and southwards; the corps artillery to the rear of the latter; the 8th Rifle battalion in Villers-Brétonneux; General Dohna's combined brigade in the same quarter, for the purpose of watching Corbie and the upper Somme.

Thus, the 1st Army had assembled 5 brigades of infantry and a division of cavalry at Amiens. In face of the army was the French Army of the North, behind the Somme and the Hallue. General Faidherbe's Head-Quarters were said to have been at Corbie since the 18th of December. Notwithstanding the undoubted numerical superiority he possessed, the enemy still remained inactive, and was employed, as we afterwards discovered, in entrenching his position.

On the right bank of the Somme, between Amiens and Querrieux, and on the left bank, between Corbie and Villers-Brétonneux, the outposts of both armies were in close contact.

CHAPTER XI.

The Battle of the Hallue—Reflections and Measures preceding the Battle.

IN the preceding chapter we have followed the movements of the troops nearest at hand up to the moment of their concentration at Amiens. The unexpected strength of the enemy's army made it on all accounts desirable on our part to bring as large a force as possible to the scene of action. Before entering upon the measures taken with this intention and the resolutions which followed them, it is necessary to direct attention to such other circumstances as had an influence on them.

In conformity with the instructions of the 13th December given to the 1st Army, *general* instructions for the operations in France were given by the King's Head-Quarters at Versailles on the 17th. We begin by citing them, because they give a picture of the general military situation and the opinion prevailing at the time. They ran as follows:

'General circumstances make it necessary to follow up the pursuit of the enemy after a victory only so far as is requisite to disperse the bulk of his forces, and prevent his reassembling them for some time. We cannot follow him up to his last strongholds, Lille, Havre, and Bourges, nor can we permanently occupy such provinces as Normandy, Brittany, or the Vendée; on the contrary, we must make up our minds even to withdraw from points that we have gained—for instance, from Dieppe, or, if necessary, also from Tours—so as to concentrate the bulk of our forces at a few principal points. These latter must, as far as possible, be occupied by whole brigades, divisions, or corps.

General Instructions sent from Versailles. 147

From such points flying columns must clear the country of franc-tireurs; we must wait at them until the enemy has again grouped his masses in organised armies, and then rapidly assume the offensive against the latter.

'This will in all probability afford our troops the period of rest of which they have need, to recover from their fatigue, to bring up reinforcements and ammunition, and to repair their clothing.

'His Majesty the King's commands in this respect are as follows:

'To cover the Investment of Paris towards the north, the main forces of the Ist Army will be concentrated at Beauvais (afterwards at Creil, as soon as the railways can be used for the transport of large masses of troops). Rouen, Amiens, and St. Quentin will remain occupied, the latter town by General Senden's Division, which will soon be moved there. The Ist Army will give up the left bank of the Seine. On the other hand, this stream must be watched as far as Vernon.

'In the west, the troops of the Grand Duke will be assembled at Chartres, with a strong detachment at Dreux, as soon as the present pursuit of the enemy shall have come to an end.

'In the south, the main force of the IInd Army is concentrating at Orleans. It will give up the country on the left bank of the Loire and confine itself to watching the district lying towards the Cher. If Tours be not occupied, Blois and Gien must be so. Bridges further up the river must be destroyed as far as possible.

'Care must be taken that in case the above-named principal points be attacked, they receive timely assistance; supports must, at all events, be at hand for detachments that may be driven out of them to fall back upon, and then to advance again.

(Signed) 'MOLTKE.'

In connection herewith we must now cast a glance at the *state of affairs at Rouen* at this time. Since the departure of the Commander-in-Chief, General Bentheim held Rouen with the

1st Division, and had lately re-occupied the line La Bouillée—Elbeuf—Pont de l'Arche, on the left bank of the Seine. On the right bank General Pritzelwitz continued to hold the line Duclair—Barentin—Cleres against Hâvre and Dieppe, with the 4th Brigade and the Guard Dragoon Brigade. The corps artillery was now westward of Rouen at Maromme. Small infantry detachments, with a few cavalry soldiers, guarded the railway-stations at Buchy and Forges. It was General Bentheim's intention to wait in general in this position, in readiness to assume the offensive against any advance of the enemy from Hâvre, and only to hold the aforesaid withdrawn position on the left bank. Continued reconnaissances on both banks of the Seine had failed to discover any symptoms of an advance on the part of the enemy; hostilities were confined to some desultory skirmishing between Prussian patrols and 'gardes mobiles' on the left bank of the river.

Nevertheless, the neighbourhood of Brionne and Bernay on the one, and the advanced line of defence in front of Hâvre on the other bank, were still occupied by the enemy in force. Joint operations of both hostile detachments were ere long to be expected, the more so from their being especially favoured by the locality. Whereas the only communication between both banks of the Seine open to the Prussians was at Rouen, the enemy's steam fleet, partly consisting of ironclads, gave him the command of the Seine. His vessels repeatedly disturbed our troops on the right bank, and enabled him to communicate freely from bank to bank.[1]

Taken in the abstract, the situation at Rouen offered no

---

[1] We may here briefly relate what measures General Bentheim took to protect himself, as far as possible, against the above-mentioned evils. He barred the stream at Duclair, where the Seine is above 900 feet broad, and 35 feet deep at low tide, by sinking several ships, a procedure which gave rise to the well-known complaints made by England. In order to command this point a battery was established at La Fontaine: this effectually stopped for the moment any further passage of the enemy's ships of war. In order to guard against being taken unawares by any advance of the enemy by land from Hâvre, General Bentheim also caused the railway bridge at Yvetot to be blown up.

inducement to diminish the number of troops stationed there, but the momentary state of affairs at Amiens and the tenor of the instructions of the 17th justified the determination, already formed on the 21st, to reinforce the troops at Amiens by bringing up 6 battalions per rail from Rouen. A railway official was sent on the 21st from Amiens to Rouen to make preparations for this transport. It is true, this measure reduced the number of the troops at the Seine to 13 battalions. On the other hand, according to the latest instructions, General Bentheim could now be released from the duty of sending troops to the left bank of this river. Rouen itself was still to be maintained. In case, however, superior forces of the enemy should make it necessary to evacuate the town for a time—an eventuality which, though not anticipated, still was by no means impossible—then General Bentheim was instructed not to retreat in the direction of Paris, but to seek connection with the 1st Army by way of Beauvais or Marseille. It was hoped that a flank operation of this kind would draw the enemy away from Paris, in case he should show signs of advancing by way of Rouen.

These were the instructions sent to General Bentheim, so far as they related to materially reinforcing the infantry at Amiens. We premise here that the prescribed transport was not effected with the desired expedition, in consequence of the insufficiency of the working material of the railway. Only 2 battalions of the 3rd Regiment reached Amiens in the course of the 22nd; the 4 other battalions followed on the 23rd and 24th.

The only other immediate co-operation in prospect within the next few days was that of *Prince Albrecht's Brigade of Guard Cavalry*, which reached Beauvais on the 22nd. Orders were sent to it by telegraph to set off for Amiens on the 23rd, and to arrive there on the 24th. This telegram was followed by a written *exposé* of the state of affairs at Amiens. It was hereby recommended that part of the brigade should march by way of Moreuil, in order to reconnoitre the country in the direction of the Somme, which river was commanded by the enemy from the mouth of the Hallue upwards. At the same time the brigade was to open communication with Generals Senden and Lippe in the direction of Noyon and Ham.

With regard to the last-named detachments, *General Senden* had been desired on the 21st to expedite his march as much as possible. He returned answer per telegram on the 22nd, from his quarters at Montcourt, that he would reach St. Quentin on the 24th instead of on the 25th. General Senden was then ordered to second the operations of the army by pushing forward in the direction of Péronne, retreating, if necessary, on Noyon or La Fère.

Lastly, it was telegraphed to *General Lippe* (who since the 21st had been at Beauvais with 1 brigade of cavalry, ½ battalion, and 1 battery, and with mixed detachments at Compiègne and Clermont) that an advance on his part to Ham on the 24th would afford a very desirable support to the operations at Amiens.

After this survey of the forces ready to take part, either directly or indirectly, in the approaching struggle at Amiens, we will now imagine ourselves at the Commander-in-Chief's Head-Quarters on the forenoon of the 22nd December. As was the case before the battle fought in November, the decision now to be formed was discussed at a conference which took place here, and to which General Manteuffel summoned Generals Goeben and Sperling and Colonel Wartensleben.

In face of the passive conduct of the enemy, the 1st Army might, under other circumstances, have contented itself with a mere defence of the Amiens position, the approach to which was attended with considerable difficulty, by reason of the Somme and of the citadel, which was in our hands.

Very cogent reasons, however, were opposed to such a proceeding. In the first place, the Commander-in-Chief put great faith in the moral element. To stop for several days in the present position, suffering a hostile army to remain in such dangerous and close proximity to the important town of Amiens,

Reasons for assuming the Offensive.

could not be without influence on the state of feeling of the hostile country, and must produce a depressing effect on the sense of victory which prevailed in our own army. Added to this, the situation at Rouen demanded that a decisive blow should be struck. If, for instance, hesitation on our part at Amiens left the enemy at the Seine leisure to plan and execute combined offensive operations, the 1st Army Corps, weakened as it was by the many detachments it had sent off, might in the meantime be attacked from Hâvre and Bernay at the same time, and perhaps compelled to evacuate Rouen.

Therefore, setting aside the possibility of our enemy at the Somme being also able to bring up reinforcements daily if we delayed any longer, regard for the state of affairs at Rouen prevented our waiting to bring General Senden's troops up from St. Quentin to Amiens. Thus, though our force was numerically inferior to that of the enemy, the determination to assume the offensive was firmly adhered to, in accordance with the spirit in which the whole war had been conducted and in unbounded confidence in the superior firmness of our troops. There were, however, different ways of so doing.

An *attack from the south* across the Somme, a river so difficult of passage, appeared scarcely feasible, and, if successful, would, supposing the Somme to mark the front of the enemy's position, only force the enemy back in the direction of his natural line of retreat. There still remained two alternatives: either to march from Amiens to the right, keeping possession of the citadel, and then, after being joined by General Senden's Division, to attack the enemy from *the east*, or to debouch from Amiens and attack his *right flank*.

Opinions differed with regard to the two last-mentioned plans of attack. The operations seemed more securely based if the attack were made from the east, and then reinforcements might be brought up for the day of battle. But in that case the enemy might also be able to derive the same advantage, and a temporary evacuation of Amiens could not be avoided. If, on the other hand, we assumed the offensive *forwards, or beyond Amiens*, there need be no hesitation in diminishing the garrison of the town in rear of the army. After fully discussing and carefully weighing all circumstances, the Commander-in-Chief pronounced in favour of the latter alternative.

In the course of the preceding discussion it had been remarked that the enemy's position behind the Hallue might just as well be merely the flank of his main-position behind the Somme as the main-position itself. It was with a view to this eventuality that the following general plan of attack was discussed and fixed to take place on the 23rd.

General Goeben was to advance with the VIIIth Army Corps and 3 regiments of the Cavalry Division by the roads leading to the Hallue. His right flank division would, if possible, first drive the enemy back behind the Hallue, then establish itself on this line and hold the enemy fast in the front. His left flank division and the cavalry would take the road to Acheux, and then press and attempt to turn the enemy's right flank, which was expected to be in that quarter. The Commander-in-Chief would hold the remaining troops in reserve, and employ them as circumstances might demand.

In conformity with this verbal arrangement the following army orders were issued on the afternoon of the 22nd:

'To-morrow we shall march against the enemy who stands close before us. I need say no more to the 1st Army.

'My orders are as follows:

'1. The VIIIth Army Corps and 3rd Cavalry Division will start at 8. A.M. to-morrow. General Goeben has already received his instructions. The VIIIth Army Corps will provide for the necessary number of bridges above and below the town.

'2. The 3rd Regiment, 5 battalions of the 3rd Brigade, with both batteries of the latter, and 1 regiment of cavalry will form my reserve.[1]

'A detachment of this reserve, consisting of the 3rd Regiment

---

[1] The regiment in question was the 5th Regiment of Lancers.

Disposition for the Attack of the Enemy. 153

of Infantry, lately arrived from Rouen, 1 squadron, and 1 battery, will be at La Motte Brébière[1] by 10 A.M. The 5 battalions of the 3rd Brigade, 3 squadrons, and 1 battery, under command of General Mirus, will leave Amiens at 11 A.M. and take up a covert position south of the wood on a line with the Ferme les Allenbons (on the road to Querrieux).

'3. There will remain at Amiens, at the disposal of the Commandant:

'*a*. The garrison of the citadel.

'*b*. The " Etappen " Battalion.

'*c*. The foot-sore men of the VIIIth Army Corps formed as a battalion.

'*d*. The battalions of the 1st Army Corps that will begin to arrive early to-morrow morning.[2]

'4. Until further orders no baggage is to be taken across the Somme.

'5. The crossing of the lines of march of the troops in the interior of the town must be avoided.

'6. I shall march with the leading battalions of General Mirus's detachment; all reports to be sent there until further orders.

(Signed) ' MANTEUFFEL.'

The following instructions were, in the first instance, given to the detachment which was sent to La Motte:

'At 10 A.M. to-morrow the detachment will occupy the bridge at La Motte Brébière, and defend it against any attack of the enemy proceeding from the right bank of the Somme; covering itself at the same time against any advance of the enemy on the left bank. If possible, the artillery will take up a position on the left bank from which it can fire on the enemy's flank during the advance of our troops. The detachment must, however, on no account engage in any combat that may lead to further

---

[1] Passage over the Somme between Amiens and the mouth of the Hallue.
[2] These battalions were afterwards brought up to the battle-field.

consequences, but must only hold the passage over the river. It will remain there until it receives direct orders from Head-Quarters of the Army.

(Signed) 'SPERLING.'

The results of the arrangements made on the 22nd, and the determination to assume the offensive, were telegraphed to Versailles the same evening.

The reconnaissances were repeated on the 22nd, and confirmed the observations previously made in all essential points. All bridges over the Somme, between Pont St. Christ (south of Péronne) and Vecquemont, at the mouth of the Hallue, with the exception of a few foot-bridges, were destroyed and occupied by the enemy. The enemy's line then followed the course of the Hallue from Vecquemont past Querrieux to Beaucourt. Advanced detachments were seen in the wood near Allonville and at St. Gratien.

December the 23rd.

The weather, which had become milder since the 15th December, had gradually changed to frost after the 20th. When day broke on the 23rd, the thermometer stood at 8 degrees below zero. The weather was calm and clear.

At 8 A.M. the 15th Division, the horse-artillery Division of the corps artillery, and General Dohna's Brigade of cavalry, crossed the Somme on bridges thrown over the river above Amiens, at Camons, and La Neuville. The troops then advanced on and to the right of the Albert road. The debouché was delayed for about an hour in consequence of the sinking of the bridge at Neuville. The Rifle Battalion had received orders to wait opposite Corbie until 9 A.M.; it now came up also by way of La Motte, and advanced on the extreme right wing in the direction of the Vecquemont—Daours group of villages. The 16th Division, and the field batteries of the corps artillery, passed through Amiens. They were ordered by General Goeben to take the road to Rainneville and Pierregot, and then to turn to the right against the enemy's flank. General Dohna's Brigade (8th Cuirassiers and 14th Lancers) kept up the connection between both Divisions. Lieut.-Col. Pestel, with the 7th Lancer Regiment, scoured the country towards Abbeville, in order to cover Amiens in this direction also. He stood at Picquigny during the 23rd, his advanced detachments watching the enemy's troops that showed themselves near Longpré and in other places. General Goeben accompanied the 15th Division.

At 11 A.M. the Commander-in-Chief followed at the head of the Reserve on the high-road to Albert. The passage at La Motte was occupied in the prescribed manner.

We have already mentioned that the country on the right bank of the Somme was perfectly open, and commanded by the citadel to a considerable distance. Four miles and a half further on towards Albert, the high-road passes through some woods of no considerable dimensions. A mile before reaching Querrieux, the plateau again becomes perfectly open, and falls in gentle slopes down to the Hallue, in itself an unimportant rivulet, but accompanied by wet meadows, and therefore in general only to be crossed by the bridges in the numerous villages. The latter form groups of villages lying partly on both banks of the stream. On the opposite bank of the Hallue the eastern slopes of the hills rise without break, and often in very steep ascents, to a considerable height. From thence every part of the west side, the one on which the Prussian forces were then advancing, was commanded. Beyond those eastern heights, between the upper Hallue and the Encre rivulet, which falls into the Somme eastward of Daours, a broad plateau, for the most part open and with very few impediments, extends up to the neighbourhood of Albert.

The enemy had only a few outposts in the country west of the Hallue. The foremost line or advanced-guard of the French Army occupied the villages on the Hallue, especially those on the east bank, in force. To judge by the prisoners we took afterwards, the best troops of the army seem to have been stationed here. Behind this line of 6¾ miles length, reaching from Daours to Contay, stood the masses of the French reserves, on the high ground eastward of the valley. They were placed partly behind the summit of the heights and partly filled the rifle-pits in front of the batteries which were placed in entrenchments along the whole line. These latter were, for the most part, armed with heavy marine guns of considerable range.[1]

The advance of the 15th Division very soon drove back the weak outposts of the enemy, and the leading troops of the division reached the Hallue at 11 A.M. They found Querrieux evacuated by the enemy, but the opposite village of Pont Noyelles, as well as the villages Bussy and Daours, were occupied

[1] Appendix No. 3 shows the order of battle of the French Army of the North at the end of December, copied from a Cambrai newspaper : it tallys tolerably accurately with the statements made by a Belgian paper somewhat later. According to these accounts the French Army numbered about 57 battalions, forming 3 divisions, a very small force of cavalry, and an uncertain number of batteries. According to General Faidherbe's work these statements require the following additions : During the period which preceded the battle of the Hallue, the Army of the North had been already formed into 2 Corps, the XXIInd and XXIIIrd, each of which contained 2 divisions of 2 brigades each. General Lecointe commanded the XXIInd Corps, of which General Derroja commanded the 1st, and General Bessol the 2nd Division. The XXIIIrd Corps was commanded by General Paulze d'Ivoy. The 1st Division of the Corps was originally Admiral Moulac's 3rd Division ; the 2nd was a newly formed division of 'gardes mobiles' under General Robin. The XXIInd Corps had 6, the XXIIIrd nominally 7 batteries, probably also the heavy guns. For some days previous to the battle the XXIInd Corps stood along the Hallue from Daours to Contay ; the XXIIIrd, with Admiral Moulac's Division, in and round Corbie ; General Robin's Division, at Albert and farther to the south-east, covering the railway from Arras to Corbie. Detachments were stationed at Bray-sur-Somme. When the Prussian Army advanced, the French troops took up the following positions : Division Moulac on the heights of Daours and Bussy, Division Bessol opposite to Pont Noyelles and Fréchencourt ; adjoining it was General Derroja's Division, which reached to Contay. To the rear of the XXIInd Corps was General Robin's Division, in the neighbourhood of Béhencourt. According to General Faidherbe's work, he attached no great importance to holding the villages on the Hallue, a statement which is somewhat contradicted by the events of the day. It is possible that the original accounts, fixing Faidherbe's Army at 60,000 men, may have been exaggerated ; yet, according to the statements we have cited above, its 4 complete divisions cannot have contained less than from 40,000 to 45,000. If, on the Prussian side, we count all the battalions brought up from Rouen, even including those that arrived after the battle was over, taking into consideration the weak effective strength of the battalions at that time, the Prussian Army at the Hallue numbered very little more than 20,000 fighting men.

Battle of the Hallue. 23rd of December. 157

in force. Other hostile troops were visible at a wood which jutted out like a bastion on the high hills north of Pont Noyelles. These heights commanded the whole foreground to a considerable distance, and were soon crowned by the enemy's batteries. Whilst the Prussian Artillery established itself on the west side of the valley, opposite to the French batteries, the 29th Brigade (Col. Bock) proceeded to attack the line of the Hallue. An obstinate struggle ensued for the possession of the villages, during which the enemy was repeatedly reinforced by troops from Corbie. However, first Pont Noyelles, and then Bussy were both taken by Col. Bock's Brigade.

At mid-day the Commander-in-Chief arrived at the hill, south of the Allenbons wood. The reserve, under General Mirus, was further to the rear in its appointed position. At 1 P.M. Col. Witzendorff, Chief of the Staff of the VIIIth Army Corps, came up and announced the taking of Pont Noyelles. At the same time he asked for reinforcements for the right wing at Daours. In this carefully entrenched village, which was defended by 'gardes mobiles,' troops of the line, and sailors, a sanguinary combat had been raging for hours. The Prussian Rifle Batallion, coming up from La Motte, now, however, successfully joined in the fight. The troops engaged at this spot were commanded by Col. Loe.

Daours lies on the direct road from Corbie to Amiens: a bridge which crosses the Somme here had not been destroyed by the enemy. This point was, therefore, evidently of very great importance. The action having hitherto progressed favourably, it was not necessary to leave the detachment stationed at La Motte any longer at this spot; therefore the Commander-in-Chief ordered Major Lewinski, of the General Staff, to lead it to Daours. As the commander of the regiment to which the detachment belonged would not arrive until the last battalion came up from Rouen, the Commander-in-Chief desired Major Lewinski to take temporary command of these troops, and to lead them to the assistance of the troops fighting under Col. Loe for the possession of Daours. At 3 P.M. Major Lewinski reached the neighbourhood of Daours, and immediately joined in the fight. He first brought forward his artillery, and soon compelled the enemy's guns on the opposite side of the valley to withdraw, with considerable loss of horses and men. For the present he kept his 2 battalions together, so as to be able to use them as a reserve for Col. Loe's battalions, which were fighting in loose order from house to house. After a sanguinary fight, we got possession of the whole of Daours between 3 and 4 P.M. From the heights north of Daours the enemy continued to shower bullets of a large calibre from his far-ranging American and tabatière muskets on the skirts of the village. This prevented our properly occupying the outskirts; therefore, at 4.40 P.M., Major Lewinski made an attempt to advance beyond Daours with his two battalions. The enemy's position on the steep hills which rise immediately behind Daours was, however, too strong. The impossibility of gaining ground here without suffering heavy losses soon became evident, the intended advance was therefore not pushed farther than the skirts of the village.

We now turn to the centre of the battle. The station which the Commander-in-Chief had chosen, on the hill east of the wood of Les Allenbons, afforded a view over the greater part of the battle-field of the 15th Division. The above-mentioned wooded height, which projects westward of Fréchencourt on the enemy's side of the valley, shut out the view of the ground on which the 16th Division was engaged.

Even if higher orders had not been given merely to hold the enemy fast in the front, the formidable strength of the enemy's position behind Pont Noyelles would in itself have made it appear not advisable to press the attack farther at this spot. On the other hand, General Kummer hoped to be able to turn that projecting wooded height by moving more to the left, and by that means also to draw nearer to the 16th Division. He had as yet still held back the 30th Brigade (General Strubberg) in reserve; two of its battalions were now brought up to

Battle of the Hallue. 23rd of December. 159

Querrieux to support the troops in Pont Noyelles if this should prove necessary. To General Strubberg he gave orders to march to Fréchencourt with the remainder of his brigade. The enemy was just upon the point of descending the hill and advancing upon this village with large bodies of troops. General Strubberg, nevertheless, succeeded in reaching the village before the enemy and in holding it against his attacks.

The bastion-like wooded hill, however, proved to be unassailable from this side also. It was surrounded by densely-lined rifle-pits and by batteries firing from behind parapets, whilst the terraces on the face of the hill made it very difficult to ascend. After a brief but fruitless attempt the assault had to be given up. The line of the Hallue was thus in our hands from Daours to Fréchencourt, but the 15th Division was spread out over this whole line of $4\frac{1}{2}$ miles length without any reserve of its own.

General Goeben had not yet received any report from the 16th Division. Somewhat after 2 P.M., however, it seemed to him as if the operations of the division began to make some impression upon the enemy. Movements which the latter made towards his right wing tended to prove this. When this state of affairs was reported to General Manteuffel, he moved the reserve more to the front, so as to have them nearer at hand, either to support the 15th Division or to assume the offensive if these impressions were confirmed. General Manteuffel and his staff then joined General Goeben on the windmill hill at Querrieux.

Whilst these events were occurring on the right wing and in the centre, the 16th Division had marched from Rainneville upon Beaucourt, pursuant to General Goeben's orders. Here also the enemy's outposts retreated on all sides. The division reached the Hallue and took the villages and other places on the bank of the stream (Montigny, Beaucourt, Béhencourt). The heights behind Béhencourt were, however, equally strongly occupied and as difficult of access as those in front of the 15th Division. It was not only impossible to turn the enemy's flank in this quarter, but, thanks to his twofold superior numbers, the enemy was even able to outflank our line from Contay.

Thus, by 4.30 P.M., after a hard and in many cases sanguinary struggle, the VIIIth Army Corps had gained possession of the whole line of the Hallue from Beaucourt to Daours. On the other hand, the isolated attacks made upon the other side of the valley had proved unsuccessful. The result expected from the flank movement of the 16th Division had been frustrated by the superior numbers of the enemy having enabled him to outflank our line. However, our having gained possession of the passages over the Hallue barred the road to Amiens to the enemy. The principal object of our attack was, therefore, attained, so long as we were to hold our ground there in face of the superior forces of the enemy. As the evening twilight set in all our efforts had to be strained to accomplish this task. About this time movements were made by the enemy which seemed to denote his intention to assume the offensive. In consequence, General Mirus was ordered to advance with the reserve, which had in the meantime been reinforced by a battalion just arrived from Rouen, to a dell near the Querrieux windmill. By this time the enemy's artillery had set fire to all the villages on the Hallue that were occupied by our troops. A long line of burning villages threw a lurid glare over the Prussian positions, affording a sure mark for the enemy's batteries, whilst the deepening gloom of the evening hid the hostile masses from our sight.

About 5 P.M., when darkness had completely set in, an advance of the enemy took place along the whole line. It was heralded in by the horn-signals so well known from former battles, and accompanied by the noise which the French always make when they attack. At first a strong column advanced between Daours and Querrieux, trying to gain the passage over the Hallue and intercept the communication between both villages. It was a critical moment. The Commander-in-Chief immediately sent forward the 1st Battalion of the 4th Regiment from the reserve to meet the enemy. The latter was repulsed with considerable loss by the file-fire of the battalion, which only lost its leader, Captain Grumbrecht, who was killed in the immediate vicinity of the spot where the commanding generals were stationed, and 6 men wounded.

After a desperate struggle, but with only a trifling loss to themselves, Colonel Loe and Major Lewinski beat off the very determined attack which the enemy made upon Daours, although the latter advanced to within 30 paces of the village. The enemy suffered very considerably at this spot, especially during his retreat, from the fire of the Rifle Battalion, which was ensconced in the enclosure of the village.

The most violent collision took place at Pont Noyelles. Here also the enemy pressed on to the enclosure of the village, but was driven back with considerable loss. The battalions of the 29th Brigade having spent all their cartridges, General Manteuffel sent forward two more battalions from the reserve to hold the enclosure of the village until their ammunition was replenished. The enemy's attack on Fréchencourt was also decisively repulsed by General Strubberg.

In like manner the 16th Division held its ground on the west bank of the Hallue, and beat off a flank attack which the enemy made from the direction of Contay. Thus, by 6 P.M., the attacks made by the enemy with great vehemence and bravery along the whole line were victoriously repulsed at all points.

After such a result, no fresh attack on the part of the French was to be expected during the night. Besides—with the exception of the momentary participation of the reserve—the VIIIth Army Corps had shown itself capable of parrying the enemy's attack single-handed. General Manteuffel therefore ordered that the VIIIth Army Corps should hold the positions it had taken to-day from Daours to Beaucourt, and make them capable of the most obstinate resistance. Suitable positions were especially to be provided on the west bank of the Hallue.

The reserve, under General Mirus, went into alarm-quarters in

Allonville and Cardonette. If not suddenly called out earlier, it was to hold itself ready for action next morning between St. Gratien and Querrieux. The detachment of the reserve stationed at Daours was to hold this village until further orders. Colonel Legat, commander of the 3rd Regiment, had in the meantime arrived there from Rouen with the 3rd Battalion of his regiment. It was thus possible to put the greater part of the troops under shelter for the night, whereas the enemy, in expectation of *our attacking him*, was obliged to bivouack with almost the whole of his troops on the heights which formed his position, and on which there was a scarcity of villages. As soon as these arrangements were made and the troops had gone to their quarters, Generals Manteuffel and Goeben went to Amiens for the night. Thus ended the 23rd of December.

December the 24th.

The course of yesterday's events had shown that the enemy's forces were numerically too superior to admit of our carrying out our previous intentions of turning his right flank, and that the mere local strength of his position was too great to be forced by an attack in front without too heavy a loss. To expose the army to such a loss would have been all the more unjustifiable because, in consequence of their loss from fatigue and fighting, and the vacancies not being always able to be filled up regularly, our battalions did not at that time upon an average number more than about 500 fighting men each. On the other hand, the firmness and brilliant bravery of our troops justified unbounded confidence in their power of *endurance* and *tactical mobility*, in both of which qualities they were superior to the enemy. It was, therefore, determined to hold for the present the whole extent of ground which we had conquered yesterday. If the enemy should also keep in his position after the 24th, it was then intended to proceed to attack him by way of Corbie. The dispositions made for this attack will be described hereafter.

Battle of the Hallue. 24th of December.

At day-break of the 24th December, the frost had increased in intensity. An icy north-east wind blew in the men's faces the whole day long.

When the Commander-in-Chief came on the field at 9 A.M. of the 24th, and took his station on a hill to the north-west of Querrieux, the enemy still held in the main his previous positions. In the front he kept up a fire, principally of artillery, against our line, but it was, on the whole, of but little importance, and of no effect. The 16th Division only was attacked from Contay, but repulsed the enemy. In the course of the forenoon movements were already remarked on the part of the enemy, the object of which could not as yet be discerned. Columns seemed to be retiring from the ridge of the hill, whilst others were advancing in the contrary direction. The French artillery remained in its entrenched positions. About mid-day Prince Albert, Junior, arrived. He had ridden on in advance of his brigade to announce its approaching arrival on the field. The brigade was, in the first instance, placed on the right of the reserve, which had in the meantime been brought up nearer to Querrieux. Since 2.15 P.M. reports kept coming in from the Rifle Battalion at Daours, stating that considerable detachments of the enemy were marching both to and fro in the direction of Corbie and Arras. It was as yet not clear whether they were reinforcements coming up, or troops leaving the field. At all events, the enemy seemed to attach great importance to Corbie. Colonel Witzendorff, who had ridden to Daours, thought for certain that he discerned signs of the commencement of a retreat on the part of the enemy. About 4 P.M. continued reports made this still more evident.

Evening twilight, however, soon set in and prevented any further observation. It was not thought advisable to push an attack in the dark, because we had often been deceived by similar movements on the part of the enemy.

It had, as we have heard, become evident on the 23rd that the whole course of the Hallue formed the real front of the enemy's line. But it had also been proved that Corbie, so important as the terminus of the enemy's railway traffic, lay behind his left flank, and must, therefore, be to him a most dangerous point of attack. This explained the great tenacity he displayed in defending Daours. To-day's observations confirmed this opinion. Under these circumstances, the Commander-in-Chief's orders on the afternoon of the 24th had to be given with a view to the two contingencies of the enemy either standing his ground or retreating. In the former case, it was intended to attack Corbie on the 25th; in the latter, to set out in pursuit of the enemy from our present position. The army orders, given at 4 P.M. on the hill south of Querrieux, were, in the first instance, as follow:

1. The whole of the Army Reserve, under General Mirus, including the detachment at Daours and the corps artillery of the VIIIth Army Corps, was to cross to the left bank of the Somme this same evening as soon as darkness had completely set in, was to advance against Corbie at day-break next morning, and attack the enemy from the south with the utmost vigour. This attack was to be prepared by the fire of the strong force of artillery. The necessary *matériel* for bridging the Somme at Corbie was placed at General Mirus's disposal.

2. The VIIIth Army Corps was first to move the 16th Division nearer to the 15th. Next morning one division was to follow General Mirus to the left bank of the Somme, at the same time keeping hold of Daours and covering all passages over the Somme between this place and Amiens. The other division of the corps was to cover Amiens.

3. In consideration of the fatiguing marches it had lately made, Prince Albert's Cavalry Brigade was quartered in Amiens for the night, after which it was to be placed at General Goeben's disposal. After this brigade had passed Bréteuil on its way hither, the Prince had despatched Lieutenant-Colonel Hymmen, with 2 squadrons, over Moreuil in his right flank, to reconnoitre the country up to the Somme.

4. In the course of the forenoon, and in conformity with this march to the right, the probability of which had been then already foreseen, orders had been sent to General Senden to march from St. Quentin to Ham. The object of this was to enable the division to join the army sooner, and to prevent all possibility of any collision ensuing between this weak detachment and the enemy.

Towards evening the symptoms of the enemy's retreat became more and more evident, whereupon the Commander-in-Chief ordered that the movements which the VIIIth Army Corps was instructed to make the next morning should not be commenced until the state of affairs on the enemy's side was quite clearly defined. If the latter should have retreated, the VIIIth Army Corps was immediately to start in pursuit, in which case General Mirus was to occupy Corbie and then advance on the left bank of the Somme, for the present, as far as Bray. This was a step towards investing Péronne, the eventuality of which had been already taken into consideration. At 6 P.M. General Mirus commenced his march with the reserve. The 15th Division remained in its previous position, whilst the 16th was moved nearer to the former in the prescribed manner. Head-Quarters of the Commander-in-Chief and of the VIIIth Army Corps remained for the night in Amiens.

The losses of the 1st Army in the battle of the Hallue were almost all suffered on the 23rd of December.

They were:

VIIIth Army Corps	4 officers,	80 men	killed.
"	33 "	724 "	wounded.
"	. .	93 "	missing.
Army Reserve	1 officer	.	killed.
"	.	20 "	wounded.
Total	38	917 men	

The enemy's loss was undoubtedly much heavier; on clearing up the battle-field 291 dead French soldiers were buried. His loss in unwounded prisoners amounted to 20 officers and 1,100 men, among whom were 1 lieutenant-colonel, 1 naval captain, and above 400 men of the line and the marines. The Prussian 70th Regiment captured a flag when Beaucourt was taken.

Two French cannons were also for a time in the hands of the 33rd Regiment (Colonel Henning), when 6 companies of this regiment pressed on in pursuit of the enemy on the heights beyond Pont Noyelles on the afternoon of the 23rd. However, 6 hostile battalions advanced against them, and they were obliged to leave the guns behind, after spiking one of them.

By day-break of the 25th of December, the French Army was in full retreat northwards. As the movements had already commenced the day before, the enemy had a whole night's start, which sufficed to save him from any immediate pursuit. Under these circumstances the retreat was, upon the whole, effected with order. We need not lay any great stress on the roads having been strewed by the arms which the less disciplined parts of the army had thrown away, nor on the number of stragglers captured during the pursuit. We also fully acknowledge the conduct of the newly-organised French Army, and the way it was handled in the battle; and we are far from calling the latter a defeat of the enemy, if this expression be understood to denote a catastrophe in which the tactical order of the beaten troops is more or less broken.

Nevertheless, for us the battle of the Hallue had the value of an important and decisive victory.

This is proved by its immediate tactical results; it is shown by the villages which we stormed in sanguinary combats, and then successfully defended against the violent attacks of the enemy, and also by more than 1,000 prisoners that fell unwounded into our hands. These are, however, matters of secondary consideration. The battles of modern times are no middle-age tournaments for the mere purpose of fighting and mutual homicide: these can never be more than the means wherewith to attain a higher purpose. In gaining or frustrating the latter

Results of the Battle.

lies the true criterion of victory or defeat. The primary object which the Prussian leaders had in view in the battle of the Hallue was to secure their possession of Amiens, and to dislodge the enemy from positions which he occupied in dangerous proximity to the town, thereby at the same time fulfilling the task assigned to the 1st Army, viz., the protection of the rear of the Army of the Meuse. Both objects were achieved in every sense of the word. We believe that the French leaders had also a higher aim in view than that of bearding us in their positions on the bleak hills eastward of the Hallue valley. General Faidherbe may not, perhaps, have aimed at raising the siege of Paris, or even at disturbing the north front of the investment of Paris, but the very least object he can have had in view must have been to regain possession of Amiens, and to keep a firm footing on the Somme as a basis for future offensive operations. The battle of the Hallue, in the first instance, threw the French back to a considerable distance from Amiens; in the sequel, it was the cause of the French losing their last stronghold on the Somme, the fortress of Péronne.

We now enter upon the Fourth Period of the operations.

FOURTH PERIOD.

OPERATIONS AND COMBATS FROM THE BATTLE OF THE HALLUE TO THE FALL OF PÉRONNE.

(DECEMBER 25TH TO JANUARY 10TH.)

CHAPTER XII.

Advance of the VIIIth *Army Corps to Bapaume—Investment and Bombardment of Péronne—Actions at Longpré, Busigny, &c.—Surprise of Souchez—Advance of the Enemy against Rouen—Actions at the Seine—Storming of the Chateau Robert le Diable.*

(DECEMBER 25TH TO DECEMBER 31ST.)

THE reports received from the VIIIth Army Corps on the morning of the 25th of December confirmed the enemy's retreat. The steps resulting herefrom, and taken by Army Head-Quarters during the last days of the month, had the following objects principally in view:

Firstly: To pursue the hostile army, for the purpose of ascertaining its line of retreat, inflicting as much injury upon it as possible, and keeping it in view.

Secondly: If possible, to capture Péronne, but at the same time, also,

Thirdly: To secure the possession of Rouen by the timely return of such troops as had been withdrawn from thence.

Bearing in mind these main objects, we will now follow the course of events day by day.

The 25th of December.

Preparatory steps towards commencing the pursuit of the enemy had, as we have heard, already been taken on the afternoon of the 24th, at the moment when the enemy's retreat seemed to be impending. The cavalry, the greater part of which it was intended to employ on the left wing, was reinforced by the Guard Cavalry Brigade, but the hard frozen ground, in many parts covered with snow, greatly reduced the efficiency of this arm. On the morning of the 25th, General Goeben put himself at the head of his corps. Advancing with the 15th Division by the high-road to Albert, and with the 16th in the direction of Contay, he reached the former town at 4 P.M. with the 30th Brigade, and pushed the advanced-guard of the 16th Division forward to Avelay. The horse-artillery batteries of the VIIIth Army Corps which had accompanied General Mirus, now rejoined the corps by way of Corbie, in pursuance of orders from Army Head-Quarters.

In all villages which the corps passed on its march many hundreds of the enemy's dead and wounded were found. French surgeons said the losses of the latter during the action had been 'immenses.'

The 7th Lancer Regiment, which was employed in scouring towards Abbeville, had found the neighbourhood of Longpré, Quesney, and the course of the rivulet at Hangest, occupied by franc-tireurs on the 24th. On the morning of the 25th, General Goeben, therefore, despatched the Fusileer battalion of the 70th Regiment to Hangest, and ordered Lieutenant-Colonel Pestel to operate with this battalion and his own Lancers as a flying column, and in particular to intercept the enemy's communications between Abbeville and the north.

Whilst General Goeben pursued the enemy towards Arras, the Commander-in-Chief decided on moving the remainder of his troops in the direction of Péronne. According to the latest accounts received, the enemy's troops were still to be seen at the Somme; therefore his army might have retreated over Péronne to Cambrai as well as to Arras. To judge from the reports sent in by the VIIIth Army Corps, it was to be supposed that General Mirus had, in the meantime, gained possession of Corbie without opposition. Orders were therefore despatched to Corbie on the forenoon of the 25th, ordering him 'to march with the 5 battalions of the 3rd Brigade, the 5th Regiment of Lancers, and the 6 batteries that remained at his disposal now that the horse-artillery batteries had been withdrawn, on the left bank of the Somme as far as Bray, and to commence rebuilding the bridge over the Somme which the enemy had probably destroyed there. The general was also to open communication with General Senden's detachment, which might be expected to be on the march from St. Quentin to Ham.'

In the meantime a detachment of the Saxon Cavalry Division (1 regiment of cavalry and 1 battery, under General Senfft) had also reached Ham from Compiégne on the 24th. Besides this, Major Strantz had been for some time stationed between Bray and Chaulnes, where he was watching Péronne with 2 squadrons of the 14th Lancers.

On the forenoon of the 25th General Mirus reached Corbie with part of his troops; the remainder were left at Villers-Bretonneux as reserve. The enemy had blown up the Corbie bridge previous to retreating; it was repaired by the afternoon. The written order to advance eastward did not reach General Mirus until between 3 and 4 P.M., so that all he could do on this day was to push forward his advanced-guard to Warfuse—Abancourt. It was at first said that Bray and Cerisy were still occupied by the enemy, but a patrol of the 5th Lancers, which pushed on north of the Somme in the direction of Bray, brought back the news that the enemy's troops, said to be 8,000 men, had withdrawn from there in a northerly direction. On the south bank of the Somme General Mirus opened communications with Major Strantz. The latter had fallen back from Méharicourt to Vauvillers on the afternoon of the 25th, because superior forces of the enemy had advanced from Péronne to the neighbourhood of Lihons.

Four out of the 6 battalions of the 2nd Brigade that had been brought up from Rouen, had been with General Mirus since the 24th of December; the other 2 were in Amiens, where the 6th Battalion of the 3rd Brigade was also stationed. The latter battalion was moved to Corbie on the 25th, and the Commander-in-Chief drew the 4 battalions of the 2nd Brigade back to Amiens on the 25th in consequence of *the reports received from Rouen.*

The state of affairs on the left bank of the Seine had induced General Bentheim, even before the battalions were sent to Amiens, to move his line of defence, La Bouille—Elbeuf, nearer to Rouen. In consequence, he caused the passages over the Seine at Elbeuf and Pont du Gravier to be destroyed; but kept that at Pont de l'Arche intact for his own offensive purposes. The patrols sent forward to the Rille found, in the beginning, no signs of the enemy in the direction of Louviers and Pont d'Audemer; in the direction of Brionne, however, they were compelled to fall back before superior forces, which pursued them to beyond St. Philbert. When the reinforcements had left for Amiens, and deducting the detachments in Gisors, Buchy, and Forges, General Bentheim had not more than 12 battalions at his disposal.

On the right bank of the Seine, it is true, the enemy's attitude showed as yet no signs of an intended attack. The Prussian patrols advanced without opposition as far as Yvetot and Caudebec; and ever since the Seine had been barred at Duclair the enemy's ships of war did not come farther up the stream than Gainneville. On the left bank, however, the enemy seemed to have offensive intentions. Our patrols were fired at, and suffered some loss in the forest between Grande Couronne and Bourg-therolde, as well as at St. Ouen on the road to Bourgachard, at no great distance, therefore, from Rouen. Unless he could reckon on his detached battalions soon returning, General Bentheim had great doubt as to the possibility of his fulfilling his task at Rouen, in case the enemy should assume the offensive on both banks of the Seine at the same time.

Upon the receipt of this report General Manteuffel gave orders that the 2nd Brigade should return to Rouen. In the first instance, 4 battalions were to be conveyed there by rail, the transport commencing on the 26th; the 2 other battalions were to remain as garrison in Amiens until relieved by other troops. Interruption of the railway traffic, especially the absconding of all the French engine-drivers, delayed this transport so considerably, that only 1 battalion reached Rouen on the 26th, the 3 others not before the 28th and 29th.

With reference to these circumstances we have a few brief remarks to make. If, at the time when the above-mentioned reports arrived from Rouen, General Faidherbe had still been before our front at Amiens with an unbroken army, we should have been placed in the alternative of either again weakening the army on the eve of decisive operations, or of being, perhaps, compelled to give up Rouen. This alone proves it to have been correct on our part to bring on the decisive general action at a time when the enemy did not wish for it himself. On the other hand, this event also shows what continual difficulties the task assigned to the 1st Army involved. With a comparatively small force, the army had to maintain possession of the two important points, Amiens and Rouen, 5 heavy marches distance from each other, and at the same time to cover the North Investment of Paris. This required the army to hold itself in a continual state of readiness to front to three different sides, so as to be able to assemble the bulk of its forces in whichever direction the enemy's operation threatened the greatest danger.

The 26th of December.

The reports sent in to General Goeben from his left wing showed the whole country, as far as Doullens, to have been evacuated by the enemy. On the 26th of December the general continued his advance on the roads leading to Arras, and established himself, with

Movements preparatory to investing Péronne. 173

3 combined brigades, at Bucquoy, Achiet-le-Grand, and Bapaume, and with a fourth, further to the rear, in reserve. General Dohna's Brigade of Cavalry, accompanied by infantry on country carts, scoured the country on the left wing in the direction of Beaumetz. The Guard Cavalry Brigade, with a horse-artillery battery and a Fusileer battalion, was on the right wing at Sailly. From here communications were to be kept open with the troops at Péronne, and reconnaissances made up to the Péronne—Cambrai road. General Goeben moved his own Head-Quarters to Bapaume, where he arrived at 3 P.M. of the 26th, and where a number of hostile stragglers were taken. According to information obtained here, it seemed that the enemy had retreated beyond Arras to Douai, and also partly to Cambrai.

General Mirus also pursued his prescribed march on the south bank of the Somme on the 26th. After a trifling skirmish with franc-tireurs and men in blouses at Vermandovillers and Estrées, the advanced-guard established itself at the latter place, the main-body in the neighbourhood of Faucancourt. A detachment was sent with the bridge-train to Bray, and repaired the bridge which the enemy had destroyed there. Major Strantz reported that the enemy's troops that had advanced to Lihons on the 25th, had retreated to Péronne. General Senden's detachment, which had made a very fatiguing march from Mézières, halted at Ham. The Saxon General Senfft was at Chaulnes.

Army Head-Quarters were transferred from Amiens to Bray-sur-Somme on the 26th, to which place they were followed by the battalion of the 3rd Brigade which had been moved from Amiens to Corbie the day before. When the reports had come in, the Commander-in-Chief gave the following orders for the 27th:

'General Goeben will remain in his position in the neighbourhood of Bapaume, keeping the enemy, who has retreated to Arras, etc., in sight; he will thus cover the Investment of Péronne, which has been planned for some time already, and will be now effected in the following manner:

'Pushing forward a small detachment on the left bank of the Somme opposite Péronne, General Mirus will cross the river with his main-body at Bray, and march in the direction of the north front of the fortress. General Senden will advance from Ham with his whole detachment (5 battalions, 3 batteries, and General Strantz's Brigade of Cavalry), and invest Péronne on the south and east, including the Roisel—Péronne road, which will form the boundary between his detachment and that of General Mirus. In the course of the forenoon of the 27th General Strantz's Brigade must, in connection with the Guard Cavalry Brigade at Sailly, have obtained command of the Péronne—Cambrai road, and thus prevent all egress of the enemy in that direction. By the afternoon of the 27th the investment must be completed, and suitable positions found for placing field-artillery.'

General Senfft was requested to join General Mirus's right flank detachment, and to keep up the communication between both banks of the river. We have now still a few remarks to make regarding the motives which led to the expedition against Péronne.

Ever since the campaign in Picardy began, the influence of this small fortress had been felt, from its disturbing our lines of communication and in every way assisting the operations of the enemy. In the beginning it was only a starting-point and support for flying columns and small surprises, but latterly it had served to cover the concentration of the enemy's army and to assist its action, which, to a certain degree, took us unawares. Being situated on the *right* bank of the Somme, it was not, properly speaking, a *tête du pont* for operations directed southwards; but, nevertheless, it favoured any sudden *debouché* of the enemy, unless it was continually watched and held in check by a body of troops sufficiently strong for the occasion. Without possessing Péronne we could not have perfect command of the whole line of the Somme from La Fère to Amiens.

The reader will have perceived that, in the first case, the operations on the Seine, and, secondly, the necessity of concentrating our forces against General Faidherbe, had as yet prevented any serious undertaking against Péronne. But, above all things, a regular siege-train was still wanting; and the maxim laid down at the commencement of the autumn campaign, viz., not to attack any fortress without being provided with the necessary means to ensure success, had as yet been proved to be correct by the results achieved at La Fère and the Ardennes fortresses. The only delay in these cases had been caused by bringing up the siege-train and establishing the batteries; when this was once accomplished, two days' fire sufficed to subdue each fortress. There had, however, also been a precedent of a contrary description. The mere display of a superior force of *field*-artillery, combined with the first impression produced by the enemy's retreat, had sufficed to cause the fall of the storm-free and well-armed citadel of Amiens. To judge from previous reconnaissances, Péronne itself seemed to have but little strength; it was, therefore, deemed possible that an unexpected attack made by field-artillery, and at a time when the garrison still laboured under the impression of the enemy's retreat, might subdue this troublesome place. At any rate, there was a chance of success, although the attempt might fail. In order, in case of failure, to be able to carry out the undertaking when once begun, we had recourse to the French artillery *matériel* found at Amiens and La Fère, so far as it could be spared there without compromising the defence of these places. As early as the middle of December Lieutenant Schmidt, the officer in command of the artillery in the citadel of Amiens, had given it as his opinion that 10 suitable siege-guns, with the necessary ammunition of 200 rounds per gun and other appurtenances, might be spared out of the armament of the citadel. We did not, certainly, expect *certain* success from the fire of such an improvised siege-train, but it would materially increase our chances against such small fortresses as Abbeville or Péronne.

Consequently, before General Manteuffel left Amiens, he had

given orders on the 25th that this small siege-train, consisting of 6 rifled twelve-pounders, 2 mortars, and 2 howitzers, was to be made ready as soon as possible and placed under the command of Lieutenant Schmidt. The Commandant of Amiens was, at the same time, desired to provide the necessary means of transport (257 horses and 53 waggons). Siege guns were also demanded from the Commandant of La Fère, but he could, at the moment, only send off 6 mortars. The gunners were to be furnished by the garrison-artillery of Amiens.

The park could not be ready to leave Amiens before the 28th; it was, therefore, determined to begin the fire at Péronne with field-guns, but without encroaching too far on the store of ammunition of the field-army. The attempt could, therefore, only be a short one. If it did not soon succeed, the small siege-train was to be brought up from Amiens and La Fère.[1]

The 27th of December.

On the 27th of December General Mirus commenced his march in the prescribed manner. The detachment on the left bank of the Somme, under the command of Colonel Tietzen, advanced to the line Villers-Carbonnel—Herbécourt. The main-body crossed the Somme at Bray, and arrived south of Combles without encountering opposition. Then, however, the advanced patrols

---

[1] To this explanation of the undertaking against Péronne we add the following remarks. In the latest publications of our western neighbours we meet with astonishing and somewhat sentimental expressions of opinion. They attempt to stigmatise our treatment of the hostile fortresses as inhuman, because the form of attack we employed against the smaller places was that of bombardment, which produces the quickest result. Setting aside the fact that this mode of attack is perfectly justified by the usages of war, we find the conduct of the French themselves inconsistent with this opinion. In point of humanity there can be no difference between the inhabitants of a town or those of a village. If, therefore, from good military reasons, the *French* General Faidherbe bombarded and burnt the *French* village of Pont Noyelles, the *German* general was surely justified in bombarding a *hostile* town defended by fortifications and troops, the possession of which was of military importance to him from the reasons we have mentioned above. Besides, it is a known fact, again proved by our recent experience, that a comparatively short bombardment causes far less loss of life, particularly among the civil population, than hunger and sickness during a long period of investment and regular siege works.

came back with the report that the villages on both banks of the Tortille rivulet—Allaines, Bouchavesnes, Aizecourt, were occupied by the enemy's troops, whose fire had forced them to turn back.

General Mirus, in consequence, formed up his advanced-guard preparatory to attacking the villages. Before they were reached the enemy had already fallen back upon Péronne. The cavalry, however, overtook and charged the rearmost troops, capturing some prisoners. In the meantime, darkness having set in, the pursuit ceased; the advanced-guard occupied the Tortille rivulet from Moislains to where it falls into the Somme; the main-body took up alarm quarters in Cléry ($4\frac{1}{2}$ miles south of Combles). Cavalry detachments were pushed forward towards the Péronne—Le Catelet road to open communications with General Senden's detachment. The bridges at St. Christ and Brie were found uninjured, and another one was thrown over the river at Ham, west of Cléry.

Very early in the morning General Strantz's Cavalry Brigade pushed on to Tincourt, with the intention of flanking the Péronne—Cambrai road from here, and opening communications with the Guard Cavalry Brigade at Sailly. When General Senden advanced from Ham he found the villages of Bruntel and Doingt, south and south-east of Péronne, occupied by the enemy. The attack was prefaced by a few shells fired at Doingt, and then both villages were taken by the advanced-guard. The enemy's troops that were dislodged here were driven back into the fortress, the guns of the latter taking part in the combat, which was prolonged until darkness set in.

General Senden then established his outposts from the west skirts of Doingt up to the Somme. The detachment itself cantoned in Bruntel, Doingt, Cartigny, and the cluster of villages Tincourt—Bouchy, where General Senden also took up his quarters.

The reconnaissances made on the north and south of the fortress had discovered two suitable positions from which the place could be bombarded by field-artillery; both were somewhat more than a mile from the centre of the place, and afforded ample room for placing several batteries. One was on a swell of the ground south-west of the Péronne—Cléry road, the other on a hill to the west of Doingt.

On the 27th General Senfft advanced from Chaulnes to the neighbourhood of Villers-Carbonnel and Brie, where he was in communication with General Senden and Colonel Tietzen. In the meantime, in consequence of the message previously sent to General Lippe, requesting his co-operation, the latter had arrived at Roye on the 26th with 2 regiments of cavalry, 1 battalion of rifles, and 1 horse-artillery battery, and advanced on the 27th to Nesle.

Whilst the troops were executing these movements in the course of the 27th, the Commander-in-Chief rode from Bray to Combles and established his Head-Quarters there at mid-day. Before leaving Bray army orders were issued, giving the command of all troops now assembled in front of Péronne to General Senden as senior officer. On the other hand, Major Strantz was ordered to rejoin the Cavalry Division with his 2 squadrons of Lancers, and General Lippe was requested to advance from Nesle to St. Quentin on the 28th, so as to cover the east flank of the investment and to reconnoitre in the direction of Cambrai. On the afternoon of the 27th further orders were sent to General Senden from Combles, desiring him to place his field-batteries in position, on the 28th, under cover of the investing troops. Simultaneously with this, the garrison of Péronne was to be peremptorily summoned to surrender on the terms of the Sedan capitulation; if it refused to do so, the bombardment was to commence immediately.

On the 27th General Goeben remained in general in the positions he occupied the day before near Bapaume. The detachments sent forward towards Arras found the nearest villages west of the fortress unoccupied. The enemy was said to have retreated altogether to the neighbourhood of Douai. General Goeben thereupon determined to move his troops also more to the right. It was his intention to move a brigade to Sailly on the 28th, and the detachment now there, under the command of General Groeben, to Fins on the Péronne—Cambrai road.

December the 28th to December the 31st.

The first orders given by the Commander-in-Chief on the 27th reached General Senden the same evening, when the fight was over; the second at an early hour of the 28th. As his own detachment was not provided with ammunition columns, he requested Head-Quarters to send him one, and a column was ordered to proceed from Bapaume next day.

Pursuant to his orders, General Senden placed his troops and batteries in position at mid-day of the 28th, and summoned the Commandant of Péronne to surrender. The latter at first announced his intention of sending a flag of truce; none such, however, arrived, therefore the batteries opened fire on all sides at 3 P.M. The fire was returned by a few guns only, and fires broke out in all parts of the town, but the fortress showed no signs of surrender. The Commander-in-Chief then telegraphed to the Commandant of Amiens to send off the siege-train, which was just ready to start, by way of Villers-Brétonneux on the 29th, so that it should reach Villers-Carbonnel on the 30th. It was to be placed, in the first instance, on the *left* bank of the Somme, this side being the most secure, thus leaving the troops of investment on the right bank greater freedom of action. General Senden was ordered not to continue the bombardment with field-guns after the 29th. If the fortress had not capitulated by the evening of the 29th, the general was to withdraw his batteries, send his troops into cantonments, and wait for the arrival of the siege-train.

The hostile Army of the North being now known to be between Arras and Douai, behind the Scarpe, the moment had arrived to provide for the execution of the Versailles orders of the 13th and 17th, by virtue of which the bulk of the

1st Army was to be concentrated at Beauvais. Before, however, this position could be taken up, two other tasks, which the course of events had imposed upon the army, had to be fulfilled, viz., to take Péronne and defeat the enemy now commencing *offensive operations on the Seine*.

During the march towards Péronne, Head-Quarters received further news from Rouen on the 26th and 27th. A telegram of the 16th reported that the enemy was advancing from the Rille, and had already established a line of outposts eastward of Bourgtherolde. On the right bank of the Seine Lieutenant-Colonel Plötz had, on the 24th, driven back the advanced posts which the enemy had stationed at Rouville and Roncherelles in front of Hâvre to beyond Bolbec, but had then encountered a superior force of 7,000 men of all arms, and been obliged to fall back to Bolbec. There were growing symptoms of the enemy's intention of assuming the offensive on both banks of the Seine at the same time. General Bentheim's requests for reinforcements became more and more pressing. With a view to enabling him to shake off his adversaries by a short, energetic offensive, the Commander-in-Chief determined to send the 3rd Brigade also to Rouen.

After the completion of this offensive on the Seine, and as soon as Péronne was taken, the Commander-in-Chief intended the 1st Army to take up the following positions: half of the 1st Army Corps, with the Guard Dragoon Brigade, at Rouen; half of the VIIIth Army Corps, with the Cavalry Division and General Senden's Division, at the Somme; the remainder or smaller half of the Army at Beauvais. The departure of the troops of the 1st Army Corps that were still at the Somme would be the first step towards taking up this position.

It was the Commander-in-Chief's intention personally to convince himself of the state of affairs at Rouen.

General Goeben, upon whom the command of the group of the army at the Somme would in that case devolve, was called to a conference on the subject at Combles, and arrived there from his Head-Quarters at Bapaume on the forenoon of the 28th. The following orders were then issued the same day:

'A brigade of the VIIIth Army Corps, with 2 batteries, will relieve the 3rd Brigade in front of Péronne on the 29th; the latter will then leave for Rouen on the 30th with both its batteries. The battalion of the brigade now attached to Head-Quarters will accompany the latter to Amiens. The 2 battalions of the 2nd Brigade at present at Amiens, will also be relieved there by troops of the VIIIth Army Corps. After the breaking up of General Mirus's present detachment he will rejoin the 3rd Cavalry Division with the 5th Regiment of Lancers.'

As a sequel to these orders, General Manteuffel wrote to Generals Goeben and Bentheim on the 29th, setting forth the tasks now before the army.

The purport of these letters, which were couched in the same terms, was:

'General Goeben will hold the line of the Somme as his principal line of defence, and will endeavour to secure this position still further by taking Péronne and Abbeville. For this purpose the siege-train now on the road to Villers-Carbonnel will be placed at his disposal. General Goeben will post a strong force at Amiens and in the region of St. Quentin and Ham, and will repair the bridges over the impassable valley of the Somme which have been destroyed by the enemy between Péronne and Amiens. The strong castle of Ham must be placed in a state of defence. Added to this, as far as can be done without fatiguing the troops, flying columns must be pushed forward northwards for the purpose of disarming the country they pass through, and destroying railway and telegraph north of the Somme, and also, if possible, north of Arras.

'These columns will afford the means of ascertaining in due time when the enemy advances again, and will prove the direction of his march, which may possibly be either towards the Somme or upon Soissons or Mézières.

'General Bentheim's task will remain the same as was pointed out when the brigade left for Amiens, at the time of the battle of the Hallue, viz., to keep hold of Rouen and watch the enemy on the right bank of the Seine from Hâvre to Vernon. It is advisable that the position on the left bank, as an immediate protection to the town of Rouen, be somewhat refused; that on the right bank more advanced towards Hâvre, and that flying columns be frequently pushed forward in the latter direction.

'As soon as the army of the Grand Duke of Mecklenburg shall have taken up its position at Chartres, communications will be opened with it by a safe road.

'Army Head-Quarters will be alternately in Beauvais, Rouen, and Amiens; the Inspection-General of "Etappen" will be moved to Creil or Chantilly.'

The formation of the army, a sketch of which accompanied this letter, was based on the supposition mentioned above, that it would afterwards become necessary to move the smaller half of the army to Beauvais.

This, however, did not come to pass. The Commander-in-Chief had sent a telegram to Versailles on the evening of the 28th, setting forth his opinion of the momentary state of affairs and stating what his next intentions were. An answer to this telegram reached General Manteuffel at Albert on the forenoon of the 29th, bringing the decision he had asked for. General Moltke first of all signified his approval of the expedition against Péronne, and then modified his former instructions, because, in the meantime, the Rouen—Amiens—Gonesse railway had been put in working order. He said that if the bulk of the 1st Army were concentrated at Amiens it would henceforth be able to hold both the line of the Seine and that of the Somme, and if necessary to support the investment of Paris also. At the same time, General Moltke recommended a short expedition to be made against Vervins.[1]

---

[1] The country round about Vervins had been a source of much annoyance to the Government-General of Rheims; not long ago a detachment of the Government-General's troops had encountered a superior force of the enemy there.

The nearest force available for this expedition was General Lippe's detachment at St. Quentin. At his request, General Senfft's detachment was also placed under his command. In consequence of the Versailles telegram, General Lippe was now requested to advance against Vervins with his whole force. Generals Goeben and Bentheim were informed of these new instructions, and that, in accordance with them, the army would now not take up the position at Beauvais, but remain with its main force at the Somme. In consequence, the following troops were placed under the General Goeben's command : the VIIIth Army Corps, General Senden's Division, the 3rd Cavalry Division, and the Guard Cavalry Brigade; and, *for the time being*, the 1st Army Corps and the Guard Dragoon Brigade, under the command of General Bentheim. The former general thus had 31 battalions, 40 squadrons, and 20 batteries, the latter 25 battalions, 16 squadrons, and 14 batteries at his disposal.

These arrangements were made on the evening of the 29th at Albert ; on the 30th Head-Quarters went to Amiens.

We will now follow the course of events with each group of the army up to the end of the year.

On the 20th December, General Kameke had arrived in front of *Mézières* with the 14th Division, and had completed the investment of the place by the 23rd. The ensuing week was spent in building batteries and other preparations for attacking the fortress. Some detachments of franc-tireurs, based on Givet and Rocroi, disturbed the north section of the investing troops, from which a few trifling encounters ensued. The last artillery companies and ammunition arrived on the 30th, and the bombardment commenced on the 31st.

In the meantime, General Kameke had been summoned to Versailles on the 25th, His Majesty the King having entrusted him with the direction of all the engineering works against Paris. His successor in command of the 14th Division was General Senden ; until he arrived, General Woyna assumed the command in front of Mézières.

The bombardment of *Péronne* was continued but feebly on the 29th, in order to economise the field ammunition. It produced no result, nor did the troops of the investment suffer any loss worth mentioning from the fire of the fortress. The town had, however, suffered considerably, and, as the VIIIth Army Corps had promised to send a second ammunition column, General Senden hoped to force the place to capitulate by re-commencing the bombardment on the 30th. In this, however, he was disappointed. The fire from the field-batteries was then continued until the siege-park was ready to open fire on the left bank of the Somme. The park reached Villers-Carbonnel on the 30th, according to orders. At La Fère, in addition to the 6 mortars, 3 twelve-pounders and 2 howitzers were ready for transport, but had not yet left. The 3rd Brigade had started for Amiens on the 30th, a brigade of the 16th Division having arrived to relieve it the day before. On the 29th *General Lippe* pushed forward 2 squadrons from St. Quentin to Le Catelet, to watch Cambrai; on the 30th he marched to Le Catelet himself, and moved the 2 squadrons on to Masnières. A sub-division of the 17th Lancer Regiment, under Lieutenant Milkau, rode into Cambrai and heard from the towns-people that the hitherto small garrison had that day been increased to 2,000 men by reinforcements arrived from the north. The Lancers did not turn back until fired upon by the enemy's infantry. It was General Lippe's intention to commence the expedition to Vervins, which he had been requested to undertake on the 31st. It was, however, reported to him that a detachment (1 company of rifles and 1 squadron) sent by him to break up the railway at the junction north of Busigny, had encountered a large body of 'gardes mobiles' and was engaged with them. The superior numbers of the enemy prevented the detachment from accomplishing its mission, and it fell back to a position at Sérain, after taking 40 of the enemy prisoners. General Lippe occupied Montbréhain, further southwards, but, under the circumstances, postponed his march to Vervins for the purpose of watching

Reconnaissances in Directions of Cambrai and Arras.

Cambrai until other troops arrived at Le Catelet to relieve him. He had already given orders to General Senfft to march by way of St. Quentin to Origny, intending to unite both detachments at Vervins.

We now turn to the troops under General Goeben's command and to the events that occurred in that quarter. We have already heard that General Groeben's detachment had been stationed at Fins, on the right wing of the army since the 28th, and was employed in watching the neighbourhood of Cambrai. Up to the 29th the country seemed to be as good as forsaken by the enemy. A patrol of the Guard Hussars rode into the weakly garrisoned town on that day, and did not turn back until attempts were made to close the gates of the fortress in its rear. On the 30th, however (the same day on which Lieutenant Milkau rode into Cambrai and ascertained that reinforcements had arrived there), troops of the enemy were also perceived southwest of the place in the hamlet Marcoing on the Schelde. In order to obtain further information, the 4th Squadron of the Guard Hussar Regiment set off from Fins at 7 A.M. of the 31st. Making a circuit eastward of Cambrai, the squadron reached Jouy and blew up the railway bridge between Cambrai and Bouchain with a hundred-weight of powder. After a ride of more than 45 miles, the squadron brought back the news that Bouchain and Cambrai were occupied by a few thousand men, but that French troops were said to have retreated from Cambrai to Maubeuge during the last week.

In the neighbourhood of Arras the enemy had pushed detachments forward south of the town since the 29th, viz., to Achicourt and Beauvais, villages that had been hitherto unoccupied. The villages on the Scarpe, between Arras and Douai, were also now found to be strongly occupied. Cavalry patrols, on approaching the railway here, were met by whole battalions of the enemy. Nevertheless, on the 29th a patrol of the 7th Hussar Regiment succeeded in breaking up the rails at Feuchy, between Arras and Douai, and in cutting the telegraph wires there. A flying column under Colonel Wittich, composed of the 9th Hussar Regiment and some infantry in carts, scoured the country on General Goeben's left flank. This detachment entered Avesnes le Comte on the 28th December, and advanced from here on the 29th in a north-easterly direction against the Arras—Béthune railway. At Souchez (5¾ miles north of Arras) Colonel Wittich surprised a hostile detachment of 'gardes mobiles,' and took 5 officers and 150 men prisoners. Advancing still farther, he met very superior forces in the strongly occupied country south of the Arras—Béthune railway, and was therefore not able to reach the Lens railway-station.

It has been already mentioned that another flying column, under Lieutenant-Colonel Pestel (7th Lancer Regiment and Fusileer Battalion of the 70th Regiment), had been assembled at Picquigny on the 25th, and was in the neighbourhood of Longpré, in face of hostile troops from Abbeville.

Lieutenant-Colonel Pestel now undertook a successful expedition. Keeping possession of the bridge at Hangest, on the direct road from Amiens to Abbeville, he marched with the main body of his detachment (3 squadrons and 3 companies) to the neighbourhood of Molliens Vidame. From thence he marched to beyond Airaines on the 28th, and then turned sharply to the right on Longpré, where 3 battalions of 'gardes mobiles' were stationed. The battalions, taken by surprise, were defeated and utterly routed after a fight of two hours. The enemy lost above 50 killed and wounded, besides 3 flags and 2 officers, and 250 men taken prisoners unwounded. The Prussian loss only amounted to 5 wounded. All other detachments of the enemy in this region now retreated to Abbeville. In the following days Lieutenant-Colonel Pestel marched by way of Domart and St. Ricquier upon Abbeville, and tried to induce the garrison to capitulate while still under the influence of this defeat. Negociations commenced on the night of the 30th December, but did not produce any result. General Goeben opened communi-

Advance of the Enemy upon Rouen.

cations between his left wing and Lieutenant-Colonel Pestel's detachment, by way of Bernaville.

All these events, and the observations made north of the Somme, did not as yet show any offensive intentions on the part of the enemy. The troops at Douai did, certainly, seem in general to be drawing nearer to Arras and Cambrai ; but, on the other hand, the cavalry patrols and flying columns had been able not only to get close up to the enemy's cantonments, but also to destroy railways within his lines, surprise a whole cantonment in his rear, and even to ride into the fortified town of Cambrai.

The accounts which came in from *Rouen* were of a more serious nature. The report of the 26th had already stated the enemy's outposts on the left bank of the Seine to be eastwards of Bourgtherolde, and that a gradual advance of the enemy from Havre was perceptible. The next news received by Head-Quarters reached Albert on the 29th. A telegram of the 27th reported the enemy to be pressing forward on the left bank. Strong hostile columns had been on that day seen advancing on Bourgachard. This telegram was followed by one recounting the events of the 29th. The enemy on the left bank, said to be 10,000 men strong, had pushed the heads of his columns up to our previous line of defence, La Bouille—Elbeuf. On the right bank he had 8,000 men at St. Romain, between Bolbec and Harfleur. During the last few days there had been continual combats between the outposts, in which the 1st Army Corps had lost about 80 men. In the course of the evening and night of the 30th, the Commander-in-Chief received further reports in Amiens. The enemy on the left bank had assumed the offensive on this day, but the troops of the 1st Army Corps had maintained their positions at Grande Couronne. On the right bank our patrols met the enemy at Fauville and Héricourt, therefore already between Bolbec and Yvetot. All information received indicated the enemy's intention to assume the offensive on both banks of the Seine, because it was known to him that troops had lately left Rouen. The reports sent in by the 1st Army Corps, and the statement they contained that the enemy's forces now on the left bank of the Seine amounted to 20,000 men, were corroborated in every respect by a communication from the King's Head-Quarters at Versailles, which reached the Commander-in-Chief about the same time. According to it, the French troops assembled near Bernay under General Lauriston consisted of 6 battalions of the line and 1 of marines, besides 12,000 'gardes mobiles.' and franc-tireurs, 600 cavalry soldiers, and several batteries. It was asserted that the satisfactory news he had received from Rouen had induced General Lauriston to start from Bernay towards Rouen on the 26th December, in order to lend a hand to the 12,000 to 15,000 men that were advancing from Havre. He had pushed forward his foremost troops as far as Bourgtherolde on the 26th. All this unmistakeably showed that an attack on Rouen was impending. In the meantime, with the exception of 1 battalion, the 2nd Brigade had returned there. It was to be followed by the 3rd Brigade, which was then on the march from Corbie to Amiens.

On the forenoon of the 31st, General Manteuffel, accompanied by part of his staff and a small infantry escort, was conveyed by a special train to Rouen.[1] The last battalion of the 2nd Brigade followed by the next train. When the enemy's attack, which was expected on the 31st, did not take place, General Bentheim advanced himself with those troops which were on the south of Rouen, in order to gain more room by making a dash at the enemy. A strong detachment of the latter was found at Moulineaux, at the neck of the Seine peninsula, westward of Grande Couronne. The detachment was routed and partly forced to take refuge in the old ruined castle of Robert le Diable, perched on a steep hill. The castle was then taken by storm. In addition to a number of dead and wounded, the

[1] Although there was no railway telegraph along this line, still the 67½ miles between Amiens and Rouen were accomplished in little more than two hours.

enemy lost about 100 prisoners, the arrival of which in Rouen had a very calming influence on the hopes which had been already excited there. Although the enemy continued his advance on the right bank of the Seine, he was still westward of Yvetot. Thus ended the year 1870 in the north.

In grateful remembrance of the events which had taken place during the past year, the Commander-in-Chief issued the following army orders on New Year's Day:

'I wish a happy New Year to the 1st Army. I feel pride in being at the head of this army. It has gained the victory single handed in four battles: before Metz,[1] at Noisseville, Amiens, and the Hallue; in three other battles, Saarbrücken, Vionville, and Gravelotte, it has taken a decisive part and helped to achieve the victory. The army has had a glorious share in the fierce and protracted struggle during the investment of Metz, and had the distinction of being the first to enter this ancient, re-conquered German fortress. The army has besieged and subdued the fortresses Thionville, La Fère, and Montmédy, and entered the populous cities of Amiens and Rouen after victoriously fighting for the possession of them. Not including the battles fought, and the sieges carried through in company with the IInd Army, the 1st Army has taken 15,000 prisoners and captured 500 guns and vast quantities of war *matériel* in its independent operations. It has always been the lot of the 1st Army to fight against superior numbers of the enemy, because its manifold and extensive labours seldom allowed it to be concentrated. The fatigues the army has undergone and the difficulties it has surmounted were of no common kind, and even now it has still been fighting and bivouacking amidst ice and snow.

'The confidence which our former Commander-in-Chief, General of Infantry Von Steinmetz, expressed when he assumed the command of the army, and which he again expressed when,

---

[1] Battle of Borny, on the 14th of August 1870.

after leading the army from success to success, he was appointed to another post by His Majesty the King—this confidence has been in every way verified by the 1st Army; again and again it has succeeded in earning the satisfaction of His Majesty the King. I feel authorised to thank the army at the close of the year in the name of its former Commander-in-Chief as well as in my own. May God's blessing rest on our standards in the new year also, and grant them new victories! That is my prayer.

(Signed) 'MANTEUFFEL.'

FINAL CHAPTER.

Capitulation of Mézières on the 1st, and of Rocroi on the 6th of January—The 14th Infantry Division leaves the 1st Army—Defeat of the French troops on the left bank of the Seine on the 4th of January—Advance of the French Army of the North to raise the Siege of Péronne—Battle of Bapaume — Operations of Count Lippe's Cavalry Division against Vervins (January 2nd to January 6th)—General von Goeben takes the command of the 1st Army—Capitulation of Péronne on the 9th of January.

THE New Year's wish of the Commander-in-Chief was soon fulfilled. In consequence of the bombardment, which had only been commenced the day before, the fortress of Mézières capitulated on New Year's day, with 2,000 men and 193 guns. General Manteuffel now hoped to be able to bring the 14th Division up to the Somme to reinforce the field-army, and gave the necessary orders to this effect. The Division had, however, been otherwise disposed of at Versailles, and had received orders from thence to attempt in the first instance to take Rocroi by a *coup de main*. General Senden, who arrived at Mézières on the 3rd January, appointed 5 battalions, 2 squadrons, 6 batteries, and a company of pioneers, under General Woyna's command, to make this expedition. The undertaking was crowned with complete success. On the 6th of January, a foggy day, the small fortress was suddenly invested and bombarded by field-guns. The effect produced by 'this fire not being immediately perceptible, General Woyna was on the point of giving up the attempt, but Lieutenant Foerster, Adjutant of the Division, who had been sent into the fortress with a flag of truce, made use of his opportunity so cleverly and with so much energy, that he persuaded the commandant to capitulate. 300 men and 72 guns again fell into our hands, and the small fortress of Givet, situated in the extreme northern corner of the country, was now completely isolated. In the meantime, the railway transport of the 14th Division and its siege-train to Mitry had already commenced. The latter was intended to reinforce the artillery attack on the north front of Paris. In consequence of the menacing turn affairs had taken in the southeast of France, the Division was sent to Chatillon-sur-Seine, to form part of the South Army, and thus definitely left the 1st Army. The pontoon-train of the 1st Army Corps, hitherto employed at Mézières, was sent by way of Rheims to Rouen on the 7th of January. Part of the Mézières siege-train and 1 artillery company were to be employed against Péronne, but were not made use of there because the fortress had surrendered before they arrived.

Having on the 31st of December gained more room in the immediate neighbourhood of *Rouen*, General Bentheim then waited for the arrival of the 44th Regiment from Amiens. When the Commander-in-Chief granted these reinforcements he said, from the very first, that it would only be for a time, because, although for the moment there were no signs of the enemy again assuming the offensive against the Somme, this might ere long be expected to take place. General Bentheim was therefore instructed to make a short but vigorous attack on the enemy on the left bank of the Seine as soon as the reinforcements arrived, so that immediately afterwards not only the 44th Regiment but even more troops still might be quickly moved from Rouen to Amiens. After settling these matters with General Bentheim, General Manteuffel returned to Amiens on the afternoon of the 1st of January.

General Falkenstein having fallen ill, General Bergmann, of the Artillery, took command of the 1st Division and of the troops on the left bank of the Seine. The enemy had made no farther advance on the right bank since the 1st of January.

Defeat of French troops on left bank of the Seine. 193

The Prussian detachment that was pushed forward in this direction went to Yvetot, and remained there without being molested during the 3rd of January. The enemy had retreated on the 2nd January as far as Languelot, on the Bolbec—Yvetot road, and had not advanced beyond Anguetierville in the direction of Caudebec.

The 44th Regiment having arrived at Rouen, the proposed attack on the left bank of the Seine was commenced at an early hour of the 4th of January. To all appearances the foremost line of the enemy's troops, which were commanded by General Roye, consisted of three different groups, viz.: about 1,500 men at La Londe (west of Elbeuf), 2,500 at Bourgtherolde, and 4,000 at Bourgachard. Foggy weather and the intricacy of the country had prevented seeing what reserves were farther to the rear.

General Bentheim started at 4 A.M., and advanced in the first instance against Moulineaux. The moon was hidden by a thick fog, and it was impossible to see farther than a few paces. The enemy's line of defence and barricades at Moulineaux were found unoccupied. A flank detachment attacked the ruin Robert le Diable, which the enemy had in the meantime occupied again. Almost all the French found there were either killed or taken prisoners. Shortly after daybreak our troops reached the position and road-junction at la Maison Brûlée. The enemy defended this position, and received the advancing troops with a sharp fire of musketry, two guns at the same time sweeping the Moulineaux road. Taking advantage of a wood immediately in front of the position, our troops succeeded in gaining possession of the latter by a flank attack. The greater part of its defenders were taken prisoners in the houses, and the two guns were captured.

General Bentheim's farther advance was made in 3 columns. The right column (Colonel Legat, with 2 battalions of the 3rd Regiment) kept on the road to Bourgachard; the centre (Colonel Busse, with 1 battalion of the 43rd and the whole 44th Regiment) marched on Bourgtherolde; and the left column

O

(Lieutenant-Colonel Hüllessem, with the 41st Regiment) followed a road through the forest which led straight to La Londe.

Colonel Legat met with considerable resistance at St. Ouen. The enemy opened fire with 8 guns here, and tried to turn the Prussian left wing. For a time the action took a serious turn, our left wing being hard pressed by a French column. In the meantime, however, the Prussian artillery was brought to the front and arrested the enemy's advance. It was, in particular, the timely arrival of Captain Hoffbauer's battery that disengaged our left wing. Debouching from St. Ouen he drove the enemy back by a well-aimed fire of grape at a moment when the latter had advanced to within 300 paces. At all other points the enemy was also forced to give way, and our troops then advanced to Bourgachard, which was taken before dark. The enemy retreated in disorder still farther. A small detachment under Colonel Preinitzer (1 squadron, 2 guns, and a company of infantry on carts) followed in pursuit, and overtook the enemy at Rougemontier ($5\frac{3}{4}$ miles west of Bourgachard). Being again attacked here, the enemy lost 2 guns and numerous prisoners, and fled in the direction of Pont Audemer. The centre column, under Colonel Busse, came upon the enemy in the neighbourhood of Bourgtherolde, in front of the south-west edge of the large forest of La Londe. After a short musketry action the enemy was routed, and then Bourgtherolde taken without much opposition. The fog favoured the enemy's retreat, which he apparently effected both in the direction of Bourgachard and of Brionne.

Our left column, which advanced on La Londe, and with which a detachment coming from Pont de l'Arche over Elbeuf was to co-operate, did not encounter the enemy, who seemed to have avoided the attack by making a timely retreat.

The trophies of this day consisted of 4 rifled cannons, 3 flags, and about 500 unwounded prisoners. The enemy's total loss was, of course, much higher. He now retreated on both banks of the Seine to a considerable distance from Rouen, and from this time forth no further engagement of any importance took place

Position of the troops at the Somme.

in this part of the theatre of war. We shall show, by-and-by, what other advantages were derived from these events.

We now turn to the *group of the Army at the Somme*. When General Senden left, General Barnekow, commanding the 16th Division, took the command in front of Péronne on the 1st of January. The direction of the artillery attack was entrusted to Colonel Kameke. With His Majesty's sanction, the infantry and artillery of General Senden's former Division and the Guard Cavalry Brigade were combined, and placed under the command of Prince Albrecht, Junior, by virtue of an army order of the 31st December. General Strantz's Cavalry Brigade was attached to the 3rd Cavalry Division. On the 1st of January, before these changes were carried out, the troops were in general distributed as follows:

General Senden's former Division (1 battalion of which was still at La Fère) and the greater part of the 16th Division were in front of Péronne. General Goeben had changed his former position, facing northwards, to one farther to the right, in consequence of further information he had received respecting the transport of French troops from Douai to Cambrai. A mixed detachment under Prince Albrecht was stationed at Fins, on the right wing. After some trifling skirmishing with troops pushed forward from Cambrai, the detachment had succeeded in blowing up the bridges at Noyelles, Marcoing, and Masnières; the latter one was, however, only imperfectly destroyed. On the left wing at Bucquoy was General Groeben, with 3 regiments of the 3rd Cavalry Division (General Mirus had rejoined the division with the 5th Lancer Regiment on the 31st December), 1 battalion, and 1 battery. The centre was occupied by the 15th Division at Bapaume, with General Strubberg's Brigade pushed forward to Sapignies; the left flank of the brigade was covered by a detachment in Achiet-le-Grand. The 70th Regiment—belonging to the 16th Division—was partly employed as garrison in Amiens and at other railway stations, and partly with Lieutenant-Colonel Pestel's detachment.

The latter was still occupied in scouring the country on the west flank of the army. After having in vain summoned Abbeville to surrender, Lieutenant-Colonel Pestel had proceeded to the neighbourhood of Nouvion with the intention of intercepting the enemy's communications between Abbeville and Boulogne. On the 1st of January he destroyed the telegraph and iron railway-bridge over the Maie canal.

The Inspection-General of 'Etappen' left Amiens for Chantilly on the 2nd January.

General Lippe's Division was still at Le Catelet; General Senden now intended sending a detachment there, so that the former might be able to commence the expedition to Vervins on the 2nd. On the afternoon of the 31st December, General Goeben had moved his Head-Quarters from Bapaume to Combles, in order to be nearer to Péronne. The Amiens siege-train was established on the left bank of the Somme, and was now ready for action. With its assistance the bombardment, which had ceased since the 31st December, was resumed on the forenoon of the 2nd January.

In the meantime, the news of our operations against Péronne had moved General Faidherbe to decide on making an attempt to raise the siege of the beleaguered fortress. On the 2nd of January he advanced with 2 divisions on the roads to Bucquoy and Bapaume. The Prussian left wing, under General Groeben, fell back behind the Encre rivulet, and the small detachment of the 15th Division stationed at Achiet evacuated this place also on the approach of the enemy from Bucquoy. On the other hand, on the road to Bapaume, General Strubberg's Brigade at Sapignies repulsed all attacks of the enemy's superior forces. The Prussian grape fire was of very great effect here, and a squadron of the 7th Hussars also had an opportunity of making a successful charge. General Strubberg's losses were moderate; those of the enemy considerably greater, and included 250 unwounded prisoners. Towards evening, however, the patrols that were sent out in all directions reported the advance of fresh

Advance of the French to raise the siege of Péronne. 197

hostile columns from the directions of Douai and Arras; General Kummer therefore withdrew General Strubberg's Brigade nearer to Bapaume, and concentrated his whole division there. Next morning he was reinforced by 2 horse-artillery batteries from Le Transloy.

When the news of the action at Sapignies reached Combles, General Goeben sent orders to General Kummer to hold his position at Bapaume on the 3rd January, and General Groeben was desired to assemble his troops farther westwards at Pys, and, if an attack were made on Bapaume, to try and fall upon the enemy's flank and rear with the greater part of his cavalry and artillery. Prince Albrecht's detachment, which now consisted of 3 battalions, 3 regiments of cavalry, and 3 batteries, marched on the morning of the 3rd from Fins to Bertincourt. Three battalions of the troops investing Péronne were ordered up to Sailly as reserves. General Goeben himself rode early on the 3rd from Combles to Le Transloy, where, for the moment, 2 battalions and 2 horse-artillery batteries were in reserve. Of these the two latter were very soon placed at General Kummer's disposal.

On the forenoon of the 3rd, the enemy advanced to the attack with the 2 whole army corps which he had meanwhile concentrated. The 15th Division disputed the ground north of Bapaume against these three to four-fold superior numbers until mid-day. The fight raged with great fury round the villages of Favreuil and Bièfvillers. General Kummer then withdrew his troops, and stationed the 30th Brigade on the heights south of Bapaume, with the 29th Brigade deployed in front of it. In the meantime, Prince Albrecht had advanced from Bertincourt to Frémicourt and arrived there at the moment when General Kummer withdrew his troops from the ground in front of Bapaume. The Prince immediately joined in the action and advanced against the enemy's left flank. Although he did not gain much ground himself, still he checked the enemy's progress. The Prince's detachment then established itself between Bapaume and Frémicourt, adjoining the 15th Division and covering its right flank.

The enemy now endeavoured to turn the left flank of the division, at the same time attacking Bapaume in the front. The town was, however, held, and the reserves being ordered up to the left wing, succeeded in wresting, at the point of the bayonet, part of the ground which had been lost there, in particular the village of Tilloy, from the enemy. They then held their ground in the neighbourhood of Ligny in an obstinate struggle, in which they were seconded by General Groeben's left flank detachment, until the enemy broke off the engagement at about 7 P.M.

In a sanguinary fight of nine hours duration, Bapaume and the main position behind the town had been gloriously and successfully defended. The enemy had to-day lost 300 unwounded prisoners; but our own loss was also heavy.[1] The troops were exhausted after the two days' fight, and the stores of ammunition had so much diminished that they needed replenishment. Under such circumstances, the immediate continuation of the struggle against such superior forces of an enemy who had maintained a firm and steady demeanour up to the last moment, might, if unsuccessful, cause a serious defeat. In correct appreciation of the general political and military situation, General Goeben, however, wished to avoid a battle in which the advantage of victory would have borne no comparison with the disadvantage of defeat. He therefore gave orders that the 15th Division should withdraw southwards at 8 A.M. on the 4th, and that Prince Albrecht's detachment should take the direction of Roisel (eastward of Péronne). The cavalry division, reinforced by the infantry that had been employed on the left

---

[1] The Prussian loss on the 2nd and 3rd of January amounted to:

	officers		men	
	11		117	killed
	35	,,	667	wounded
			236	missing
Total	46 officers,		1,020 men.	

About 200 of these casualties occurred on the 2nd of January.

wing of the line of battle, which raised its force of this arm to 5 battalions, was to proceed to Albert, where it would be on the enemy's flank in case he advanced on Péronne.

The stunning effects of the battle had, however, been more felt by the enemy than by the defenders of the position. In the course of the night the French already evacuated the nearest villages north of Bapaume, and retreated in good order in the direction of Douai and Arras early on the 4th.[1] This was soon perceived on the part of the Prussians. Whilst the bulk of the army was carrying out the prescribed movements, a part of the cavalry division remained in close contact with the enemy; the 8th Cuirassier Regiment attacked his rearmost battalions, and took some prisoners. On the evening of the 4th January, the 15th Division was in the neighbourhood of Bray, mostly on the left bank of the Somme; the 16th Division and Prince Albrecht's Division were on the right bank of the river, round Péronne; General Groeben's Division, reinforced by infantry, occupied Bapaume, and continued to watch the enemy's movements. General Goeben established his Head-Quarters at Becquincourt (between Bray and Péronne).

Whilst these events were taking place at Bapaume, the bombardment of Péronne had been resumed on the 2nd and continued during the 3rd and 4th of January. On the last-named day, the

[1] According to General Faidherbe's work, the French lost 53 officers and 2,119 men at Bapaume; twice as many, therefore, as the Prussians. Nevertheless, the French claimed the victory. It is true that the French Army, with its great numerical superiority gained ground in the battle, and that all this lost ground was not recovered by the Prussians in the battle itself, but only by the *immediate results of the battle*. To form a judgment on this question we must again seek the criterion elsewhere Had Faidherbe really gained the victory, an energetic general like he was would have carried out his openly avowed purpose of raising the siege of Péronne, instead of retreating. The reasons which he gives as his motives, viz., want of shelter for his troops in the villages full of dead and wounded, a report that the bombardment of Péronne had been discontinued, the severe cold and the fatigue of his troops, etc., etc., are all more adapted to veil a defeat than to illustrate a victory. The truth is, perhaps, that the *tactical* victory remained undecided, because *neither side* was disposed to *renew the struggle immediately;* both felt themselves little capable of doing so, and therefore each wished some distance to intervene between him and his adversary. The *strategical* victory, however, consisted in the attempt to raise the siege of Péronne having been frustrated, and was therefore decidedly on the side of the Prussians.

siege-train of 11 guns prepared at La Fère left this place for Villers-Carbonnel. At that time, however, affairs seemed to take a turn that might, perhaps, lead to the investment being temporarily suspended; General Barnekow, therefore, ordered the 11 guns to return to La Fère. An artillery company brought up from Mézières arrived at La Fère the same day.

Lieutenant-Colonel Pestel had returned from his expedition in the west to his former position between Amiens and Abbeville, and was at Picquigny on the 4th.

This was the general course of affairs on the line of the Somme up to the evening of the 4th January. We now only have to recount the operations of *General Lippe's Cavalry Division* during this period.

On the 2nd January, General Lippe marched from Le Catelet eastwards, in the first instance to Bohain. A flank detachment, which was to march by way of Busigny, drove the enemy out of Maretz, but on advancing farther encountered superior forces, and therefore took up a position at Maretz and observed the enemy's movements. The French then advanced from Busigny in the wooded district north of Bohain, between Fremont and Becquigny, and General Lippe, in consequence, recalled 2 squadrons that were stationed at these villages and the Maretz detachment to his own position at Bohain. The whole day long the roar of artillery had been audible in the direction of Péronne and farther northwards. This induced General Lippe not to proceed with the expedition against Vervins until he had assured himself of the state of affairs on his left flank by pushing forward to Busigny. For this purpose, General Senfft, who had reached Origny on the 2nd, was also brought up to Bohain on the 3rd. It was discovered on this day that the enemy had evacuated Maretz and Busigny, and had retreated the night before, it was said, to Cambrai. Patrols that scoured the country farther northwards found no signs of the enemy either. The destruction of the railway near Busigny, which, though previously intended, had not yet been feasible, was now thoroughly effected.

On the 4th the division marched to Guise. Town and neighbourhood were occupied by swarms of 'gardes mobiles,' who received the advanced-guard with a sharp fire, but were apparently already making preparations to retire, partly on carts. The Saxon artillery drew up on the high ground westward of Guise, and opened fire on whatever was to be seen of the enemy, thereby accelerating his retreat. Guise was then entered from the south, and the defile west of the town cleared of the enemy. The Guard 'Reiter' Regiment pursued the latter in the direction of Vervins, the 17th Lancers northwards. The former regiment captured 20 stragglers at Beauvain, and then patrolled towards Vervins and Merle, both of which places were apparently not occupied by the enemy. The Lancers found about 1,000 'gardes mobiles' posted behind a rivulet near Iron, so that the battery and a company of rifles were obliged to be sent forward to support them. The enemy attempted to advance again, but was checked by the fire of the artillery, and the fight ceased when darkness set in.

Early on the 5th a mixed detachment of all arms was pushed forward beyond Etreux to reconnoitre in the direction of Landrecies, and the Guard 'Reiter' Regiment advanced again to Vervins and Merle. The enemy was nowhere to be seen. All French troops hitherto in this quarter seemed now to be endeavouring to rejoin the Army of the North, in the direction of Douai and Arras. After attaining these results, General Lippe marched to St. Quentin on the 6th.

We now turn again to the west.

On the afternoon of the 4th, the news of the issue of the battle of Bapaume arrived at Amiens, and General Goeben was, in consequence, desired to follow up the hard-won victory with those troops that were still in contact with the enemy, and in particular to continue the siege of Péronne.

On the 5th the ammunition was replenished, and the cavalry that was pushed forward beyond Bapaume reported the complete retreat of the enemy, after which part of the 15th Division was moved in the direction of Albert on the 6th, and the siege-train ordered up from La Fère. Lieutenant-Colonel Pestel was desired to draw nearer to the left wing; he, in consequence, marched to Villers-Bocage on the 6th, and to Acheux on the 7th January. One squadron remained at Picquigny, and the battalion of the 70th Regiment rejoined the 16th Division.

General Goeben reported these measures to Amiens on the 6th and then remarked, with regard to his future plans, that in order to avoid being again placed under the necessity of fighting a defensive battle with his front to the north, he now intended to take up the following positions :

1. The 15th Division at Albert and along the Arras railway.

2. Prince Albrecht's Division and the corps artillery in the neighbourhood of Combles.

3. The 3rd Cavalry Division, with 2 battalions, at Bapaume.

4. The 16th Division and General Strantz's Cavalry Brigade in front of Péronne, with orders to cover the investment of the fortress in the direction of Cambrai.

If another attempt were to be made to raise the siege of Péronne, General Goeben intended to leave the Bapaume road open to the enemy, and then to fall upon his flank and rear with the troops named above, sub. 1, 2, and 3, i.e., with 18 battalions, 24 squadrons, and 90 guns.

On the 7th of January accounts came in from divers quarters speaking of considerable reinforcements received by the Army of the North. Twenty thousand men were said to have disembarked at Boulogne, of whom part had been thrown into Abbeville. It was then stated that General Faidherbe now intended to attack Amiens with 3 army corps, and that large masses of troops were already assembled at Hamelincourt, halfway between Arras and Bapaume, on the 6th January. If this information should prove correct, the numerical superiority of the enemy would be overwhelming, and in this case General Goeben intended to withdraw his troops wholly behind the Somme, and to await the enemy's attack there. The cavalry division would then alone remain at Bapaume to feel the enemy, but would retire southwards if pressed by superior numbers.

General Goeben's intentions and arrangements coincided perfectly with the opinion which prevailed at Head-Quarters. Although the latter laid great stress on gaining possession of Péronne, for reasons we have already mentioned, still it was evident that we must not risk losing a battle northwards of the Somme. We had to make up our minds, if the necessity arose, to raise the investment of that fortress on the right bank of the Somme for a time, and only to continue the bombardment from the left bank, which was more secure, and where the siege-train was for this reason established. A correspondence, carried on between the Commander-in-Chief and General Goeben on the 6th and 7th of January, entered fully into all these questions.

It is fitting that we now refer to some other arrangements made by the Commander-in-Chief. We know, from the preceding pages, that four important reports had reached Amiens at different times within the course of the last few days. First, that the 14th Division had definitely ceased to belong to the 1st Army, which precluded all hope of receiving reinforcements from that quarter. Then came the report on the issue of the battle at Bapaume; somewhat later, the news that considerable reinforcements were joining the Army of the North. It was, therefore, doubly welcome when news reached Amiens of General Bentheim's successful operations against General Roye, which had rendered it again possible to bring up from the Seine the reinforcements that were so desirable at the Somme.

At that moment 9 battalions of the 1st Army Corps were on the left bank of the Seine, on the line Bourgachard—Pont de l'Arche; 6 on the right bank, on the line Pavilly—Duclair; 6 garrisoned at Rouen, and 1 was at Gisors and other small stations. Three battalions (the 4th Regiment) and 2 batteries still remained at Amiens. A telegram was now despatched to General Bentheim, ordering him to send 6 battalions and 2 batteries per rail to Amiens. The transport of these troops, which raised the strength of that part of the 1st Army Corps which was detached to the Somme to 9 battalions and 4 batteries, commenced on the afternoon of the 7th January.[1]

On the same day Lieutenant-Colonel Pestel's march to Acheux was reported at Amiens, and news also arrived there that the enemy, who had remained perfectly inactive at Abbeville ever since the action at Longpré, had pushed forward troops to Pont Rémy (between Abbeville and Longpré) at mid-day of the 5th. This was connected with the rumours of reinforcements having arrived from Boulogne. To protect the Amiens—Rouen railway, General Manteuffel gave orders on the 7th that a battalion of the 4th Regiment and a squadron of the Guard Hussars, that had hitherto remained at Amiens, were to march to Molliens-Vidame, and when there to keep up communications with the squadron at Picquigny.

These troops arrived at Molliens-Vidame on the evening of the 7th, and pushed forward a detachment towards Airaines without encountering the enemy. Lieutenant-Colonel Pestel also scoured the country between the Amiens—Arras railway and the Arras—Doullens high-road on the 8th without meeting with any opposition, and even pushed his patrols forward as far as the road which leads from Arras over Avesnes to Frévent. Neither did the advance of the enemy's army on Bapaume take place on the 7th, as was expected. Hamélincourt was even said to have been evacuated. All that now remained of the above-mentioned rumours was that the Army of the North, after having been re-victualled under shelter of the fortresses, had now extended its cantonments somewhat more to the south. The French line of outposts was established about on the line Douchy—Ervillers—Croisilles; the army cantoned behind it in the neighbourhood of Boisleux and Boyelles, about half-way between Arras and Bapaume.

Under these circumstances, General Goeben remained in his

---

[1] As the enemy still continued inactive in Normandy, still more troops were afterwards moved from Rouen, which was not without influence on the brilliant issue of the battle of St. Quentin.

General Goeben takes command of the 1st Army. 205

previous position on the 7th: 15th Division between Bray and Albert; Prince Albrecht at Combles; 16th Division and General Strantz's Brigade round Péronne; Head-Quarters at Becquincourt.

No change took place in the situation on the 8th. The bombardment of Péronne was continued with vigour. On the morning of the 9th the fortress ceased firing, and late in the evening of the same day capitulated, with 3,000 men and 47 guns. For a time, however, it seemed doubtful whether the capitulation would be completed. Hostile troops had advanced from Cambrai, forcing Colonel Wittich to fall back from Fins to Nurlu on the 9th. Added to this, on the forenoon of the 10th the Army of the North was reported to be advancing over Bapaume to Sailly. By this time, however, the Cambrai detachment had already retired northwards of Fins, and the rumour of an approach of the Army of the North proved to be exaggerated.[1] Péronne was occupied by Prussian troops at 1 P.M. of the 10th January.

With this event the object which General Manteuffel had held in view ever since the battle of the Hallue was now attained, viz., secure possession of the line of the Somme from La Fère to Amiens. But the news of this event did not reach him at Amiens. On the evening of the 7th a telegram had arrived here summoning the general to Versailles to take command of the newly-formed South Army, consisting of the IInd, VIIth, and XIVth Army Corps. From the 9th January on, the command of the 1st Army devolved upon General Goeben. Before leaving on the 9th of January, the late Commander-in-Chief issued the following farewell orders:

'His Majesty the King has appointed me to another command and ordered me to hand that of the 1st Army over to General of Infantry Von Goeben. With the fullest confidence I place this fine command in the hands of so experienced a general.

---

[1] According to General Faidherbe's work, it was determined to make another reconnaissance of the state of affairs at Péronne, in consequence of which the French took up cantonments round Ervillers ($5\frac{3}{4}$ miles north of Bapaume) on the 10th January.

'General of Infantry Von Goeben will take command of the 1st Army to-morrow; but I cannot part from the army without repeating the final words of my New Year's wish.

'To-day, but to-day in my own name alone, and from my innermost heart and soul, I also express my deep-felt thanks to the army, and most heartily wish it further laurels. I thank the Head-Quarter's staff; I thank the generals, commanders of regiments, and officers; I thank each individual soldier of the army. I thank the surgeons, who have fulfilled their duties with equal devotion both in and out of fire; and hereby especially thank both consulting surgeons-general, whose unremitting labours have also saved the king the life of many a brave soldier. I thank the chaplains, who also never shunned fire in the exercise of their vocation; I thank all officials of the army, and remark, in acknowledgment of their services, that the officials of the Intendance have at all times known how to provide the supplies for the army, and that the officers and soldiers who did duty with the train and the 'Etappen' effectually assisted them in this service.

'And thus I say to all of you, farewell! And, in saying farewell, I at the same time think with fervent gratitude of our fallen and wounded comrades, the shedding of whose blood has contributed so greatly to the glory of the 1st Army.

'May God be with your standards henceforth.

       (Signed) 'MANTEUFFEL.

'Amiens, 8th of January, 1871.'

POSTSCRIPT.

Herewith we close this narrative. It was only intended to continue it so far as the author had had the advantage of personally witnessing events, and of knowing perfectly how they worked together. It will be the duty of another pen to describe the final period of the French campaign in the north, in which General Goeben crowned the successful labours of his predecessors by the brilliant victory of St. Quentin.

APPENDIX.

MOVEMENTS of troops, combats and battles, indeed all the outwardly visible signs of war, excite in themselves general interest. But other agencies besides these contribute their share towards the results of a campaign whose labours, when superficially regarded, remain more or less in the background, and yet exercise a prominent influence on the issue. In their totality they form, as it were, the inner cogs and wheels of the great army machinery; experience has shown how much depends on their working regularly.

It was an act of justice on the part of the Commander-in-chief when he expressed his thanks to these branches of the service also in his farewell orders of the 8th of January. 'If we would understand and fully appreciate their meritorious labours, we should have to enter into the minutest detail of them. This would, however, not be an appropriate theme, as it would be somewhat dry both to the writer and the reader. We therefore confine ourselves to making a few statements regarding the supply of ammunition and provisions, so far as this subject came under the immediate cognizance of Head-Quarters. They are, moreover, based on information received from friends and competent judges of the subject.

1. *Sketch of the arrangements which Head-Quarters of the 1st Army made for providing supplies during the war with France.*

At the commencement of the French campaign the 1st Army consisted of the VIIth and VIIIth Army Corps and the 3rd Cavalry Division. Its system of supplies was in the first instance naturally based on the Rhine. Sufficient provisions to cover the daily consumption of the army for six weeks and a fortnight's reserve were stored in the first place at Coblenz and Cologne, under the supposition that when the army advanced the Rhine-Nahe line of railway would be available for its traffic, or that the Call-Trèves line would soon be in working order. Neither one nor the other, however, was the case. The army had to rely solely on land transport for its supplies, and the insufficiency of this mode of transport already became evident during the march of the army over the Eifel and Hundsrück mountains, and the period of its subsequent concentration eastward of the Saar.

Therefore, when the army advanced beyond this river, at which time the Inspection-General of 'Etappen' commenced operations, the base of supply was moved forward from the Rhine to the Saar, and principal depôts, together with the necessary bakeries, were established at Trèves and Saarlouis. For this purpose all articles of provision still in the 'Etappen' magazines previously established on the Eifel and Hundsrück, as well as all those stored at Coblenz and Cologne, had to be moved forward to Trèves and Saarlouis, all of which had to be done by means of land transport. The Inspection-General of 'Etappen' was therefore transferred to Saarlouis, and established a waggon-park of 2,000 carts there, which were impressed by requisitions made in the Government district of Trèves.[1] The Inspection-General also provided for the erection of field-baking ovens, which were soon in working order, field-bakers having been furnished by the field-bakery columns of the army corps for this purpose.

The troops had, however, been already compelled to draw upon their 'iron rations,'[2] without having been able to replenish them immediately, according to rule. It seemed necessary that this should be done previously to entering France, and yet the stores that had been meanwhile conveyed to Saarlouis were not sufficient for the purpose, especially as the army had been lately reinforced by the 1st Army Corps and the 1st Cavalry Division. With permission of higher authorities, recourse was had to the provision stores of the fortress of Saarlouis, under the condition, however, of their being speedily returned in kind. This made it possible to refurnish the troops with their 'iron' portions and rations.

As long as the army was on the move forwards it was not possible to push forward any magazine beyond Saarlouis from which the Army Corps could draw their supplies. All that could be done was to load carts with as many of the daily necessaries as could not be procured by direct requisition, and to let them follow the army. After having made due arrangements to this effect at Saarlouis, the Inspection-General of 'Etappen' followed one day's march behind Army Head-Quarters.

---

[1] 'Regierungs-Bezirk.' The Rhenish provinces are divided into five Regierungs-Bezirke, or Government districts, viz. : Düsseldorf, Cologne, Aix-la-Chapelle, Coblenz, and Trèves.

[2] Each Prussian soldier carries a three days 'iron' ration, which must be immediately replenished whenever it is made use of.

About the middle of August the army drew near to the Forbach-Metz line of railway, whereupon the Intendant-General ordered that of the two 'Etappen' magazines established on this line for the IInd Army, the one at Courcelles should be given up to the 1st Army. As long, however, as the army was on the march it was but little able to profit by this circumstance. Now, as before, waggon-park columns laden with provisions still had to follow the army from Saarlouis. The last of these columns, consisting of about 600 waggons, arrived at Gravelotte on the 19th and 20th August. Their contents furnished the troops with provisions on the day after the battle, and the empty waggons were then used to convey the wounded to various railway stations.

As soon as the army had taken up its positions in front of Metz, the Inspection-General of 'Etappen' brought up the necessary stores from the Saarlouis magazine to Courcelles, from whence the different army corps transferred what they had need of to their own corps magazines by means of their provision and waggon-park columns. All available conveyances were at the same time engaged in collecting as much surplus provision in the corps magazines as the waggons the troops were possessed of would have been able to carry, in case of a sudden move.

This transport service was managed with most praiseworthy perseverance and energy during the whole time that the blockade of Metz lasted. This was equally the case in bringing up the supplies from Saarlouis, and in drawing them from the advanced magazines. The latter often changed their position, in consequence of alterations in the distribution of the army corps, rendering it in most cases necessary to transfer their contents to the new corps magazines. When the 3rd Reserve Division was added to the army, the daily consumption became so great that it would have been impossible to convey the supplies to Courcelles by land transport, especially as the waggon-park of the Inspection-General had dwindled down to half its original dimensions, in consequence of the transport of the wounded after the battle of Gravelotte, and other circumstances.

As soon as the purely military railway traffic caused by this battle and the preparations for the blockade of Metz ceased, a partial use of the Forbach line of railway was granted to the 1st Army for its supplies. The Inspection-General of 'Etappen' also succeeded in discovering new purveyors, who delivered their goods direct to the principal depôt at Saarlouis. Thus, such waggons as had been hitherto appropriated to this service were now available for conveying supplies to the army.

Added to this, several railway-trains laden with provisions of all kinds were handed over to the IInd Army at Ars-sur-Moselle. Probably originally intended for the IIIrd Army, these trains had been in the first instance despatched to Nancy, but not being as yet able to proceed any farther, they now had to be unladen in order not to encumber the line. Their contents were given to the IInd Army, but the Ist Army also participated in them to a certain degree. By these means the stock of provisions in the different magazines was gradually increased, and it thus became possible, not only to feed 50,000 of the Sédan prisoners and the troops escorting them, but also to send 100 waggons a day laden with provisions of all kinds to the Crown Prince of Saxony's detachment during its operations in the Argonnes forest.

Towards the end of August, on the other hand, a great and general calamity ensued, seriously affecting the supplies of the army. It was an epidemic disease that broke out almost simultaneously in all the cattle-parks of the army at Saarlouis, Courcelles, Ars-sur-Moselle, and Jouy-aux-Arches, and which the veterinary surgeons pronounced to be the veritable 'rinderpest.' In consequence of this, about 1,000 Podolian oxen were obliged to be immediately slaughtered, and a sanitary cordon was established to prevent the passage of any living cattle. In order, notwithstanding, to provide the army with fresh meat, the sphere of requisition was extended farther and farther to the rear of the army, and this system more rigorously enforced. Nevertheless this measure did not suffice to provide for the wants of the army. All that could be done under the circumstances was to give the troops mutton and pork as often as possible, to increase the supply of bacon, and to buy up salted and smoked beef and pork in the large seaport towns. Fresh beef cannot, however, be entirely dispensed with for any length of time; slaughter-houses were therefore erected at Mayence, and meat was preserved there by boiling, drying, and rubbing with pepper and salt, then packed in straw and sent to the army.

Thus everything that could be thought of was done to meet these adverse circumstances, and we may say that, on the whole, this heavy calamity passed over without any injurious influence on the health of the troops. In the meantime, in order to be prepared in case the army advanced, the work of accumulating provisions in the magazines was continually progressing. When the capitulation of Metz took place, however, it became evident that all these precautionary measures barely sufficed to meet the contingency. For, whilst the IInd Army had only to provide for the inhabitants of the beleaguered city, it fell to the lot of the Ist Army to feed about 150,000 prisoners of war during their transport to the frontier. This exhausted the stock of provisions, and fresh supplies had to be provided at a moment when the army was on

Appendix.

the eve of marching. The magazine of the army had been transferred from Courcelles to Herny about the middle of October. The Inspection-General of 'Etappen' now moved it to Metz to disencumber the line of railway. This facilitated the drawing of supplies from the magazine by the corps, and went a great way towards enabling all demands to be promptly satisfied.

The next question now was how to prepare for the coming march. The Intendant-General assigned to the 1st Army, which was in the first instance to march to the Oise, the line Réthel—Rheims as its base of supplies. In order to be perfectly prepared for the time when the troops would have consumed the provisions they carried with them, officials were sent on in advance as early as the 2nd November, with orders to prepare, within twelve days, magazines containing fourteen days' provisions at Laon and Réthel for the 1st Army Corps, and in Rheims and Soissons for the VIIIth Army Corps and the 3rd Cavalry Division. The Government-General of Rheims was requested to give its assistance, and the Intendant-General had sent a similar request to the Army of the Meuse to afford as much help as its own surplus stores admitted of. In particular, measures were to be taken to establish a large magazine at Soissons.

The result of these requests was that a store of oats at Clermont was placed at the disposal of the army, and was made use of by the Cavalry Division during its advance, but for the moment no further help could be given.

The army orders of the 4th of November, from which we give the subjoined extract, made the following arrangements for provisioning the army during its advance:—

'Within two days before starting, the Army Corps will draw their necessary supply of provisions, by which is to be understood that they complete their three days' iron portions and rations, load their provision-columns with rations and bread-stuffs for four days' consumption, and the waggon-park of 400 carts attached to each corps with oats for six days, and a reserve of flour and biscuit. The Inspection-General of " Etappen " will then assemble all waggons at its disposal, of which it is expected that it will have 1,000, within the next few days, load them with a three days' supply of oats and provisions, and send them after the army in such manner that supplies for one army corps are pushed forward on the northern " Etappen " line, and for one army corps and a cavalry division on the south line. The Inspection-General of " Etappen " will report the number, freight, and line of march of the waggons it sends off. As a rule the troops must claim to be fed by their hosts. They will only have recourse to the stores in cases of emergency, and will then, in the first instance, fall back upon the provision and waggon-park columns. The empty waggons must be assembled daily, and, until further orders are given, be sent to the Inspection-General of "Etappen" at Metz, in order that they may be reloaded there and sent after the army again.

'Provisions are not to be requisitioned during the advance of the army, but they may be purchased; and it is at the discretion of the corps to make arrangements for opening markets for the sale of them. The 1st Army Corps is informed that there is a magazine in Sédan from which it may perhaps be able to draw supplies, if the corps apply to the commandant and send an official on in advance. If the magazines on the "Etappen" line of the Army of the Meuse should be available, the VIIIth Army Corps will be apprised of it. Every possible care must be taken to establish magazines when the enemy advances farther.'

These arrangements were suited to the circumstances, and on the whole answered their purpose. When Verdun capitulated, the VIIIth Army Corps received a quantity of oats from the stores of this fortress, and shared also in those that the Cavalry Division obtained from the Army of the Meuse at Clermont. By these means the army crossed the Argonnes mountains and entered Champagne without experiencing any want of supplies either for man or horse. In Champagne the army found the magazines that had been prepared beforehand, and so thoroughly replenished its stores from them that it was amply provided with provisions when it continued its march to the north-west of France. Henceforward the labour principally consisted in bringing up the supplies from the magazines in the rear. Those established at Rheims and Soissons were the most convenient ones for the army, on account of their situation and the existing railway communication. It was, however, found that these magazines could not be filled on the spot, but only by bringing up supplies from the home country. Therefore the principal depôt of the army was moved from Saarlouis to Metz, where goods could be delivered on the spot. From here the supplies were pushed forward in the first instance to the magazines at Rheims and Soissons. Thus, the latter were divested of the character of principal depôts, and remained during the whole period of their existence mere branch magazines.

During the first period of the operations of the army beyond the Oise its supplies were moved forward from Soissons to Compiègne; all further transport had to be effected by the army corps themselves. But when traffic was opened on the Crépy-Creil line of railway on the 1st

Appendix.

December, all stores were moved from Rheims and Soissons to Compiègne, and branch magazines were then established at Beauvais and Creil. In Beauvais the stores of the Army of the Meuse were also placed at the disposal of the 1st Army. The French system of railways was, on the whole, favourable to bringing up our supplies from the home country; but the lines that had been broken up in parts occupied by our troops had to be repaired, besides which the necessary rolling-stock, especially locomotive engines, had to be procured and put in order before we could use them for moving our supplies to the most important points. The traffic over Crépy and Creil to Amiens and Rouen was attended with peculiar difficulty, for the Oise had to be crossed by a temporary bridge. For this reason the line could not be used for any very heavy traffic, but only for bringing forward such articles as were absolutely necessary for the daily consumption of the army.

On the other hand, when the Rheims-Laon-La-Fère-Ham-Amiens railway began to be worked, this line, although it was certainly from a military point of view somewhat exposed, afforded a direct line of communication with the home country, on which heavy trains could run from Metz to Amiens and Rouen without discharging their freight. After leaving Metz such trains proceeded direct to the corps magazines, without it being previously necessary to store their contents in the magazines of the Inspection-General of 'Etappen.'

2. *Sketch of the mode in which the ammunition of the army was completed.*

The ammunition expended by the field armies during the campaign 1870–71 must be classed under the following heads, according to the regulations existing at that time:

1. In the foremost line the pouch-ammunition of the fighting troops, and that contained in the limbers and ammunition waggons.
2. The ammunition columns of the army corps.
3. The reserve ammunition columns of the army.
4. The reserve ammunition depôt of the army.[1]

The troops completed their ammunition from the corps ammunition columns, if possible from those of their own corps. The course to be taken

---

[1] The corresponding classification in the British army is:
   1. In possession of the troops and regimental reserve.
   2. Field Reserve with the Artillery (1st and 2nd reserve).
   3. Military store reserve field arsenal (3rd reserve).
   4. Military store reserves, grand depôt and intermediate reserves.

with regard to bringing up reserve ammunition and completing the ammunition reserve of the corps was determined by the Head-Quarters Staff of the army, and was the special duty of the officer commanding the artillery of the army. For this purpose the latter disposed of the reserve ammunition columns and the reserve ammunition depôt. In the former the ammunition was laden on waggons without teams, in the latter it was packed in boxes. As a rule, the ammunition columns completed their supply from the reserve columns, and these from the reserve depôt. The depôt was established at some point at a suitable distance behind the army, and was moved forwards as the latter advanced. According to the regulations, the reserve columns had either to fetch their supply themselves from the depôt, or the latter sent it to them per rail. The latter mode being the simplest and quickest, attention was turned to adapting it in refilling the corps ammunition columns direct from the depôt. It was found in this case also to work well whenever it was possible to bring the ammunition per rail close up to the army.[1]

The supply of the 1st Army with ammunition was effected under the superintendence of General Schwartz according to the foregoing general principles. During the first period of the campaign and the blockade of Metz the reserve ammunition columns were stationed at Saarlouis under the command of Major Rosenzweig; Captain Boettcher was at the head of the reserve depôt which was also at Saarlouis.

When Metz fell, part of the reserve columns were in the first case pushed forward to this place. Towards the end of November, when the army set off from the Oise to the Somme and the Lower Seine, all the reserve columns were moved forward to Laon. The telegraphic order for this removal was despatched on the 20th November; they arrived at Laon between the 27th November and the 2nd December. Then followed the transport of the reserve depôt from Saarlouis to Soissons by means of impressed relays of horses. The reserve columns and the depôt remained there until the end of the campaign.

The lines of railway which ran westward from Soissons afforded the means of sending the necessary supply of ammunition to within the sphere of the corps ammunition columns, sufficiently near, therefore, to

---

[1] If no railway was available for the transport of the ammunition, then the reserve ammunition columns, not being horsed, had first to be made fit for the road by impressing relays of horses, and then despatched to meet the empty waggons of the corps ammunition columns on their way towards them. Experience had, however, shown during the French campaign that the impressment of any considerable number of horses was always attended with difficulty and delay, and expectations founded on this measure were seldom realised within the given time.

the troops in the field. The necessary rolling stock for the transport of the reserve columns (without teams) could not be obtained, and the railway transport of heavy trains was a difficult and uncertain matter on account of the unsafe parts of the line. But, even if it had been possible to push the columns forward by rail, they would have greatly encumbered the line at the stations and absorbed a considerable quantity of rolling-stock for several days.

This made the advantage alluded to above of replenishing the corps ammunition columns direct from the reserve depôt still more palpable, for a few trucks attached to the trains sufficed for the transport of the boxes of ammunition. With very few exceptions this mode was therefore adopted for the transport of ammunition to the Somme and the Seine.

The general mode of proceeding was as follows :—As soon as a general action was to be expected, orders were telegraphed to Soissons to hold ammunition in readiness to be sent forward. Thanks to this timely precaution, even when the expenditure had been very great, the ammunition of the army was always promptly completed. It was despatched from Soissons on the receipt of a second telegram. This one was sent off immediately after the battle, without waiting for any application on the part of the troops. A rough estimate of the necessary quantity was formed on the battle-field from enquiries made by the adjutants of Head-Quarters Staff on the spot. If it afterwards turned out that more was required, a supplementary quantity was ordered up later; but if the supply received in the first instance was in excess of the demand, the surplus was returned to the depôt per rail as soon as it was known for certain that the ammunition of the whole army was sufficiently completed. The railway trucks containing the ammunition were always shunted on to side lines at the stations, so that they were easily accessible to the ammunition-waggons, which would drive close up to them and receive their loads without impeding the traffic on the line.

By degrees, as the operations of the army advanced, in addition to the main depôt at Soissons, intermediate depôts were established at Laon, Creil, Beauvais, Bréteuil, Nesle, and Longueau, near Amiens. The ammunition expended in the battle of Amiens on the 27th November was replenished from Laon between the 2nd and 4th December.

Subsequently the convoys of ammunition were sent from Soissons in the direction of Amiens for that part of the army that was operating at the Somme, and to Beauvais for the troops at the Seine. In either case the ammunition had to pass the Creil station; this spot was therefore selected to form an intermediate depôt for the supply of both halves of the army. It was especially adapted to the purpose by reason of its situation, which was secure from attacks of the enemy, and yet not at too great a distance from the army. When more ammunition had been sent forward than the troops wanted, it was deposited here for the time; it was easily sent forward again if a fresh demand occurred, and could be replenished from Soissons in a very short time.

On the 22nd December, the eve of the battle of the Hallue, the commander of the artillery sent warning to Soissons to get an ammunition transport ready to be sent off in the direction of Amiens. On the evening of the first day of the battle the quantity to be sent was fixed according to a rough estimate made of the expenditure, and on the evening of the second day, the 24th, Bréteuil was named as the station to which the empty ammunition waggons would be sent from the battle-field to receive their supply.

In the course of the following days the first replenishment of the ammunition was effected, and the surplus sent for the present to Creil, from whence it was conveyed to Longueau, near Amiens, on the 28th December. Here the ammunition of the army was fully completed; the quantity necessary to satisfy the increased demand occasioned by the bombardment of Péronne, having been ordered per telegram from Soissons, had arrived very speedily at Longueau. The ammunition spent in the battle of Bapaume was also completed from here, so that notwithstanding the great expenditure in the bombardment of Péronne and the battle of Bapaume, the army never felt the want of reserve ammunition. Part of what was expended at Bapaume was completed by the reserve ammunition column attached to the 3rd Cavalry Division, the column then replenishing its own store from the depôt at La Fère.

The ammunition that was not issued to the army remained at Longueau till the 14th January, and was then returned to the intermediate depôt at Creil.

The next demand arose on the 19th January, the day of St. Quentin, after which battle the ammunition was completed with especial promptitude. The order for sending a supply from Creil to Nesle could not be telegraphed earlier than the night after the battle. Nevertheless, the convoy reached Nesle the very next evening; at the same time that part of the empty columns appointed to receive its supply at Nesle arrived there also, General Schwartz having given orders on the battle-field that only one-half of the empty columns was to complete its ammunition at Nesle; the other half was ordered to proceed to Soissons. The object of this was, in case of any irregularity occurring in the railway traffic, to be sure of receiving half of the necessary supply at Soissons, even though the waggons could not get back from there for some days. However, the transport to Nesle was effected without any delay, so that sufficient ammunition to replace that expended in the battle was in the immediate neighbourhood of the army by the evening of the 20th, and the troops could immediately begin to complete their supply.

For the troops operating on the Seine only two trifling transports of ammunition were sent per rail from Soissons to Beauvais, to which place the empty waggons were despatched from Rouen. Every shot fired by the army was replaced in the course of the armistice.

The annexed table shows the amount of ammunition issued from the reserve stores and distributed to the 1st Army at the different intermediate stations.

In addition to the foregoing ammunition, 450,000 rounds of needle-gun ammunition were sent from the reserve ammunition depôt to the citadel of Amiens, but were not expended.

The store of ammunition in the reserve depôt was completed from the artillery depôts at Coblenz, Cologne, Minden, and Spandau on direct requisition of the former. The requisitions were always promptly answered, but the transport to Soissons often consumed a long time. For instance, a transport from Minden took seven, one such from Spandau fourteen days.

Ammunition column or depôt which made the issue	Intermediate station at which the ammunition was distributed to the Corps columns	Shells		Needle-gun ammunition	Needle carbine ammunition	Ball cartridges for cavalry[1]	Columns which received the ammunition
		4-pounder	6-pounder				
				rounds	rounds	rounds	
Reserve ammunition column of the 1st Army	Laon	4,055	1,552	121,155	800	628	Ammunition columns of Ist and VIIIth Army Corps
,,	Soissons	...	1,457	...	...	...	,,
Reserve ammunition depôt of the 1st Army	,,	1,931	...	...	...	...	,,
,,	Bréteuil	2,949	1,131	227,500	21,290	12,000	VIIIth Army Corps
,,	Amiens (Longueau)	2,490	3,323	10,460	...	...	Ist and VIIIth Army Corps
,,	Nesle	5,212	3,550	549,265	1,500	17,688	,,
,,	Beauvais and Creil	1,105	486	256,984	59,622	19,281	,, Ist Army Corps
,,	La Fère	1,054	896	162,530	8,660	6,000	13th column of the reserve ammunition park attached to the reserve division
Total of reserve ammunition issued to the 1st Army during its operations in the north of France	...	18,796	11,395	1,227,894	91,872	55,577	

[1] The Cuirassier and Lancer regiments, and the non-commissioned officers of the Hussars and Dragoons, carried pistols instead of carbines.

ORDER OF BATTLE
OF
ARMY CORPS

ORDER OF BATTLE OF THE 1ST ARMY

AT THE TIME OF LEAVING THE MOSELLE (7TH NOVEMBER).

Commander-in-Chief . . . GENERAL OF CAVALRY BARON VON MANTEUFFEL.
Chief of the Staff . . . MAJOR-GEN. VON SPERLING (absent commanding 29th Infantry Brigade).
Chief of the Staff (ad interim) . QUARTERMASTER-IN-CHIEF COLONEL COUNT VON WARTENSLEBEN.
Quartermaster-in-Chief (ad interim) . MAJOR VON LEWINSKI.
Commander of Artillery . . . LIEUTENANT-GENERAL SCHWARTZ.
Commander of Engineers . . . MAJOR-GENERAL BIEHLER.

a. FIRST ARMY CORPS.

General of Cavalry . . BARON VON MANTEUFFEL
    (afterwards Lieutenant-General VON BENTHEIM).
Chief of the Staff . . LIEUTENANT-COLONEL VON DER BURG.
Commander of Artillery . . MAJOR-GENERAL VON BERGMANN.

1st Division—Lieut.-Gen. von Bentheim (afterwards Major-Gen. Baron von Falkenstein).		2nd Division—Major-Gen. von Pritzelwitz.	
1st Brigade—Colonel von Boecking, commanding 44th Regiment. 1st Regiment. 41st Regiment. 1st Rifle Battalion.	2nd Brigade—Major-Gen. Baron von Falkenstein (afterwards Col. von Massow). 3rd Regiment. 43rd Regiment.	3rd Brigade—Major-Gen. von Memery (*ad interim* Col. von Busse, commanding 43rd Regiment). 4th Regiment. 44th Regiment.	4th Brigade—Major-Gen. von Zglinitzky. 5th Regiment. 45th Regiment.
1st Regiment of Dragoons. 1st Field Artillery Division.		10th Regiment of Dragoons. 3rd Field Artillery Division.	

CORPS ARTILLERY.
2nd Field Artillery Division.
2 Batteries of the Horse Artillery Division.

b. SEVENTH ARMY CORPS.

General of Infantry . . . VON ZASTROW.
Chief of the Staff . . . COLONEL VON UNGER.
Commander of Artillery . . MAJOR-GENERAL VON ZIMMERMANN.

13th Division—Lieut.-Gen. von Bothmer.

25th Brigade—Major-Gen. von der Osten-Sacken.
  13th Regiment.
  73rd Regiment.
  7th Rifle Battalion.

26th Brigade — Major-Gen. Baron von der Goltz (*ad interim* Col. von Barby, commanding 55th Regiment).
  15th Regiment.
  55th Regiment.

8th Regiment of Hussars.
3rd Field Artillery Division.

14th Division—Lieut.-Gen. von Kameke.

27th Brigade—Col. von Pannewitz (*ad interim* Col. von Conrady, commanding 77th Regiment).
  39th Regiment.
  74th Regiment.

28th Brigade—Major-Gen. von Woyna.
  53rd Regiment.
  77th Regiment.

15th Regiment of Hussars.
1st Field Artillery Division.

CORPS ARTILLERY.

2nd Field Artillery Division.
2 Batteries of the Horse Artillery Division.

c. EIGHTH ARMY CORPS.

General of Infantry	. . VON GOEBEN.
Chief of Staff	. . COLONEL VON WITZENDORFF.
Commander of Artillery	. . COLONEL VON KAMEKE.

15th Division—Lieut.-Gen. von Kummer.		16th Division—Lieut.-Gen von Barnekow.	
29th Brigade—Major-Gen. von Sperling (*ad interim* Col. Mettler, commanding 70th Regiment, afterwards Col. Bock, commanding 65th Regiment). 33rd Regiment. 65th Regiment.[1] 8th Rifle Battalion.	30th Brigade—Major-Gen. von Strubberg. 28th Regiment. 68th Regiment.	31st Brigade — Major-General Count Gneisenau. 29th Regiment. 69th Regiment.	32nd Brigade—Col. von Rex (*ad interim* Col. Beyer von Karger). 40th Regiment. 70th Regiment.
7th Regiment of Hussars. 1st Field Artillery Division.		9th Regiment of Hussars. 3rd Field Artillery Division.	

CORPS ARTILLERY.

2nd Field Artillery Division.
Horse Artillery Division.

---

[1] The 65th, 68th, and 70th Regiments replaced the 60th, 61st, and 72nd Regiments, which had hitherto belonged to the VIIIth Army Corps. The 65th Regiment was still with General Gayl's detachment in front of Verdun, so that the change with the 60th Regiment was not effected until the army reached the neighbourhood of this fortress on the 9th November.

Appendix. 223

d. THIRD RESERVE DIVISION.

(Hitherto Lieutenant-General von KUMMER.)

a. Combined Infantry Brigade . . MAJOR-GENERAL VON BLANKENSEE.
        19th Regiment.
        81st ,,

b. Landwehr Division . . . MAJOR-GENERAL SCHULER VON SENDEN.
The 12 Landwehr Battalions returned home as escort of prisoners. Of the troops originally composing this division there still remained :

  3rd Reserve Cavalry Brigade . . MAJOR-GENERAL VON STRANTZ.
        5th Reserve Regiment of Lancers.
        3rd ,, ,, of Hussars.
        2nd ,, 'Reiter' Regiment.
        1st ,, Regiment of Dragoons.
        3rd Garrison Pioneer Company of the IXth Army Corps.
        1 Light Reserve Battery of the 11th Artillery Regiment.
        3 Reserve Batteries.

e. 3rd Cavalry Division . . . LIEUTENANT-GENERAL COUNT VON DER GROEBEN.

6th Cavalry Brigade—Major-General von Mirus.	7th Cavalry Brigade—Major-Gen. Count Dohna.
8th Regiment of Cuirassiers (Col. Count Roedern).	5th Regiment of Lancers (Col. von Reitzenstein).
7th Regiment of Lancers (Lieut.-Col. von Pestel).	14th Regiment of Lancers (Col. von Lüderitz).

Horse Artillery Battery of the 7th Field Artillery Regiment.

ORDER OF BATTLE OF THE 1ST ARMY CORPS

ON THE 9TH DECEMBER.

General Commanding	LIEUTENANT-GENERAL AND DIVISIONAL COMMANDER VON BENTHEIM.
Chief of the Staff	LIEUTENANT-COLONEL VON DER BURG.
Commander of Artillery	MAJOR-GENERAL VON BERGMANN.
Commander of Engineers	MAJOR FAHLAND.

1st Infantry Division—Major-Gen. von Falkenstein.		2nd Infantry Division—Major-Gen. von Pritzelwitz.	
1st Infantry Brigade—Col. von Böcking, commanding 44th Regiment.	2nd Infantry Brigade—Col. von Busse, commanding 43rd Regiment.	3rd Infantry Brigade—Major-Gen. von Memerty.	4th Infantry Brigade—Major-Gen. von Zglinitzky.
1st Regiment—Col. von Massow.	3rd Regiment — Col. von Legat.	4th Regiment — Col. von Tietzen and Hennig.	5th Regiment — Major von der Dollen.
41st Regiment — Lieut.-Col. von Meerscheidt-Hüllessem.	43rd Regiment—Lieut.-Col. von Rosenberg.	44th Regiment—Major Bock.	45th Regiment — Col. von Mützschefahl.
2nd and 3rd Company of Pioneers, with entrenching-tool column.	1st Rifle Battalion—Lieut.-Col. von Plötz.		
6th Regiment of Dragoons.—Major Oettinger.		10th Regiment of Dragoons—Col. von der Goltz.	
1 Field Division of 1st Artillery Regiment—Major Preinitzer.		3rd Field Division of 1st Artillery Regiment—Major Müller.	
		1st company of 1st Pioneer Battalion.	

CORPS ARTILLERY.

COLONEL JUNGÉ.

2nd Field Division of 1st Artillery Regiment, Lieutenant-Colonel von Gregorovius.
Horse Artillery Division of 1st Artillery Regiment, Major Gerhards.
Ammunition columns of 1st Artillery Regiment, Major von Kaunhoven.
Pontoon train of xiith Army Corps.

TRAINS.

MAJOR VON HOFE,

ORDER OF BATTLE OF THE VIIITH ARMY CORPS

ON THE 9TH DECEMBER.

General Commanding	GENERAL OF INFANTRY VON GOEBEN.
Chief of the Staff	COLONEL VON WITZENDORFF.
Commander of Artillery	COLONEL VON KAMEKE.
Commander of Engineers	LIEUTENANT-COLONEL SCHULZ.

15th Infantry Division—Lieut.-Gen. von Kummer.

29th Infantry Brigade—Col. von Bock.	30th Infantry Brigade—Major-Gen. von Strubberg.
33rd Regiment—Lieut.-Col. von Henning.	28th Regiment — Col. von Rosenzweig.
65th Regiment—Lieut.-Col. Baron von Dörnberg.	68th Regiment — Col. von Sommerfeld.

8th Rifle Battalion.
7th (King's) Hussar Regiment—Col. Baron von Loe.
1st Field Division of 8th Artillery Regiment—Major Mertens.

16th Infantry Division—Lieut.-Gen. Baron von Barnekow.

31st Infantry Brigade—Major-Gen. Count von Gneisenau (*ad interim* Col. Mettler, 70th Regiment).	32nd Infantry Brigade — Col. von Rex (*ad interim* Col. Beyer von Karger, 69th Regiment).
29th Regiment — Lieut.-Col. von Blumröder (*ad interim* Major von Elern).	40th Regiment—Lieut.-Col. Reinicke.
69th Regiment—Col. Beyer von Karger (*ad interim* Lieut.-Col. Marschall von Sulicki).	70th Regiment—Col. Mettler (*ad interim* Major Erni).

9th Hussar Regiment—Col. von Wittich.
3rd Field Division of 8th Artillery Regiment—Lieut.-Col. Hildebrand.

CORPS ARTILLERY.

COLONEL VON BROECKER.

2nd Field Division of 8th Artillery Regiment, Major Zwirnemann.
Horse Artillery Division of 8th Artillery Regiment, Lieutenant-Colonel Borkenhagen.
Ammunition columns of 8th Artillery Regiment.—Captain Eggers.

8TH TRAIN BATTALION.

COLONEL VON DER MARWITZ.

Copied from the '*Gazette de Cambrai*' of the 30th December, 1870.

ARMÉE DU NORD.—22ND ARMY CORPS.—GENERAL FAIDHERBE.

1st Infantry Division—Gen. Lecointe.
1st Infantry Brigade—Col. Derroja.
2nd Marching Battalion of Chasseurs.
1st, 2nd } Battalions of 75th Marching Regiment.
1st Battalion of 65th Marching Regiment.
1st, 2nd } Battalions of 67th Marching Regiment.
5th, 6th, 7th } Battalions of Gardes Mobiles du Pas de Calais.
2nd Infantry Brigade—Col. Moynier.
10th Marching Battalion of Chasseurs.
1st, 2nd } Battalions of 24th Marching Regiment.
1st Battalion of 64th Marching Regiment.
1st, 2nd, 3rd } Battalions of 68th Marching Regiment.
1st, 2nd } Battalion of 46th Regiment of Gardes Mobiles (du Nord).
3rd 8-pounder Battery of 12th Artillery Regiment.
1st 4-pounder Battery of 15th Artillery Regiment.
2nd 4-pounder Battery of 15th Artillery Regiment.

Total, 20 battalions, 3 batteries.

2nd Infantry Division—Gen. Paulze d'Ivoy.
1st Infantry Brigade—Col. de Bessol.
20th Battalion of Chasseurs.
1st, 2nd } Battalions of 43rd Regiment of the Line.
1 Marine Battalion.
1st, 2nd, 3rd } Battalions of 69th Marching Regiment.
1st, 2nd, 3rd *bis* } Battalions of Gardes Mobiles du Gard.
1st, 2nd, 3rd } Battalions of 44th Regiment of Gardes Mobiles.
2nd Infantry Brigade—Col. Thomas.
18th Marching Battalion of Chasseurs.
1st, 2nd } Battalions of 91st Regiment of the Line.
1st, 4th } Battalions of 33rd Regiment of the Line.
1st, 4th *bis* } Battalions of Gardes Mobiles de la Somme.
2nd Battalion of Gardes Mobiles de la Marne.
2nd *bis* 4-pounder Battery of 15th Artillery Regiment.
3rd *bis* 4-pounder Battery of 15th Artillery Regiment.
3rd *bis* 12-pounder Battery of 15th Artillery Regiment.

Total, 20 battalions, 3 batteries.

3rd Infantry Division—Admiral Moulac.
1st Infantry Brigade—Naval Capt. Payen.
19th Marching Battalion of Chasseurs.
1st, 2nd } Battalions of Marine Fusiliers.
3rd, 7th, 8th, 9th } Battalions of 48th Gardes Mobiles Regiment (du Nord).
2nd Infantry Brigade—Commandant de la Grange.
1 Battalion Mobilisés du Pas de Calais.
1st, 2nd, 3rd } Battalions of 47th Regiment of Gardes Mobiles.
4th, 5th, 6th } Battalions of Gardes Mobiles du Nord.
10th, 11th, 12th } Battalions of Gardes Mobiles du Nord.

Total, 17 Battalions.

Appendix.

TROOPS ATTACHED TO HEAD-QUARTERS.

1st ⎫ 12-pounder Mounted Battery.
2nd ⎭
2 companies of Engineers.
Engineer park.
2 squadrons of Gendarmes.
2 squadrons of Dragoons.
1 peloton of Dragoons as Head-quarters' escort.

Total 2¼ squadrons, 2 batteries, 2 companies of engineers.

SUMMARY.

1st Infantry Division, 20 battalions, — squadrons, 3 batteries.
2nd Infantry Division, 20 battalions, — squadrons, 3 batteries.
3rd Infantry Division, 17 battalions, — squadrons, — batteries.
Reserve, ½ battalion, 2¼ squadrons, 2 batteries.

Total, 57½ battalions, 2¼ squadrons, 8 batteries.

INFANTRY.

1 Chasseur Battalion of the Line.
4 Marching Chasseur Battalions.
5 Battalions of the Line.
4 Battalions of Marines.
14 Marching battalions.
29 Battalions of Gardes Mobiles.

Total, 57 battalions.

ARTILLERY.

4 4-pounder batteries.
1 8-pounder battery.
3 12-pounder batteries.

Total, 8 batteries.

Operations of the 1st Army under General von Manteuffel.

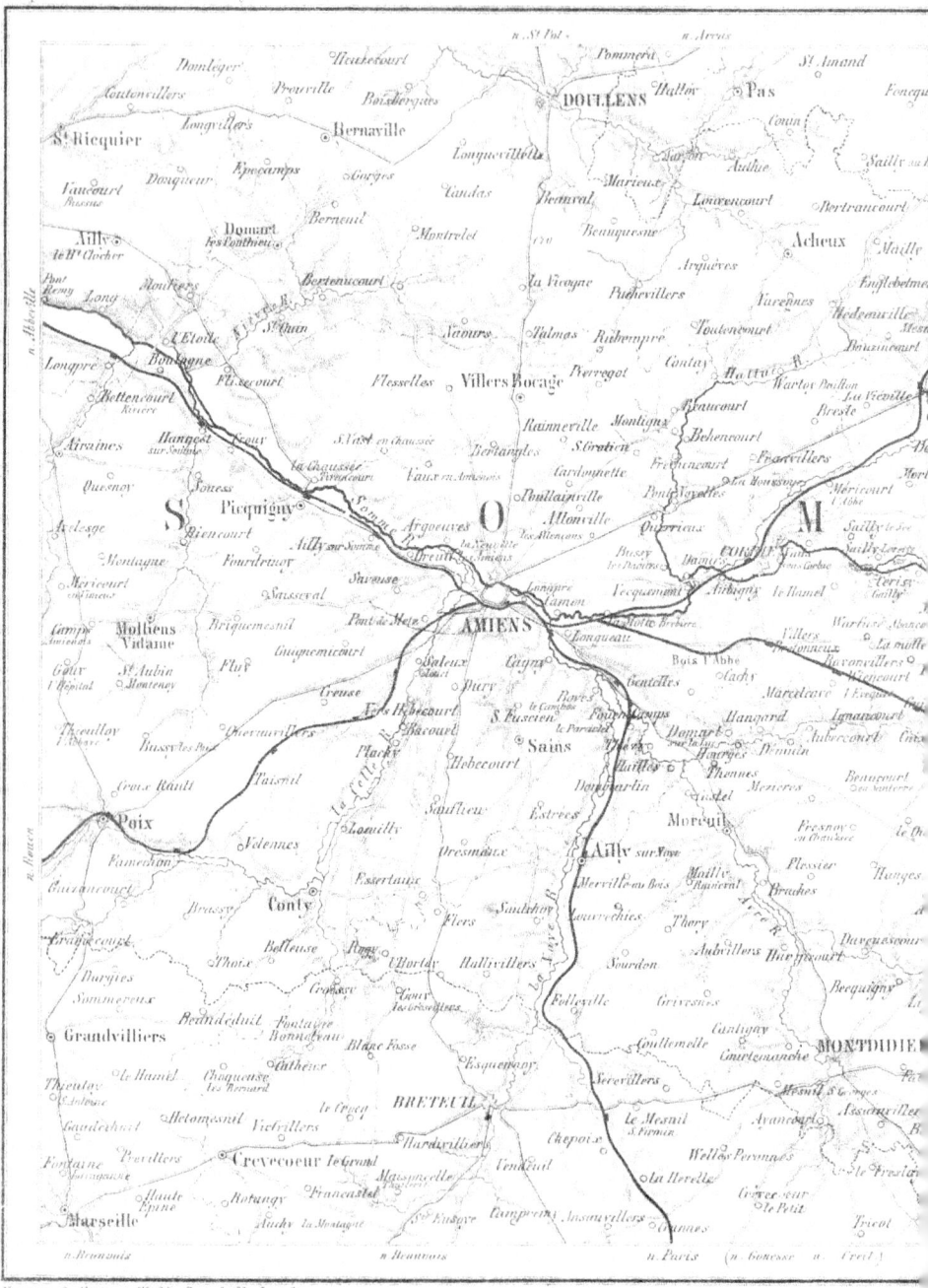

Henry S. King & Co 65 Cornhill, London

N.

Map II.

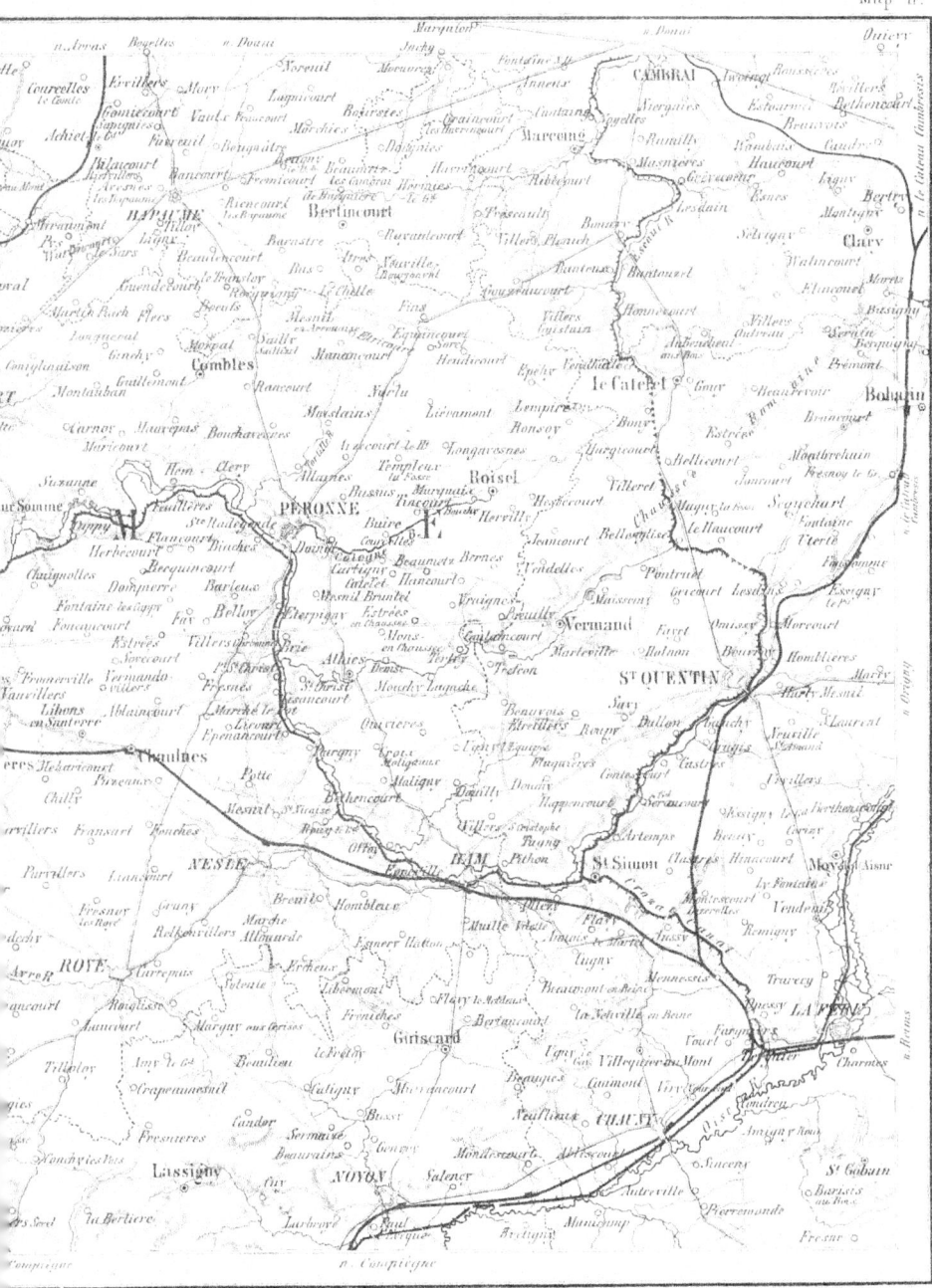